"THE TRUTH SHALL MAKE YOU FREE"

"Open ye the gates, that the righteous nation
which keepeth the truth may enter in."
—Isaiah 26:2.

PUBLISHERS
WATCHTOWER BIBLE AND TRACT SOCIETY, INC.
International Bible Students Association
Brooklyn 1, New York, U. S. A.

First edition
ONE MILLION COPIES

Dedicated
to

JEHOVAH

"A God of truth
and without iniquity,
just and right is he."
—Deuteronomy 32:4

and to

JESUS CHRIST

"I am the way,
and the truth, and
the life."— John 14:6

CONTENTS

"THE TRUTH
SHALL MAKE YOU FREE"

"THE TRUTH
SHALL MAKE YOU FREE"

CHAPTER I

T WAS the 22nd day of the month Ethanim, the month which the Romans called October. Great were the multitudes that thronged the areas for the common people in the temple of Jerusalem. The seven-day feast of the harvest ingathering had just been celebrated, the most joyous event of the year to the people of the nation. Its celebration was a happy expression of the people's conviction that there would be freedom from want for at least the year to come.

Today was the eighth day. The people had not yet dispersed to their homes throughout Palestine and other provinces of the Roman Empire, because this eighth day was a further day of festive gathering, a sabbath of refraining from work, and hence a holiday. It was called the "last day, that great day of the feast". That morning one of the temple priests had gone forth, trailed by a rejoicing multitude waving branches of palm and other trees, and had fetched water from the fountain of Siloam. The golden pitcher of water was brought into the temple's court of the priests amid the shouts

9

of the worshipers and the sound of cymbals and trumpets, and was then poured over the great copper altar of sacrifice. The ceremony recalled the time when their forefathers dwelt in tabernacles in the wilderness for forty years and divine power caused water to issue forth miraculously from a flinty rock to refresh the thirst-crazed people. More than this, now the seed-time of the farmers was approaching, and the offering of Siloam's water to the God who had performed that miracle was a petition for his blessings of the rain upon the seed sown. The due season of the year for the early rain was at hand. The people looked to the great Rain-maker to keep them free from want.

Pontius Pilate was then Rome's governor of its province of Judea. During the great feasts of these Judeans it was his custom as procurator to remove from Caesarea, on the Mediterranean seacoast, and to come up to Jerusalem and reside there. Pilate had taken up his duties in Judea some six years previously, in A.D. 26. His family name, or cognomen, suggests that he was descended from a freedman, who had been given the *pileus* or cap of liberty.

From the household of Tiberius Caesar, the Roman emperor, Pilate came, to govern for ten years, trying to keep the Pax Romana in Palestine. He little understood the Jews. Under him they appeared to enjoy freedom of religion. This, however, was not without a struggle, for Pilate quarreled with them almost continuously. Hence they did not altogether enjoy freedom from fear. They remembered how at the very beginning of his administration Pilate had transferred the headquarters of his army from Caesarea to Jerusalem. Of course, the soldiers took with them their standards bearing the image of the emperor and brought them into the hallowed city, whose God had given his people the command: "Thou shalt not make unto thee any graven image, or any likeness of any thing that is in heaven above, or that is in the earth beneath, or that is in the water under the earth: thou shalt not bow down thyself to them, nor serve them."[1] Cautiously the soldiers took in their standards by night.

No former governor had attempted such a thing which to the Jews was a desecration of the sacred city. Their rage and indignation were great on discovering those flags or image-bearing standards in the midst of Jerusalem. In large crowds they streamed down to Pilate, then at Caesarea, and implored him to remove the images. The fifth day of the discussions Pilate treacherously planted soldiers in places of concealment. At a given signal he caused them to surround the petitioning Jews and to put them to death if they refused to break off their entreaties. This only made them stronger in their determination. They declared themselves ready to die rather than to give in to such idolatrous encroachment upon the sacred realm of worship. Only then did Pilate yield and order the military standards cleared out of

[1] Quoted from Exodus 20: 4, 5, in the Holy Scriptures.

Jerusalem and returned to Caesarea. Yet later he caused some inscribed shields to be hung up in Jerusalem, and it was finally by order from Emperor Tiberius himself that those things esteemed defiling were removed from the city. These and other unwise moves stood out as sore spots in the struggle for freedom of worship according to the dictates of Jewish conscience. Continual vigilance was the price of their liberty from defilement.

Now another thing had appeared to disturb, and that from their own midst. A man had suddenly risen up from Galilee. "A Nazarene" they called him. For this reason the "holier than thou" religious leaders despised him. It was known he had been baptized in Jordan river. It was thought that he had thereby acknowledged himself to be a sinner. For three years he had gone about Palestine, tramping from place to place and preaching and teaching in the synagogues, in the homes of the people, in the mountains, at the seaside, and in the temple. Indeed he was in the temple this very day.

The whole nation was in a ferment religiously. This unusual man from "Galilee of the Gentiles" had come out for the worship of God clean and pure, not only from Gentile defilements such as image-bearing standards and inscribed shields, but also from all religion. He had taken issue with the religious practices of the Jewish elders, scribes, Levites, priests, Sadducees and Pharisees. A number of these were members of the Sanhedrin, the Supreme Court, having power over the Jews which was limited only by the Roman governor. These high-ranking men were strong advocates for what one of them called "the Jews' religion", or "Judaism". They were ever on the lookout for false prophets, subject to trial before the Sanhedrin.

One day a number of scribes and Pharisees from Jerusalem came to this wonder-working preacher from Galilee with the question: "Why do your disciples transgress the tradition of the elders by not washing their hands before meals?" To this he retorted: "Why do you, too, transgress God's commands for the sake of your tradition? God said, 'Honour thy father and thy mother'; and 'Let him who reviles father or mother be put to death'; but you say: 'If a man says to his father or mother, "This thing is consecrated, otherwise you should have received it from me," he shall be absolved from honouring his father'; and so you have rendered futile God's word for the sake of your tradition." Then this Galilean made bold to call them religious hypocrites and to apply against them a verse from God's prophet Isaiah. He said: "Hypocrites! Well did Isaiah prophesy of you, 'This people honours me with their lips, while their heart is far from me; in vain do they worship me, while giving as doctrines the mere precepts of men.' "[1]

On another occasion this Galilean openly taught the people from a mountainside and ex-

[1] Quoted from Matthew 15:2-9, Weymouth's translation, 5th edition.

posed religion and its widely advertised works
of charity, self-inflicted fasts and other exhibitions. He said: "Beware of doing your good
actions in the sight of men, to attract their
gaze; if you do, there is no reward for you with
your Father who is in heaven. When you give
in charity, do not blow a trumpet before you
as the hypocrites do in the synagogues and
streets in order that their praises may be sung
by men. I solemnly tell you that they have received in full their reward. But when you are
giving in charity, let not your left hand perceive
what your right hand is doing, that your char-
ities may be in secret; and your Father—He
who sees in secret—will recompense you.

"And when praying, you must not be like
the hypocrites. They are fond of standing and
praying in the synagogues or at the corners of
the wider streets, in order that men may see
them. I solemnly tell you that they have received in full their reward. But you, whenever
you pray, go into your own room and shut the
door: then pray to your Father who is in secret,
and your Father—He who sees in secret—will
recompense you. And when praying, do not use
needless repetitions as the heathen do, for they
expect to be listened to because of their multitude of words. Do not, then, imitate them; for
your Father knows what things you need before
ever you ask him. . . .

"When you fast, do not assume gloomy looks
as the hypocrites do; for they disfigure their
faces that it may be evident to men that they

are fasting. I tell you in truth that they have received in full their reward. But, whenever you fast, pour perfume on your hair and wash your face, that it may not be apparent to men that you are fasting, but to your Father who is in secret; and your Father—He who sees in secret —will recompense you."[1]

Such speech was decidedly antireligious to the high priests, scribes, and Pharisees of Jerusalem and the members of their Supreme Court. To them, it was unreligious conduct when this Galilean performed miraculous cures of sick and afflicted people on the weekly rest-day, the sabbath. The common people heard him gladly. This fact robbed the religious leaders of their freedom from fear; more so when the people came to look upon this ambulating teacher as one of God's prophets. The question then arose, and was openly discussed, as to whether this was the mighty Prince that was foretold to come, the Messiah, whom Greek-speaking Jews at that time called "Christ". It was hoped that the Messiah, or Christ, would destroy the yoke of Rome from off the necks of those who worshiped the Most High God. He was to set up the kingdom of God, which would be a blessing to men and women of all nations, the Gentiles, and would usher in a free world without end. Now on that "great day of the feast" the people who listened to the Galilean teaching at the temple were heard to discuss among themselves. Some said: "Of a truth this is the Prophet"; that is,

[1] Quoted from Matthew 6:1-18, Weymouth's translation.

the prophet who should arise after Moses and be like Moses. Others said: "This is the Christ."[1]

The religious leaders began to think that freedom of speech was not a good thing for this bold young man, who was "not yet fifty years old", only thirty-three years old, in fact. They wanted to kill him, but were afraid to lay hands upon him because of the people. How they despised the people for listening to him! They called such people *am ha-arets* (*people of the earth*) and said they were unworthy of a resurrection to life eternal. That day, while the Galilean was instructing the people, they said: "This people who knoweth not the law are cursed." So the chief priests and Pharisees sent out officers of the law to arrest him at the temple and break up his preaching in public. The officers were more honest than their religious dictators and came back without the preacher. Asked why, they replied: "Never man spake like this man."

"This man" did not ask the political or the religious rulers for the right or guarantee of the freedom of speech to preach the message he gave. He already possessed that right as a right given to him by the One who had sent him to preach and teach "the kingdom of heaven". That One, he said, was his Father above. No one could, therefore, properly interfere with his right of freedom of speech for the Kingdom. Fear of death—that he did not have; for he said: "When ye have lifted up the Son of man,

[1] Quoted from John 7: 26, 37, 40, 41.

then shall ye know that I am he, and that I do nothing of myself; but as my Father hath taught me, I speak these things. And he that sent me is with me."[1]

Why did this Galilean speak thus boldly, with complete freedom from fear of religionists who attempted to mob him, to arrest him and to kill him? There he stands, speaking in the temple to those believing on him. Listen to him! Hear for yourself his own answer to the question: "If ye continue in my word, then are ye my disciples indeed; and ye shall know the truth, and THE TRUTH SHALL MAKE YOU FREE."

Here is the secret of the Galilean's courage to speak out plainly against religion and religious hypocrites and their sins. He had the truth, and knew it, and spoke the truth uncompromisingly for the sake of the freedom of the people. He recognized that the religious leaders and their dupes were in a worse bondage than they realized, a bondage to their worst adversary, the Devil. Some of these religionists objected and said that they were the seed or descendants of the faithful patriarch Abraham and hence were never in bondage; and how, then, could the Galilean make *them* free?

The Galilean answered: "Verily, verily, I say unto you, Whosoever committeth sin is the servant of sin. . . . If the Son therefore shall make you free, ye shall be free indeed. I know that ye are Abraham's seed; but ye seek to kill me, because my word hath no place in you. I speak

[1] Quoted from John 7: 32, 45-49; also John 8: 28, 29.

that which I have seen with my Father: and ye
do that which ye have seen with your father.
. . . Ye do the deeds of your father." Thereupon the self-righteous religionists slurred the
Galilean's birth and said: "We be not born of
fornication; we have one Father, even God."
They trusted in the "fatherhood of God", at
least for their nation out of all the nations.

Who needed to be told the truth more than
they, that they might realize their bondage and
learn the path to freedom? Therefore the Galilean, this one named *Jesus,* said straightfor-
wardly to the religionists: "If God were your
Father, ye would love me: for I proceeded forth
and came from God; neither came I of myself,
but he sent me. Why do ye not understand my
speech? even because ye cannot hear my word.
Ye are of your father the devil, and the lusts of
your father ye will do. He was a murderer from
the beginning, and abode not in the truth, because there is no truth in him. When he speaketh a lie, he speaketh of his own: for he is a
liar, and the father of it. And because I tell you
the truth, ye believe me not."

Jesus was not the servant of sin or the Devil
and his lies; Jesus was free. Therefore he asked
them: "Which of you convinceth me of sin? And
if I say the truth, why do ye not believe me? He
that is of God heareth God's words: ye therefore hear them not, because ye are not of God."
Hence they were not free from blindness by the
father of lies, but were bound with his murderous spirit.

Angered by the truth from this One who spoke with perfect freedom from fear, the religionists accused him of having a devil and being in bondage to it. "Jesus answered, I have not a devil; but I honour my Father, and ye do dishonour me. And I seek not mine own glory: there is one that seeketh and judgeth. Verily, verily, I say unto you, If a man keep my saying, he shall never see death."

Remarkable, this saying; for here is promised everlasting freedom from death, and this by keeping the saying of truth. Are there believing persons now living on earth who will literally experience the fulfillment of this promise? The religionists who heard Jesus rejected the truth of his testimony concerning himself and his Father. "Then took they up stones to cast at

him: but Jesus hid himself, and went out of the temple." To their sin of unbelief of the truth they would add the devilish deed of murder. They soon died in their willing bondage, as Jesus had warned them: "I said therefore unto you, that ye shall die in your sins: for if ye believe not that I am he, ye shall die in your sins." [1]

WHAT IS TRUTH?

Today, nineteen centuries removed from the time of the utterance, "The truth shall make you free," the world is not free. Who can honestly contend that it is? The very fact that, in the 1940's, politicians of "Christendom" publish a statement to the world guaranteeing the so-called "Four Freedoms" is a blank admission that the peoples and nations are not free. Nevertheless "Christendom", which, according to her profession of the name "Christian", ought to be free, claims to have continued in the word of Jesus and to be his disciple indeed. The facts belie her claim. Instead of knowing the truth, "Christendom" is a confusion of religions, Catholic, Protestant, and Jewish, and pagan, and a confusion of political systems, democratic and totalitarian. All are now fearfully groping in darkness for some inter-religious and international arrangement whereby they can all survive and get along together.

This serious plight of "Christendom" stands as a condemnation that her political and religious leaders during the sixteen centuries of her

[1] Quoted from John 8:24-59.

existence have not continued till now in the word of Jesus and have not been his disciples indeed. Today, in "Christendom", are fulfilled the words of the ancient prophet: "None calleth for justice, nor any pleadeth for truth: they trust in vanity, and speak lies; they conceive mischief, and bring forth iniquity. . . . Judgment is turned away backward, and justice standeth afar off: for truth is fallen in the street, and equity cannot enter. Yea, truth faileth; and he that departeth from evil maketh himself a prey: and the LORD saw it, and it displeased him that there was no judgment." [1]

The most pressing need of all people who desire life and liberty in a free world is for the truth. To continue in the word of a mere man who speaks out of his own wisdom makes one a disciple of such man, but also leads to bondage. Not so, however, with the word of Jesus. To continue in His word makes us free as his disciples, knowing the truth, because his is not the word of one merely of human origin or possessed of mere human wisdom. He called upon his hearers to be honest and to examine and recognize his real identity and that of his Father. Why? Because, said he, "this is life eternal, that they might know thee the only true God, and Jesus Christ whom thou hast sent." [2] That truth is echoed by one of his disciples, who wrote: "This is the true God, and eternal life." [3]

[1] Quoted from Isaiah 59: 4, 14, 15.
[2] Quotation from John 17: 3 and [3] from 1 John 5: 20.

Jesus stuck to the word he preached, because it was the truth. He was finally arrested by religionists, held in custody and abused and derided, falsely accused, and then nailed to a tree till lifeless. But he died a free man. He died because he did not choose to fight back with powers that were at his command. He yielded to death because he knew more benefit would result from his death than to fight for further life in the flesh. He died because the interests of the truth concerning himself and his Father would be more fully served by suffering innocently unto death than by continuing to live as a man. As truth cannot for ever be crushed to earth, so neither could this faithful Truth-teller; for his Father duly freed him from death's bonds and ushered him into a freedom as wide as the universe and wherein he will "never see death".

What is his word, or doctrine, wherein we must continue in order to be his disciples and know the truth and be free? We cannot turn to any of the many conflicting religions for His word, because he told the practicers of religion they were guilty of "making the word of God of none effect through your tradition, which ye have delivered". Thereafter the religionists killed him, because his word found no place in them. Jesus did not teach like the religionists, who referred to human authorities and traditions of religious men. Hence, "the people were astonished at his doctrine: for he taught them as one having authority, and not as the scribes."[1]

Jesus revealed the source of his word of truth. He said: "My doctrine is not mine, but his that sent me. If any man will do his will, he shall know of the doctrine, whether it be of God, or whether I speak of myself." Privately he said to his disciples: "The word which ye hear is not mine, but the Father's which sent me." Then, joining with his disciples in prayer, he said to his Father: "Sanctify them through thy truth: thy word is truth."[2]

It is his Father's written Word that is the truth; which was why he repeatedly quoted it as his authority and guide during his earthly life. If we would continue in his word and be his disciples, we must likewise turn to his Father's word of truth. Then we shall come to know the truth and be made free with a God-given freedom that no human or devilish powers can take away. To find life eternal we must know in truth "the only true God, and Jesus Christ whom [He] has sent". This knowledge we can rightly acquire only by means of the written Word of God. That Word instructs the truth-seekers and freedom-lovers: "Buy the truth, and sell it not; also wisdom, and instruction, and understanding." "Have not I written to thee excellent things in counsels and knowledge, that I might make thee know the certainty of

[1] See Mark 7: 1-13; and John 8: 43, 45, 47; and Matthew 7: 28, 29.

[2] Quotations are from John 7: 16, 17; 14: 24; 17: 17.

the words of truth; that thou mightest answer the words of truth to them that send unto thee?"[1]

You must buy the truth at the cost of your time and effort spent in searching God's written Word, doing so without religious bias and prejudice. Otherwise you will be like the religious leaders, "ever learning, and never able to come to the knowledge of the truth." The divine instruction given through one of Jesus' faithful disciples who continued in His word and came to know the truth is: "Study to shew thyself approved unto God, a workman that needeth not to be ashamed, rightly dividing the word of truth."

To enable you thus to buy the truth and thereafter continue in it and "sell it not", this book is published. Through all the following pages, this book will continue in His word, and those pages will set out the scriptures in support of the truth, as quoted principally from three versions of the Bible, the Catholic Douay Version (*Douay*), the King James or Authorized Version (*A.V.*), and the American Revised Version (*A.R.V.*). Each such citation of Scripture will set out the particular book of the Holy Scriptures, then the chapter thereof, and then the verse or verses; as, for example, 2 Timothy 3: 7 and 2 Timothy 2: 15, for the two scripture texts quoted in the above paragraph. Man's chief and most vital study is God and His purpose. Rightly our consideration begins with him.

[1] Quotations are from Proverbs 23: 23; 22: 20, 21.

CHAPTER II

"A GOD OF TRUTH"

PEN your copy of the Bible at the first book thereof, which is called "Genesis", and at the first verse. It matters not whether you use the Catholic *Douay* Version, or the Jewish *Leeser* Version, or the Protestant versions, either the King James or the American Revised. They all translate the same opening Hebrew words of the original Bible, *B'reshith' bara' Elohim',* and they all read the same way: "In the beginning God created."

These inspired words put God first. They do not begin with raising the question posed by worldly scientists, Is there a God? because, all things considered, that question is foolish. "The fool hath said in his heart, There is no God. Corrupt are they, and have done abominable iniquity: there is none that doeth good. God looked down from heaven upon the children of men, to see if there were any that did understand, that did seek God." (Psalm 53: 1, 2) The course of action of those who deny or doubt the existence of God, and the outcome thereof, prove them fools. They deny the central truth, and are in bondage to error, which leads to destruction. To get free from such death-dealing error and to come to the great Giver of life and truth, man must believe that God is. There is no end of proof that He is. "But without faith it is impossible to please him: for he that cometh to God must believe that he is, and that he is a rewarder of them that diligently seek him." (Hebrews 11: 6) "The fear of the Lord is the beginning of knowledge: but fools despise wisdom and instruction." "The fear of the LORD is a fountain of life, to depart from the snares of death."—Proverbs 1: 7; 14: 27.

He is a "God of truth". It is "impossible for God to lie", and "he cannot deny himself". Hence he begins his inspired book of Genesis with the self-evident truth that God is: "In the beginning God created." This could not mean there was a beginning to God; but that he is the Beginner of all things that exist. He is the Creator, the Source of all creation. The man whom God inspired to write the book of Genesis also wrote: "Before the mountains were brought forth, or ever thou hadst formed the earth and the world, even from everlasting to everlasting, thou art God."—Psalm 90: 2.

It is only fitting of God that his eternal existence should be beyond finding out by lowly man with limited powers and who can not even search out to the bottom the secrets of the wonderful works of God round about him, and of which works man himself is one. "For my thoughts are not your thoughts, neither are your ways my ways, saith the LORD. For as the heavens are higher than the earth, so are my ways higher than your ways, and my thoughts than your thoughts." (Isaiah 55: 8, 9) Having no beginning, God the Creator is therefore the one and only Being. He is the Supreme One. "Who only hath immortality, dwelling in the light which no man can approach unto; whom no man hath seen, nor can see; to whom be honour and power everlasting. Amen."—1 Timothy 6: 16.

There was a time when God began to create. Before that he was all alone in the universe, for immeasurable time. He was not lonesome; because he is perfect, being complete in himself. Hence his pleasure is absolutely independent of creatures, although he does find pleasure in the exercise of his boundless powers of creation. Those who worship him truthfully say in adoration: "Thou art worthy, O Lord, to receive glory and honour and power: for thou hast created all things, and for thy pleasure they are and were created."—Revelation 4: 11.

There was never a time when there was chaos, that is, a formless, disorganized and confused state, throughout the universe. It is only pagan Greek mythology that claims that *Chaos* was the most ancient of the gods. Exposing the foolishness of such idea of pagan science, the divine Word of truth says: "God is not the author of confusion, but of peace." "God is not a God of confusion, but of peace." (1 Corinthians 14: 33, *A.V.* and *A.R.V.*) He did not bring order out of chaos, because chaos never existed contemporaneously with "the true and living God". The universe was never out of his control. When

He, the sole inhabiter of the universe and of eternity, began to create, he proceeded orderly. His processes of creation, whether instantaneous or progressive, operated under his regulation and according to laws which he established to govern the creative process to its perfection. Nothing can get beyond his control and mastery.

As being undeniable proof of his existence and his supremacy, unsearchable wisdom and almighty power, God calls man's attention to the works visible to man in the heavens, the earth, and the seas, which works operated before man's appearance on the earth and which continue to operate without man's aid and beyond man's power to explain or control.—Read chapters 38 to 41 of the book of Job.

The sensible man, marveling at such works of divine power and intelligence, exclaims: "I have heard of thee by the hearing of the ear: but now mine eye seeth thee. Wherefore I abhor myself, and repent in dust and ashes." That man appreciates the inspired words of the psalmist: "When I consider thy heavens, the work of thy fingers, the moon and the stars, which thou hast ordained; what is man, that thou art mindful of him? and the son of man, that thou visitest him?" (Job 42: 5, 6; Psalm 8: 3, 4) To such honest man the heavens, though silent, testify that God is and is glorious: "The heavens declare the glory of God; and the firmament showeth his handiwork. Day unto day uttereth speech, and night unto night showeth knowledge. There is no speech nor language; their voice is not heard. Their line is gone out through all the earth, and their words to the end of the world. In them hath he set a tabernacle for the sun, . . . there is nothing hid from the heat thereof." —Psalm 19:1-6, *A.R.V.*

GOD, that is what the Almighty One is. To those who transgress against this truth he says: "Remember the former things of old: for I am God, and there is none else; I am God, and there is none like me." (Isaiah 46:9) Religionists point to the fact that the word *God* here, as well as at Genesis 1:1, is the word *Elohím* in the Hebrew original, and that *Elohim* is the plural number of the Hebrew word *Elóah*. Hence they claim that here in these verses and in others *Elohim* means "gods" and that this proves that God Almighty is a trinity of persons, all three being uncreated, having an eternity of existence together, and being equal in power and glory. Not only is such teaching of a trinity of persons in one god unreasonable and beyond the ability of these trinity-teachers to explain, but not even the word "trinity", nor even the idea of such, appears in God's Word of truth. The trinity of gods, however, does appear as a teaching of pagan religions in Egypt, Babylon, Greece, China, and elsewhere long before its adoption by the religionists of so-called "Christendom". The foolishness and unscripturalness of such trinity doctrine, and its evident pagan origin, will appear more plainly as this discussion goes along. The brightening truth about the "true and living God" will make

you free of one of the greatest blasphemies and
confusing doctrines of religion.

Here let it be sufficient to say that *Elohim,*
though being plural in form, is accompanied by
a singular pronoun and a singular verb when it
refers to The Supreme and Almighty One. This
fact shows his unity and oneness of Being, there
existing none besides him, none like him, none
equal to him in power and glory and eternity.
Wherefore the plural form *Elohim,* as meaning
God Almighty, is merely the plural of excellence
and majesty and means one Person. *Eloah*
(singular) and *Elohim* (plural) are both en-
larged from the original Hebrew noun *El;* and
El is, in turn, drawn from the verb *ool,* which
means to be strong and mighty or to be before
or ahead of. Hence the plural *Elohim* fits and
describes the Supreme One as summing up all
power and might and as surpassing all and being before all in His excellency and eternal existence.

If GOD is what he is, what is his name? That
question was put long before this, even thousands of years ago, in the days of Moses. By the
miracle of the burning bush Almighty God
manifested his presence to Moses for a very de-
cided *purpose.* "Moses said unto God, Behold,
when I come unto the children of Israel, and
shall say unto them, The God of your fathers
hath sent me unto you; and they shall say to
me, What is his name? what shall I say unto
them? And God [*Elohim*] said unto Moses,
I AM THAT I AM: and he said, Thus shalt thou

say unto the children of Israel, I AM hath sent me unto you. And God [*Elohim*] said moreover unto Moses, Thus shalt thou say unto the children of Israel, JEHOVAH, the God [*Elohim*] of your fathers, the God [*Elohim*] of Abraham, the God [*Elohim*] of Isaac, and the God [*Elohim*] of Jacob, hath sent me unto you: this is my name for ever, and this is my memorial unto all generations."—Exodus 3:13-15, *A.R.V.*

Elohim here is Jehovah, and there are not three persons Jehovah; only one. In the great-

est commandment of the law the Lord God says
by his prophet Moses: "Hear, O Israel: Jehovah our God [*Elohim*] is one Jehovah: and
thou shalt love Jehovah thy God [*Elohim*] with
all thy heart, and with all thy soul, and with all
thy might." (Deuteronomy 6: 4, 5, *A.R.V.*) Thus
the argument that the title *Elohim* supports the
trinity doctrine falls flat as foolish.

By his prophet Isaiah the Lord God announces: "I am Jehovah, that is my name; and
my glory will I not give to another, neither my
praise unto graven images." (Isaiah 42: 8,
A.R.V.) At what time the Lord God revealed
this name to mankind on earth is not definitely
stated. It first appears in the Hebrew text of
the Bible at Genesis 2: 4, and occurs thereafter
six thousand six hundred times, from Genesis to Malachi. The English Bible versions, the
Catholic *Douay,* the Jewish *Leeser,* and the
King James or Authorized Version, hide this
important truth by translating *Jehovah* by the
words LORD, GOD, and *The Eternal.* The King
James Version makes only four exceptions to
this practice which obscures the truth. However,
the name *Jehovah* is found first on the lips of
the first woman, at Genesis 4: 1, *A.R.V.* The
first man shown to address Him by the name is
Abraham the patriarch, "the friend of God," at
Genesis 15: 2, 7, 8: God "said unto him, I am
Jehovah that brought thee out of Ur of the
Chaldees, to give thee this land to inherit it.
And he said, O Lord Jehovah, whereby shall I
know that I shall inherit it?"—*A.R.V.*

The Lord God also revealed himself to Abraham under another title: "And when Abram was ninety years old and nine, Jehovah appeared to Abram, and said unto him, I am God Almighty." (Genesis 17:1, *A.R.V.*) This title was to strengthen Abraham's faith in God's promise to him of a miraculous birth of a son.

That Abraham and others before Moses' day knew the name but did not appreciate its inward meaning is stated by God himself: "God spake unto Moses, and said unto him, I am Jehovah: and I appeared unto Abraham, unto Isaac, and unto Jacob, as God Almighty; but by my name Jehovah I was not known to them." (Exodus 6:2, 3, *A.R.V.*) Jehovah went on to state his purpose concerning his chosen people, then slaves in Egypt. His purpose was to fulfill a certain part of his covenant made with their forefather Abraham and to make them his covenant people. That was the occasion of making known the inward meaning of God's name. From the emphasis laid upon it on this occasion, and from God's special choice of it in announcing his purpose to vindicate himself and the word of his covenant, it is plain that the name *Jehovah* means or signifies *The Purposer*, or His purpose toward his creatures. The name does not call notice to His being the Eternal One, which he is, of course. The name is the *causative* form of the Hebrew verb *havah* (*to be*) and literally means "He causes to be", that is, he causes according to his purpose.

For many centuries, particularly after the days of Jesus and his apostles, the meaning of the name *Jehovah* has been lost to sight, and even the very name has been pushed into the background. Only in very recent years has God caused his name to be brought forth again to the light and its meaning to be made known to his faithful servants, because it is the due time and the vindication of his name *Jehovah* draws near.[1] Let none now ignore that name!

At Genesis 2:4 the designation "Jehovah God" first appears in Sacred Writ. Being God (*Elohim*), Jehovah is divine. He is The Divinity or Divine One. "Being therefore the offspring of God, we must not suppose the divinity to be like unto gold, or silver, or stone, the graving of art, and device of man."—Acts 17:29, *Douay*.

Jehovah is unseen to human eyes, but he gives mankind evidence of his divinity by his works visible to them. "For the invisible things of him, from the creation of the world, are clearly seen, being understood by the things that are made; his eternal power also, and divinity." (Romans 1:20, *Douay*) It would be improper to speak of Jehovah as having the "divine nature", because *nature* means that which is born or produced, or, that which is according to birth and growth; whereas Jehovah is without birth or beginning or growth. He is ever perfect, and produces all things righteous, good and perfect. However, to creatures who prove themselves faithful disci-

[1] See *The Watchtower*, June 1, 1928, ¶ 5; January 1, 1933, ¶¶ 4, 5, 6.

ples of Jesus, it is written by the disciple Peter: "According as his divine power hath given unto us all things that pertain unto life and godliness, through the knowledge of him that hath called us to glory and virtue: whereby are given unto us exceeding great and precious promises: that by these ye might be partakers of the divine nature [(literally) a divine nature], having escaped the corruption that is in the world through lust." (2 Peter 1: 3, 4) Such faithful disciples, together with Jesus, become partakers of "a divine nature" by reason of being specially begotten by the invisible force of the Divine One, Jehovah God.

God is invisible, beyond the power and capacity of man to see Him. To the prophet Moses he said: "Thou canst not see my face: for there shall no man see me, and live." (Exodus 33: 20) Hence human nature could never ascend to heaven and see God. In support of this a disciple of Jesus writes: "No man hath seen God at any time; the only begotten Son, which is in the bosom of the Father, he hath declared him." "And no man hath ascended up to heaven, but he that came down from heaven, even the Son of man." (John 1: 18; 3: 13) This holds true because human nature is "of the earth, earthy", but God is spirit and is The Spirit. Concerning the great Spirit and the manner of worshiping Him, Jesus said: "The hour cometh, and now is, when the true worshippers shall worship the Father in spirit and in truth: for the Father seeketh such to worship him. God is a spirit:

and they that worship him must worship him in spirit and in truth."—John 4 : 23, 24.

Is it now necessary to go to some religious temple or cathedral in order to worship God, who is spirit? His servant Paul gives the true answer: "God that made the world and all things therein, seeing that he is Lord of heaven and earth, dwelleth not in temples made with hands; neither is worshipped with men's hands, as though he needed any thing, seeing he giveth to all life, and breath, and all things; . . . Forasmuch then as we are the offspring of God, we ought not to think that the Godhead is like unto gold, or silver, or stone, graven by art and man's device. And the times of this ignorance God winked at; but now commandeth all men every where to repent."–Acts 17 : 24-30; 7 : 48-50.

Is, then, anyone worshiping God when he offers incense and bows down to an image of any kind or material and says prayers on his knees before such image? That is the practice of religion, but it is not the worship of God, the God whom Jesus worshiped in spirit and in truth. (John 20: 17) All the faithful worshipers of God from Abel to Moses did not worship God in man-made temples or before images. At Mount Horeb, in Arabia, Jehovah God gave a terrifying manifestation of his power and then called Moses up into the mountain and gave to that prophet the stone tablets of the Ten Commandments written in His own hand, "written with the finger of God." The first two of these commandments read: "I am Jehovah thy God

[*Elohim*], who brought thee out of the land of Egypt, out of the house of bondage. Thou shalt have no other gods before me. Thou shalt not make unto thee a graven image, nor any likeness of any thing that is in heaven above, or that is in the earth beneath, or that is in the water under the earth: thou shalt not bow down thyself unto them, nor serve them; for I Jehovah thy God am a jealous God."—Exodus 20:2-5, *A.R.V.*; and 31:18.

A religionist may not excuse himself by saying that he merely gives the image "relative honor and worship" and is not worshiping the image itself, but the one for whom the image stands. That is the very argument that the pagan heathen gave as an excuse for using images in their religion and worshiping the sun, moon and stars, and the "queen of heaven", as they called it. (Jeremiah 7:18; 44:17-25) Such religious practice is self-deception, and God does not excuse the use of images under this pretext, but calls it a snare and expressly forbids it to those who worship him in spirit and in truth. Even to wave the hand and give a salute and throw a kiss was forbidden by him as idolizing the image or thing.

Therefore God inspired Moses to utter and write down this warning to God's covenant people: "Take ye therefore good heed unto yourselves; for ye saw no manner of form on the day that Jehovah spake unto you in Horeb out of the midst of the fire; lest ye corrupt yourselves, and make you a graven image in the

form of any figure, the likeness of male or female, the likeness of any beast that is on the
earth, the likeness of any winged bird that flieth
in the heavens, the likeness of anything that
creepeth on the ground, the likeness of any
fish that is in the water under the earth; and
lest thou lift up thine eyes unto heaven, and
when thou seest the sun and the moon and the
stars, even all the host of heaven, thou be drawn
away and worship them, and serve them, which
Jehovah thy God hath allotted unto all the peoples under the whole heaven." Against such religious practices Jehovah God warned, saying:
"Neither shalt thou serve their gods; for that
will be a snare unto thee. The graven images of
their gods shall ye burn with fire: thou shalt not
covet the silver or the gold that is on them, nor
take it unto thee, lest thou be snared therein;
for it is an abomination to Jehovah thy God."
(Deuteronomy 4: 15-19; 7: 16, 25, *A.R.V.*) God's
Word of truth thus declares that religion is a
deadly snare.[1]

At Psalm 84: 11 is the inspired statement:
"Jehovah God is a sun and a shield." (*A.R.V.*)
But that is no justification for worshipers of
Jehovah God to kiss the hand to the sun or a
shield or to salute them and bow down to them
because they are used as symbols of God. From
such obeisance to creatures and man-made things
the pure and true worshiper of God must hold
back, as did the faithful man Job. Said he: "If I
have made gold my hope, or have said to the fine

[1] Concerning James 1: 26, 27, see pages 87-89.

gold, Thou art my confidence; if I rejoiced because my wealth was great, and because mine hand had gotten much; if I beheld the sun when it shined, or the moon walking in brightness; and my heart hath been secretly enticed, or my mouth hath kissed my hand: this also were an iniquity to be punished by the judge: for I should have denied the God that is above."
—Job 31: 24-28; 1 Kings 19: 18; Hosea 13: 2.

Nothing could be of greater importance than to worship Jehovah God in spirit and in truth, as Jesus said. This is a God-given right of all His creatures, and no human government, no matter how high it is on earth, has any right to interfere therewith and to dictate contrary to the rule and commandment of the worship of Jehovah God. Jehovah is the Supreme Power. (Ecclesiastes 5: 8) The very life of intelligent creation depends upon such true worship of the Supreme Power. "Therefore choose life, that thou mayest live, thou and thy seed; to love Jehovah thy God, to obey his voice, and to cleave unto him; for he is thy life, and the length of thy days." (Deuteronomy 30: 19, 20, *A.R.V.;* 32: 47) "This is the true God, and eternal life." (1 John 5: 20) "The gift of God is eternal life through Jesus Christ our Lord."—Romans 6: 23.

There came a time when the great Creator and Life-giver began his creative work. This was an expression of his love; for "God is love". (1 John 4: 16) What was his first creation, the beginning of the creation of God? And was it living or inanimate?

CHAPTER III

SPIRIT SONS OF GOD

CIENCE of the men of this world cannot solve the secret of the first creation of God. The secret is solvable and is, in fact, now revealed to those who fear God and who therefore have the "wisdom that is from above". The worldly and religious scientists, worshiping their own brains and the brains of other men, pass by the very source of truthful information, God's Word, or they reject its testimony. Thereby they deny God its Author and make fools of themselves. They continue to gaze into the endlessness of space with their telescopes and to peer through their magnifying glasses into the realm of microcosms and to dig into the earth for fossil bones and remains, but never learn the source of life nor come to life-giving wisdom and truth. They never get free from the bonds of their misleading human imaginations and suppositions. They go from one delusion to another, while those who trust in their theories fall into deeper darkness and humankind continues to fight and suffer and die, and the old world faces a terrible end.

The almighty, all-wise God who brought forth his first creation at an unknown time in the past is also able to create now a new world of right-

eousness wherein men who fear him and worship him in spirit and in truth may live freely
in light, peace and joy forever. His first creation has an important and vital connection with
the establishment of the hoped-for new world.
It is therefore no matter of idle speculation or
impudent curiosity for God-fearing men to examine into this question. What God has caused
to be recorded in his Word of truth is proper
for man to desire and to seek to understand. At
the due time God makes it understandable. "The
secret things belong unto the LORD our God: but
those things which are revealed belong unto us
and to our children for ever, that we may do
all the words of this law."—Deuteronomy 29:29.

God's first creative work was no experimental
model. It was his best work of creation till nineteen centuries ago. It was a perfect work and
perfectly showed forth the wisdom and knowledge and praiseworthy workmanship of the
Creator. It was deserving of bearing the name
of Jehovah its Maker. "For I will proclaim the
name of Jehovah: ascribe ye greatness unto our
God. The Rock, HIS WORK IS PERFECT; for all his
ways are justice: a God of faithfulness and
without iniquity, just and right is he." (Deuteronomy 32: 3, 4, *A.R.V.*) All Jehovah's works are
an honor and credit to him, and the study of
them in order the better to know him leads to
wisdom and the understanding of the truth.
"The works of the LORD are great, sought out of
all them that have pleasure therein. His work is
honourable and glorious: and his righteousness

endureth for ever. The works of his hands are
verity and judgment; all his commandments
are sure. They stand fast for ever and ever,
and are done in truth and uprightness.—Psalm
111: 2, 3, 7, 8.

God's first creation was living and intelligent
and was made to possess wisdom. "For Jehovah
giveth wisdom; out of his mouth cometh knowledge and understanding." (Proverbs 2: 6,
A.R.V.) Hence in the book of inspired proverbs
the Creator causes the one who is the beginning
of His creation to speak under the symbolic
figure of Wisdom and to say: "Jehovah possessed me [(marginal reading) Jehovah formed
me] in the beginning of his way, before his
works of old. I was set up from everlasting,
from the beginning, before the earth was. When
there were no depths, I was brought forth, when
there were no fountains abounding with water.
Before the mountains were settled, before the
hills was I brought forth; while as yet he had
not made the earth, nor the fields, nor the beginning of the dust of the world. When he
established the heavens, I was there: when he
set a circle upon the face of the deep, when he
made firm the skies above, when the fountains
of the deep became strong, when he gave to the
sea its bound, that the waters should not transgress his commandment, when he marked out
the foundations of the earth; then I was by him,
as a master workman; and I was daily his delight, rejoicing always before him, rejoicing in

his habitable earth; and my delight was with the sons of men."—Proverbs 8: 22-31, *A.R.V.*

Jehovah God had now set out on the purpose of endless creation. He now had beside him a "master workman" endowed with wisdom. This one had received life from God. This made him the Son of God. In begetting this Son or bringing him forth to life Jehovah was the only Producer or Creator, unassisted. His first living creature was therefore the "only begotten Son of God". He was a spirit like Jehovah his Father and could see Him and be with Him. Being a spirit and in the image of God, this only begotten Son was in the "form of God". He was perfectly subject to his Father and Creator. Not once did he meditate upon a usurpation to be equal with his Father; such equality he knew wisely is an impossibility. He recognized Jehovah as the Supreme Power and as his Head. He never turned aside from that rule. Hence the only begotten Son is spoken of as the one "who, existing in the form of God, counted not the being on an equality with God a thing to be grasped". (Philippians 2: 6, *A.R.V.*) Jehovah the Father dearly loved his only begotten Son, and the Son loved the Father and proved that love by unselfish obedience to Him and keeping His commandments. He feared Jehovah, not with a tormenting, selfish fear, but with a dread of ever displeasing his Father and God and not glorifying Him. The Son worshiped Jehovah God, which means, not idle adoration and admiration, but service actively to God and thereby honoring and exalting Him.

Did this firstborn Son possess immortality, that is, deathlessness? That he did not have this quality and was not immortal at that time is proved by later facts as well as plainly stated in the Bible. Endless life is dependent upon unending obedience to God. By faithful and perfect obedience the Son would live by his Father's approval and could live with him forever. The time came, however, that Jehovah God opened up to his Son the opportunity to gain immortality. That the Father gave the Son such opportunity is proved by the Son's statement: "As the Father hath life in himself; so hath he given to the Son to have life in himself." (John 5: 26) This also proves that Jehovah is the Lifegiver to the Son.

The Father, Jehovah God, made the Son his mouthpiece or spokesman, which in itself meant that there were to be other creatures and that toward these the Son of God would declare and execute the word of God. Therefore in this position the Son was called "The Word of God". This position of being the Chief Executive Officer of Jehovah put the only begotten Son in a superior position with respect to all other creatures that should be. The Father clothed the Son with power befitting his position, and thus the Son, this "master workman" with God Jehovah, was a mighty one, and was before others, Jehovah only excepted. Concerning the Son in the office of "The Word of God" it is written:

"In the beginning was the Word, and the Word was with God, and the Word was God. The same was in the beginning with God. All things were made by him; and without him was not any thing made that was made."—John 1:1-3.

Does this mean that Jehovah God (*Elohim*) and the only begotten Son are two persons but at the same time one God and members of a so-called "trinity" or "triune god"? When religion so teaches it violates the Word of God, wrests the Scriptures to the destruction of those who are misled, and insults God-given intelligence and reason. Note first that the above quotation of John 1:1-3 mentions only two persons, not three. The very words of the text also show that the Son, who receives life, could not be coeval or co-existent from eternity with the Father, who gives life to the Son and so begins him. Though there is no beginning of God (*Elohim*), or Jehovah, there was a beginning of speech or word; and it was God who began or produced speech or word. Thus the very title shows that Jehovah God produced or began the one who is called "The Word". "Thy word is true from the beginning"; or, according to the marginal reading of the Bible, "The beginning of thy word is true." (Psalm 119:160) God is the origin of the Word. "And God [*Elohim*] said."—Genesis 1:3, 6, 9, 11, 14, 20, 24, 26.

The confusion is caused by the improper translation of John 1:1-3 from the Greek, in which the text was originally written, into the English, such translation being made by religionists who tried to manufacture proof for their teaching of a "trinity". This fact is made plain in a book entitled "The Emphatic Diaglott", which sets out the original text of the Scriptures in Greek letters and under each line of the Greek text it presents a word-for-word translation of the original Greek. This sublinear English translation reads, as you will note in reproduction below: "In a beginning was the Word, and the Word was with the God, and a god was the Word. This was in a beginning with the God. All through it was done; and without it was done not even one, that has been done." You will also note that in the regular English in the right-hand column *The Emphatic Diaglott* emphasizes the distinction between the Creator as THE God and the Word (*Logos*) as A god by printing the word "GOD" when referring to the Creator and "God" when referring to the Word or Logos.

*[EYAΓΓΕΛΙΟΝ] ΚΑΤΑ ΙΩΑΝΝΗΝ.
[GLAD TIDINGS]   BY   JOHN.

*ACCORDING TO JOHN.

ΚΕΦ. α΄. 1.

¹'Εν ἀρχῇ ἦν ὁ Λόγος καὶ ὁ Λόγος
In a beginning was the Word, and the Word

ἦν πρὸς τὸν Θεόν, καὶ θεὸς ἦν ὁ Λόγος.
was with the God, and a god was the Word.

²Οὗτος ἦν ἐν ἀρχῇ πρὸς τὸν Θεόν.
This was in a beginning with the God.

³Πάντα δι' αὐτοῦ †ἐγένετο· καὶ χωρὶς
All through it was done; and without

αὐτοῦ ἐγένετο οὐδὲ ἕν, ὃ γέγονεν.
it was done not even one, that has been done.

⁴'Εν αὐτῷ ζωὴ ἦν, καὶ ἡ ζωὴ ἦν τὸ φῶς
In it life was, and the life was the light

τῶν ἀνθρώπων· ⁵καὶ τὸ φῶς ἐν τῇ σκοτίᾳ
of the men; and the light in the darkness

φαίνει, καὶ ἡ σκοτία αὐτὸ οὐ κατέλαβεν.
shines, and the darkness it not apprehended.

CHAPTER I.

1 In the ‡Beginning was the †LOGOS, and the LOGOS was with GOD, and the LOGOS was God.

2 This was in the Beginning with GOD.

3 ‡Through it every thing was done; and without it not even one thing was done, which has been done.

4 In it was Life; and the LIFE was the LIGHT of MEN.

5 And the ‡LIGHT shone in the DARKNESS, and the DARKNESS apprehended It not.

By remembering that the word "god", according to the Hebrew, means "mighty one" or "one who is before (others)", and by remembering the Son's power and position with reference to all the rest of creation, it is easily grasped that God's Son, the Word, was and is "a god" (*El*), or "mighty one", pre-eminent above other creatures, whereas Jehovah, the Producer of the Word, is "the God" (*Elohim*), without beginning and "from everlasting to everlasting".

By referring to John 10: 34-36 you will note that Jesus quotes from the law at Psalm 82: 6 and says: "Is it not written in your law, *I said, Ye are gods?* If he called them gods, unto whom the word of God came, and the scripture cannot be broken; say ye of him, whom the Father hath sanctified, and sent into the world, Thou blasphemest; because I said, I am the Son of God?" If those mighty men of earth against whom God directed his word of condemnation could be called "gods", much more could and do the true Scriptures speak of God's Son, the Word, as "a god". He is a "mighty god", but not the Almighty God, who is Jehovah. (Isaiah 9: 6) Certainly, then, John 1: 1-3, according to its original Greek text, is no proof that Jehovah God and his Son are "one in person, equal in power and glory", as religious catechisms say without Scripture proof. The contrary is true. God the Speaker has power over the Word, and sends forth the Word to bear and fulfill God's message. In agreement with this John 1: 18 reads: "No one hath seen God at any time; an

only begotten God, the one existing within the
bosom of the Father, He hath interpreted him."
—Rotherham's translation; see also the *A.R.V.*
translation, marginal reading.

The question now arises as to the other creatures that were produced after God's firstborn
Son, the Word. Were these other creatures each
a direct creation of God as his Son the Word
was? The firstborn Son's title "only begotten
Son" indicates that the other creatures were not
God's direct creation without any agent in between. After Jehovah God created the Word
direct, then he used this only begotten Son as
His agent or "master workman" in the creation
of everything else. To this effect John 1:3 testifies concerning the Word: "All things were
made by him; and without him was not any
thing made that was made." John 1:14 also declares that God's only begotten Son, the Word,
was the One who in due time became the "man
Christ Jesus"; it says: "And the Word was
made flesh, and dwelt among us, (and we beheld
his glory, the glory as of the only begotten of
the Father,) full of grace and truth." Also
1 John 1:1 reads: "That which was from the beginning, which we have heard, which we have
seen with our eyes, which we have looked upon,
and our hands have handled, of the Word of
life."

God's use of his Son the Word in the crea-
tion of all things after him is further stated at
Ephesians 3:9: "God, who created all things by
Jesus Christ." Also at Colossians 1:15-17 it is

written concerning the Word or Jesus Christ: "Who is the image of the invisible God, the firstborn of every creature: for by him were all things created, that are in heaven, and that are in earth, visible and invisible, whether they be thrones, or dominions, or principalities, or powers: all things were created by him, and for him: and he is before all things, and by him all things consist." God's Word, Christ Jesus, would have to be the "firstborn of every creature", to be before all other creations and to be God's "master workman" in producing them. In proof of this Christ Jesus says concerning himself: "These things saith the Amen, the faithful and true witness, the beginning of the creation of God."—Revelation 3:14.

Being the only begotten Son of God and "the firstborn of every creature", the Word would be a prince among all other creatures. In this office he bore another name in heaven, which name is "Michael". It means "Who is like God?" and marks its bearer as one who upholds the majesty and supremacy of Jehovah God and who will vindicate Jehovah's name and word against any possible false charges and misrepresentations. Other names were given to the Son in course of time. In all the principalities which were created in the invisible spirit realm Michael was "one of the chief princes", and in due time he became the invisible prince of God's chosen people of Israel. (Daniel 10:13, 21; 12:1; Jude 9; Deuteronomy 34:5, 6) As Jehovah's mighty prince and message-bearer, Michael has angels under his command, and hence he is an archangel. It is he whom Jehovah uses to clear out all rebellion from the universe, though it be attended by a time of trouble on earth such as has never before been known.—See Revelation 12:7-9; Daniel 12:1; Matthew 24:3, 21, 22; 1 Thessalonians 4:16.

For how long Jehovah God and his beloved Son were together without other companionship and enjoying each other's love the inspired Word of truth does not reveal. However, Jehovah has pleasure in the work of creation and in bestowing his loving-kindness upon creatures, and his time came for other creatures to be brought forth. Now he worked jointly with his Son, his only begotten Son being in complete harmony with his Father's purposes and acting in perfect unity and full co-operation with Him. Properly, then, the Son could say: "I and my Father are one." (John 10:30) The Son under his Father's direction proved himself a "master workman" and produced other spirit creatures who were given various rank and power and authority, namely, cherubim, seraphim, and angels.

Cherubim is understood to mean the office of *bearers*, that is, of God's throne; they are an escort of His throne and uphold His majesty in the throne as the Supreme Power of the Universe. Hence Jehovah God is addressed, at Psalm 80:1, in this manner: "Thou that sittest above the cherubim, shine forth." (*A.R.V.*) Also Psalm 18:10: "And he rode upon a cherub, and

did fly; yea, he did fly upon the wings of the
wind." Also Psalm 99: 1: "Jehovah reigneth; let
the peoples tremble: he sitteth above the cherubim."—*A.R.V.*

On the lid of the ark of the covenant which
Jehovah commanded Moses to make were two
golden representations of cherubim, one at each
end of the mercy seat. But the high priest and
people of Israel were not permitted to worship
and adore these cherubic images. To prevent
this, God commanded that, when the ark of the
covenant was carried about from place to place,
the entire ark including the cherubim must be
covered over with a cloth that they might not
even be visible to the people. (Exodus 25: 18-22;
Numbers 4: 5) Man came in contact with living
cherubim early in human history.—Genesis
3: 24; Ezekiel 28: 13, 14.

Seraphim means *fiery* or *burning* ones. The
divine revelation shows them as attending upon
God's throne at his temple of judgment, and
they are used to purge away defilement as by
fire. They declare God's holiness, and have been
used to foretell that all the earth will yet be
filled with Jehovah's glory.—Isaiah 6: 1-7.

Angels literally means *messengers*. It de-
notes not only Jehovah's message-bearers but
also his heavenly deputies sent out on errands
of service. One placed as chief or first one over
a body of angels would be an *archangel* in rank.
All these are spirit sons, invisible to man and
higher than man in form of life and organism.
Of God's creation of angels it is written: "Who

maketh his angels spirits; his ministers a flaming fire."—Psalm 104: 4; Hebrews 1: 7.

All these are bright and glorious creatures. Therefore they are likened in Scripture to the stars which man beholds in the heavens. They were all sons of God because of receiving life from Jehovah and by his only begotten Son, the Word. The Word was brought forth first in the morning of creation. Then, while creation was yet at its morn, Jehovah together with the Word created another glorious spirit son, named *Heylel,* which means *shining one, day-star,* or *Lucifer.* Being one of the early ones of God's sons, he is called a "son of the morning". (Isaiah 14: 12) The Word and Lucifer appear to have been the two described as "morning stars".

Up to this time in universal history all was joy, peace, and constructive work throughout Jehovah's realm of heavenly creatures. The Record, at Job 38: 7, describes an occasion of singing and shouting for joy among them: "When the morning stars sang together, and all the sons of God shouted for joy."

All these glorious spirit sons of Jehovah were arranged in an orderly manner and assigned to certain respective duties, to work in harmony with one another without discord and friction. Thereby all would work together without confusion for the carrying out of the righteous and holy purpose of their Creator, Jehovah. So arranged and disposed in "thrones, or dominions, or principalities, or powers", they all made up the heavenly part of a universal organization,

Jehovah's organization, over which He reigns supreme as 'King everlasting'. (Jeremiah 10:10) All were subject to Jehovah as Supreme Head. Even the Word, who became Jesus Christ, was subject to the Father: "The head of Christ is God." (1 Corinthians 11:3; 15:28) The only begotten Son and all other spirit sons of God worshiped Jehovah as God Most High and Ancient as eternity. "And the Ancient of days did sit, whose garment was white as snow, and the hair of his head like the pure wool: his throne was like the fiery flame, and [its] wheels as burning fire. A fiery stream issued and came forth from before him: thousand thousands ministered unto him, and ten thousand times ten thousand stood before him." (Daniel 7:9,10) Blessed is their portion to behold the majestic beauty of Jehovah and to be his holy ministers!

CHAPTER IV

EARTH'S CREATION

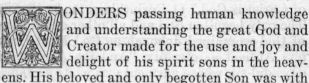ONDERS passing human knowledge and understanding the great God and Creator made for the use and joy and delight of his spirit sons in the heavens. His beloved and only begotten Son was with him in these grand creative works, and each fresh new creation caused all living creatures to praise and adore the Almighty One, "which doeth great things past finding out; yea, and wonders without number." (Job 9:10) Jehovah God and his "master workman", the Word, were The Higher Powers, and under them the universal organization of spirit creatures, seraphim, cherubim, and angels, lived and moved and served the purpose of God with perfect obedience and all to his glory.—Romans 13:1.

Then the much diversified wisdom of God was expanded to those spiritual heavens by the beginning of a new form of creation, the material creation. There were vast, fathomless depths of space, and at God's command his mighty Son, the Word, began to adorn these with awesome material things. "By the word of Jehovah were the heavens made, and all the host of them by the breath of his mouth. For he spake, and it was done; he commanded, and it stood fast." (Psalm 33:6, 9, *A.R.V.*) Glorious spiral nebulae

were formed, and globular clusters of stars,
suns and their planets and comets to move about
the suns in a well-defined orbit, all together
billions of milky ways, or galaxies of stars. The
vision of the omnipotent Creator could take in
the beautiful sight, and it was all well done in
perfect agreement with his irresistible will.
There was no chaos or wild confusion, but all
these heavenly bodies moved with orderliness
and regularity according to the hand of the
great Former of all things. The formation of
each spherical body went forward according to
the divinely fixed law. The Creator by his Word
held in control all created, forming and developing things. His invisible force, which the Bible
calls "the spirit of God", was sent forth from
him to work and fulfill his pleasure toward all
these inanimate creations in the limitless reach-
es of space.

There, in assigned places, were the heavenly
bodies Ash and Cesil and Cimah and Mazzaroth,
which men have misnamed Arcturus, Orion, and
Pleiades, and the zodiac, after the names of
false gods, or demons.—Job 9: 9 and 38: 31, 32,
marginal readings.

At this point the opening book of the Holy
Scriptures begins its matchless and truthful record: "In the beginning God created the heavens
and the earth." (Genesis 1: 1, *A.R.V.*) Whether
the mass of matter composing the earth was
originally thrown off from the fiery sun about
which it revolves, and just how long before this
the earth mass was being formed, the Divine Rec-

ord does not say. Hence the Scripture record that follows, in Genesis, chapter 1, does not describe the creation of the earth mass itself, but the ordering and preparing of it for the final purpose of its Creator.

What was and is that final purpose? The Creator's answer is the answer of truth, which truth frees the human mind and heart of all fears concerning the destiny of the earth we inhabit: "For thus saith Jehovah that created the heavens, the God that formed the earth and made it, that established it and created it not a waste, that formed it to be inhabited: I am Jehovah; and there is none else." (Isaiah 45:18, *A.R.V.*) "One generation passeth away, and another generation cometh: but the earth abideth for ever. The sun also ariseth, and the sun goeth down, and hasteth to his place where he arose." (Ecclesiastes 1:4, 5) "The earth which he hath established for ever."—Psalm 78:69.

The preparing of the earth and the disposing of things upon it for inhabitation the Creator's record divides into six work periods. These six periods are followed by a period of rest or sabbath toward earthly works, but not a sabbath toward other parts of the universe and the work there. That rest period of God toward the earth still continues, as a comparison of his Word at Genesis 2:1-3 and Psalm 95:7-11 and Hebrews 3:15-19; 4:1-11 shows. Already about six thousand years of that great rest or sabbath of God have passed, and his Word assures us definitely that there is another thousand years thereof yet

to run. Hence this great rest day of the Creator
toward the earth appears to be about seven
thousand years long. This seventh "day" being
of such length, it is but reasonable to conclude
that the preceding six work-days were each of
the same length, the six spanning a total period
of forty-two thousand years.

The record of earth's creation, being of things
before man's existence, is therefore inspired of
God. God asks man: "Where wast thou when I
laid the foundations of the earth? declare, if
thou hast understanding. . . . when the morning stars sang together, and all the sons of God
shouted for joy? Or who shut up the sea with
doors, when it brake forth, as if it had issued
out of the womb? when I made the cloud the
garment thereof, and thick darkness a swad-
dlingband for it." (Job 38: 4-9) "Who maketh
his angels spirits; his ministers a flaming fire:
who laid the foundations of the earth, that it
should not be removed for ever. Thou coveredst
it with the deep as with a garment: the waters
stood above the mountains." (Psalm 104: 4-6)
These and other Scripture statements unite in
testifying that the earthly sphere was once enveloped in a canopy of water and other materials suspended above the surface of the globe.
Great bands or belts of such enwrapped the
earth and hid its face from view.

Originally the earth was a fiery mass of matter. In this incandescent state it glowed like a
miniature sun, like a star. No seas could exist
upon its surface then, but all moisture was

driven off as steam and its hydrocarbons were vaporized and its metal and minerals were sublimated and thrown far out into space, about the boiling, burning earth-core. As the earth rotated on its axis, this thrown-off matter gradually formed into great rings about the earth at its equator, where the centrifugal force of the spinning earth was most powerful. Yet the earth's power of gravity held the rings in the vicinity of the earth's equator. According to the density and specific gravity of the materials thrown off from the molten earth, they formed into rings of water mixed with mineral substance, the densest and heaviest being nearest the earth-core, the next heavy being immediately next out beyond it, and so on, the lightest being thrown out farthest and being almost wholly a water ring. Thus an annular or ring system[1] existed, and the appearance to the eye of God was like that of a great wheel, with wheels within wheels, and with the molten earth itself as the spherical hub of them. The formation was exactly like that of the planet which astronomers call "Saturn" and which still has a ring system about it, three rings concentric yet swinging about its equator.

The planet Saturn is progressing to its final creative form according to the same divine laws that governed the earth at its early stages of creation. The evidence tends to the conclusion that these rings are composed of frozen snow

[1] See the book *The Earth's Annular System*, by Isaac N. Vail (1886).

particles. With the aid of a telescope it is notice-
able not only that Saturn has rings, but that
about the sphere there are bands of various
widths and brightness, and these are at various
latitudes above and below Saturn's equator.
However, at its north and south poles there are
no canopies, but the poles are exposed. There
the canopy belts are falling, those being the
areas of least resistance to gravitational forces.
Such belts are produced by the rings at the
equator falling one after another and then
spreading out to form belts on either side of
the equator. Each of these canopy belts revolves
about Saturn at its own specific speed, gradually slowing down as it nears the polar region.
Unseen within and beneath these canopy belts
the planet Saturn itself rotates on its axis like
a central core at its own as yet unmeasured
speed.

Likewise with the early earth. As it cooled,
its nearest and heaviest ring fell first toward
the equator. But the earth's centrifugal force
prevented its fall to the earth's surface, and the
ring flattened out and spread out like a belt, one
part to the north and the other to the south.
Ring after ring fell, and belt after belt formed.
The belts moved toward the north and the south
pole and there to a final fall to the earth itself.
At the polar points of least resistance the
earth's gravity pulled down each belt as it
reached such weak spot, and the waters and
their valuable treasures took a Niagara-like
plunge. Reaching the earth, the watery deluge

swept as a terrific inundation or flood from the poles toward the equator, carrying along its wealth of metals and minerals, together with ice. This greatly enriched the surface of the cooling earth.

At a certain stage, then, the surface of the earth, except at the poles, was completely enveloped in a canopy of mineralized and watery belts, like swaddling bands, high in suspension about the earthly globe. There was yet a series of rings riding on high at its equator, and thus the appearance of our planet was then like that of Saturn at present, whose rings are 171,000 miles across diametrically. The earth reached

this stage of annular and canopy development more quickly than Saturn, because, being a smaller body, it cooled more rapidly and its exhalations condensed sooner. No form of a continent then showed upon the earth, but there was water directly upon the bosom of the earth, as well as a watery deep swirling high up above. Then the invisible force or "spirit" of Jehovah acted upon those exterior waters, moving upon the outer face or surface of them. "And the earth was without form, and void; and darkness was upon the face of the deep. And the spirit of God moved upon the face of the waters."—Genesis 1: 2.

The earth having now cooled and solidified, it no longer glowed like a star, but was dark. "And God said, Let there be light: and there was light. And God saw the light, that it was good: and God divided the light from the darkness. And God called the light Day, and the darkness he called Night. And the evening and the morning were the first day."—Genesis 1: 3-5.

This was not some electrical light created at the earth itself, otherwise it would have shone all around the earth at the same time and there would have been no division between light and darkness. Whence, then, came the light? From the sun, which had been created unknown time prior to our tiny planet earth of the solar system.

The sunlight shone only upon the upper surface of the frozen or watery canopy high up above and around the earth. Only half of this canopy received the light of the sun at any time, the other half being away from the face of the sun and being in darkness. But, like the earth within, the belt canopy about it was also revolving around the earth's axis. Thus there was a division between the daylight period and the night period. However, the light of the sun did not penetrate through those canopy belts and reach the surface of the earth itself or reach the waters immediately upon the earth. The canopy belts were practically opaque, and between them and the earth the intervening space was dense with carbon, worse than a "pea-soup fog" in London. Note, too, that in describing this first day, as well as all following creative days, the Creator God puts the evening before the morning. He begins each creative day of seven thousand years with the evening period. At evening the final form of stable things to come is seen only in dim outline at first, if at all; and then it becomes clearer and, at last, fully distinct at the climax or "morning" of the day.

"And God said, Let there be a firmament [an expansion] in the midst of the waters, and let it divide the waters from the waters. And God made the firmament, and divided the waters which were under the firmament from the waters which were above the firmament: and it was so. And God called the firmament Heaven. And the evening and the morning were the second day." (Genesis 1: 6-8) This appears to mean a clearing up to some extent of the expanse between the waters under which earth's surface was buried and the watery belts suspended above the earth. The firmament or "heaven" was not holding up the canopy belts on high, but the establishment of the firmament

marked a clear separation between such waters
above and those under it. It was in this firmament that the winged creatures yet to be made
would fly, and which in time man himself would
invade with the airship, the airplane and the
rocket. At the close of the second creative day
the light from the sun had not yet pierced
through the canopy and reached the firmament.
All was still dark there.

"And God said, Let the waters under the
heaven be gathered together unto one place, and
let the dry land appear: and it was so. And God
called the dry land Earth; and the gathering
together of the waters called he Seas: and God
saw that it was good." (Genesis 1: 9, 10) Thus
at the beginning of the third creative day of
seven thousand years there were great convul-
sions within the bowels of the earth, very likely
caused by the falling of more belts of the canopy
at the poles of the earth and subjecting it to
new weights and pressures. At any rate, God's
directive power was operating, and bodies of
land were forced up above the surface of the
hitherto watery waste. Vast continents and
islands pushed up. They were nude of all vegetation or plant life.

"And God said, Let the earth bring forth
grass, the herb yielding seed, and the fruit tree
yielding fruit after his kind, whose seed is in
itself, upon the earth: and it was so. And the
earth brought forth grass, and herb yielding
seed after his kind, and the tree yielding fruit,
whose seed was in itself, after his kind: and

God saw that it was good. And the evening and
the morning were the third day." (Genesis
1:11-13) There was no evolution or developing
of one form or specialty of plant life through
indefinite, indistinct changes into another form
of plant life. God's manifold wisdom created
the multitude of definite forms of plants and
vegetation, each one bearing seed within itself
to reproduce and continue its own kind unchanged. All this bringing forth of the first
forms of plant life took place in the darkness
that still hovered in the firmament over the
earth and within the dense watery canopy.

"And God said, Let there be lights in the
firmament of the heaven to divide the day from
the night; and let them be for signs, and for
seasons, and for days, and years: and let them
be for lights in the firmament of the heaven to
give light upon the earth: and it was so. And
God made two great lights; the greater light to
rule the day, and the lesser light to rule the
night: he made the stars also. And God set them
in the firmament of the heaven to give light upon the earth, and to rule over the day and over
the night, and to divide the light from the darkness: and God saw that it was good. And the
evening and the morning were the fourth day."
(Genesis 1:14-19) This does not say or mean
that first during earth's fourth creative day God
produced the sun around which the earth revolves and also produced the earth's satellite,
the moon, and also the stars visible far beyond
to the naked eye. These celestial bodies existed

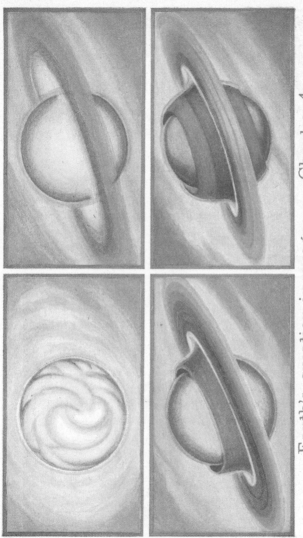

Earth's creation in progress.—Chapter 4.

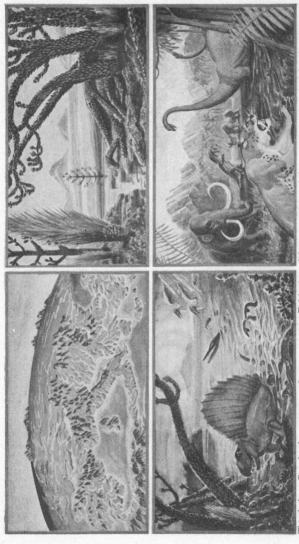

Third day: Dry land appears, and vegetation. Fifth day: Marine and amphibious creatures, and birds, appear. Sixth day: Land animals are created. – Chapter 4.

long before the earth's "fourth day" began. God had made them and hung them in the space at vast distances out beyond the rings and canopy circling the earth, and hence high above the firmament or "heaven" surrounding the earth, which "heaven" divided the waters on the earth from those above.

Now, however, for the first time the light of the sun, moon and stars appeared in the firmament of earth's heaven and that light penetrated through to the land surfaces and seas of the earth itself. Evidently by this time more of the canopy's densely-laden watery belts had reached the poles and fallen, deluging the whole earth for the time and wiping out the growing plant life. After such floods subsided, more plants sprang up and covered the protruding land surfaces with herbage. The canopy belt last falling in the course of the fourth day left only the lightest rings of almost pure water to drop at the equator and to spread out northward and southward like a tent or canopy over the earth. This remaining aqueous canopy was translucent. It therefore let the light of the sun, moon and stars far outside to stream through and light up the firmament, the air expanse which had now become relatively free of carbon. The effect of this was to produce a hothouse state upon the earth under its translucent canopy. This was very conducive to the luxuriant growth of plant life, even to the northern and southern polar regions, in the intervals between the fall of canopy belts.

Due to the aqueous canopy still enveloping the earth above the firmament the definite outline of the sun, moon and stars could not have been seen at the surface of the earth. Only their light diffused through the canopy. As time went on, the canopy would become very thin immediately above the equator of the earth, and the sunlight would penetrate through and be refracted with unusual brilliancy. What creatures would now inhabit the earth?

ANIMAL SOULS

Because the several versions of the Bible quoted from thus far do not convey the strict or inner sense of the original Hebrew in the further part of the creation account, we now quote from an authoritative version which does so. It is Rotherham's *The Emphasised Bible,* published in 1902 and based upon the most authentic of Bible manuscripts. Quotations hereafter from this emphasized Bible version will be marked (*Roth.*). Accordingly, the Record now reads: "And God said: Let the waters swarm with an abundance of LIVING SOUL, and birds shall fly over the earth, over the face of the expanse of the heavens. And God created the great sea-monsters, and every LIVING SOUL that moveth, with which the waters swarmed after their kind, and every winged bird after its kind. And God saw that it was good. And God blessed them, saying, Be fruitful and multiply, and fill the waters in the seas, and let the birds multiply in the land. So it was evening, and it was morning, a fifth day."—Genesis 1:20-23, *Roth.*

God's Word of truth as above quoted proves the existence of earthly souls thousands of years before man's appearance. God's inspired Record calls the sea monsters and other sea creatures, and also the birds, "living souls," because they lived and had a measure of intelligence. In the original Hebrew of the Bible this expression is *nephesh chayyah,* the very same expression that is applied to man by his Creator. Keeping this truth in mind will help the student of God's Word to get free from the great religious confusion and darkness on the question, What is a human soul, and can it die like the lower animals? If your copy of the King James Version or American Standard Version has marginal reference readings, you can prove the above by the references of verses 20 and 30 to the margin.

During this fifth creative day there may have been a falling of further belts of the aqueous canopy at the poles, resulting this time in the destruction of animal or creature life by the icy waters, some forms of animal life being wiped out which do not exist today. This destructive process, together with further upheavals of the earth's crust, was, no doubt, responsible for those great limestone deposits known as "shell-fish cemeteries". However, as this fifth day was thousands of years long, newer forms of creature life would be produced by divine power after each such deluge.

The final work-day was now reached. "And God said, Let the land bring forth LIVING SOUL after its kind, tame-beast and creeping thing and wild-beast of the land after its kind. And it was so. And God made the wild-beast of the land after its kind, and the tame-beast after its kind, and every creeping thing of the ground after its kind. And God saw that it was good." —Genesis 1: 24, 25, *Roth.*

What forms or kinds of animal souls were first to be created on this sixth creative day is not stated. Doubtless some forms whose fossils or petrified remains have been found imbedded deep in the earth were destroyed by further falling belts from the canopy and by the resulting inundations rushing down like tidal waves from the poles. The creative day not being twenty-four hours long, but several thousand years long, Jehovah's power would replenish the earth with animal life of like or new kinds. It was doubtless after the last of such devastating deluges on the sixth day that the description at Genesis 2: 4-6 applies: "These are the generations of the heavens and of the earth when they were created, in the day that Jehovah God made earth and heaven. And no plant of the field was yet in the earth, and no herb of the field had yet sprung up; for Jehovah God had not caused it to rain upon the earth: and there was not a man to till the ground; but there went up a mist from the earth, and watered the whole face of the ground."—*A.R.V.*

CHAPTER V

HUMAN SOULS CREATED

OD made the earth to be inhabited by man. The sixth creative day was closing. The masterpiece of God's earthly creation was yet to come, to preside over all lower animal creatures and to do so in the image of God, who presides over all creation. To this end this earthly masterwork must be intelligent above the subject animals. It must be in the likeness of the Creator by possessing the needed measure of wisdom, power, love, and justice. Again the Lord God used his only begotten Son, the Word, as a master workman, and to him Jehovah God spoke when finally ready to bring forth the climax of his earthly creatures.

"And God said, Let us make man in our image, after our likeness: and let them have dominion over the fish of the sea, and over the fowl of the air, and over the cattle, and over all the earth, and over every creeping thing that creepeth upon the earth. So God created man in his own image, in the image of God created he him; male and female created he them. And God blessed them, and God said unto them, Be fruitful, and multiply, and replenish the earth, and subdue it: and have dominion over the fish of the sea, and over the fowl of the air, and over

every living thing that moveth upon the earth."
(Genesis 1: 26-28) Here the Creator gave to the
man and his mate a mandate respecting the
earth. The mandate included more than being
in the image of God by exercising dominion over
all the earth and its living creatures. God by
his "master workman" had made the first human
pair by his direct power. He would make no
more of them directly. He gifted them with the
power to reproduce their kind by marriage
union; unlike the angels, who "neither marry,
nor are given in marriage", all of them being
God's individual creations by his Word. Therefore the most responsible part of that divine
mandate to the perfect man and woman was to
"be fruitful and multiply" their own human kind
and to fill the earth with a Godlike offspring.

The great Provider favored this beautiful human pair with perfect freedom from want and
freedom from fear. There was plenty for all,
man and beast alike. "And God said, Lo! I have
given to you every herb yielding seed which is
on the face of all the land, and every tree wherein is the fruit of a tree yielding seed; to you
shall it be for food; and to every living thing of
the land, and to every bird of the heavens, and
to every thing that moveth on the land wherein
is a LIVING SOUL, every green herb for food.
And it was so. And God saw every thing which
he had made, and lo! it was very good. So it was
evening, and it was morning, the sixth day."
(Genesis 1: 29-31, *Roth.*) A period of about
42,000 years had passed by now since God said

toward the earth, "Let there be light." After all the preparatory work of those thousands of years the loving Creator Jehovah had given man and woman a start that was "very good".

Jehovah having pronounced it "very good", it was nothing short of a perfect start. By man's faithful continuance in the carrying out of the divine mandate to him things could remain perfect for man in that free original world in which man was created. What more work of Jehovah God was needed in man's behalf? None; and so the Creator turned over to man the dominion of the earth as God's visible earthly representative. Man's work and privileges must thenceforth proceed according to the divine mandate.

"Thus the heavens and the earth were finished, and all the host of them. And on the seventh day God ended his work which he had made; and he rested on the seventh day from all his work which he had made. And God blessed the seventh day, and sanctified it: because that in it he had rested from all his work which God created and made." (Genesis 2: 1-3) It is foolish to think this means that Almighty God was exhausted or weary from his work on this small planet earth and that thereafter he was obliged to rest for personal recovery. "Hast thou not known? hast thou not heard? The everlasting God, Jehovah, the Creator of the ends of the earth, fainteth not, neither is weary; there is no searching of his understanding. It is he that sitteth above the circle of the earth, and the inhabitants thereof are as grasshoppers; that

stretcheth out the heavens as a curtain, and
spreadeth them out as a tent to dwell in."
(Isaiah 40: 28, 22, *A.R.V.*) Hence, when Exodus
31: 17 states that "on the seventh day he rested,
and was refreshed", it means he had achieved
the work he had purposed toward the earth, and
he felt the refreshing exhilaration and joy of
achievement. He rested, too, in the knowledge
that nothing that might develop thereafter could
thwart or successfully block his purpose as to
the earth. He would be equal to any emergency
that could arise, and would overcome it.

Man's time the moon would mark off into
months. The statement at Genesis 2: 1-3 does
not say that God divided time for the perfect
man and woman into seven-day periods and
commanded them to observe a rest or sabbath-
day every seventh day. As long as this perfect
pair observed the divine mandate they would
rest in their Creator and enjoy freedom of worship and freedom from fear and want, and
thereby they would enjoy God's sabbath rest
with him. They would enjoy a perpetual sabbath
by faith and obedience to him.

The account of creation of man given in Genesis, chapter one, is a general one. That in chapter two is a detailed one, filling out the shorter
account above. In this chapter two the name of
Jehovah appears for the first time, because
thenceforth the name of the Lord God becomes
involved with man on the earth. The account is
very simple and revealing as to the human soul
and how it was created. Study the language:

"And Jehovah God formed man of the dust of the ground, and breathed into his nostrils the breath of life; and man became a living soul." —Genesis 2:7, *A.R.V.*

Notice here the same expression "living soul" as in connection with the lower animals when created. In the Hebrew text the expression is *nephesh chayyah*. (Genesis 1:20, 21, 24, 30) God made the human creature, man, or Adam, to be a "living soul" by first creating the human body and then breathing into it, not a soul, but the "breath of life", the energizing power, and then combining that life force with the body. A "living soul" means a living creature; and on earth it means a creature that breathes while alive. Man, or Adam, was a living soul like the lower animals, having a material body and breathing the atmosphere of the firmament the same as did those animals; only man, or Adam, was of a higher order, having an upright form and being of far superior intelligence. He was also in God's likeness and image. The lower animal souls die. Can the human soul die? And if it can die, is it nevertheless possible for it under right conditions to live forever? The Bible gives answer.

In the section of the earth called "Eden", which means "Pleasure", and in the eastern part thereof, Jehovah God planted a garden or paradise, and there he put the man, to "dress it and to keep it". It was in truth a pleasant place, the only specially prepared place on earth, and its life-sustaining trees and watercourses are

briefly described at Genesis 2: 8-15. Though but
newly created, Adam was fully matured and
perfect in stature, and he could talk with intelligence. The Creator caused Adam to get acquainted with the animals in the garden, that he,
as one having dominion over them, might name
them. Mark carefully the reading of the account: "God had formed from the ground every
living thing of the field, and every bird of the
heavens, which he brought in unto the man, that
he might see what he should call it, and whatsoever the man should call it, any LIVING SOUL, that
should be the name thereof. So the man gave
names to all the tame-beasts, and to the birds
of the heavens, and to all the wild-beasts of the
field; but for man had there not been found a
helper as his counterpart."—Genesis 2: 19, 20,
Roth.

Here the Record again applies the term "living soul" to the birds and other animals, the
same as to perfect man in God's image and likeness. The animals were mortal souls and had
been dying prior to man, either due to the
limited span of life or due to the creative processes' yet operating about the earth, such as
falling canopy belts from above the firmament.
Is man also a mortal soul? That is, can a human
soul die? Does it perforce have to die, like the
lower animals, or can it survive forever? Is it
immortal?

True answers to these questions are revealed
in Jehovah's law to Adam. "And the LORD God
commanded the man, saying, Of every tree of

the garden thou mayest freely eat: but of the
tree of the knowledge of good and evil, thou
shalt not eat of it: for in the day that thou
eatest thereof thou shalt surely die."—Genesis
2: 16, 17.

This proves the human soul to be mortal, even
when man is perfect and sinless as Adam was
on receiving this command of God. If the human
soul were immortal God could not have said
that man's disobedience to God's law would
bring the penalty of death upon man. Adam, the
human creature, was a soul. He had no soul
within him that was separate and distinct from
his human body and that could exist independ-
ently even should the dissolution of the human
body occur. God, who had made the human soul
by the union of the earthly body with the breath
of life, could unmake that soul if it proved rebellious against God's law. Then that soul would
cease to be. It would die, forasmuch as the living creature, the man, who is the living soul,
would die. So reads Ezekiel 18: 4, 20.—Psalm
104: 29.

Nephesh, the Hebrew term for *soul,* is also
many times translated *life* in the English Bible,
whether it means the life of a beast or life of a
man. Therefore, if a creature is possessed of
life, it can be said of that creature that there is
a living soul in him. For example, Genesis 1: 30
reads: "And to every living thing of the land,
and to every bird of the heavens, and to every
thing that moveth on the land wherein is a living
soul." (*Roth.,* and the *A.R.V.,* margin) Also,

2 Kings 4:27 reads: "Her soul is vexed within her." When the prophet Elijah miraculously restored a child to life he said to God: "Let this child's soul come into him again." "And the LORD heard the voice of Elijah; and the soul of the child came into him again, and he revived." —1 Kings 17:21, 22.

Because the blood circulating within the blood vessels is the basis of human and animal life, the life is said to be in the blood: "Flesh with the soul thereof, the blood thereof, shall ye not eat; and surely your blood of your souls will I require." (Genesis 9:4, 5, *Roth.*, margin) "As for the soul of the flesh, in the blood it is, therefore have I given it unto you upon the altar, to put a propitiatory-covering over your souls; for the blood it is which by virtue of the soul maketh propitiation." (Leviticus 17:11, *Roth.*, margin) Therefore the life, or *soul,* can not survive and exist as an intelligent creature apart from the body. Like the blood drained from the body, so life or soul does not exist apart from the body. When the life forces are withdrawn from the body, the *soul* or living creature dies, and not merely the body.

In the warning to Adam of a death penalty for disobedience in eating the forbidden fruit Jehovah God made no mention of a place of conscious torment, either temporary or eternal, after death. In all the divine record of creation it says nothing of making a burning "hell" of torment to provide for torturing human souls there. No such place ever existed, and it would be hateful to Jehovah and out of harmony with his wisdom, justice and love for him to provide such a place of everlasting torment for sinners. What is more, it is impossible for sinners to be sent to such a place, because at death the sinner soul dies and ceases to be. "The wages of sin is death." (Romans 6:23) If after the disobedient partaking of the fruit God confined the human soul at death in a torment hell, as taught by religion, God would be changing the announced penalty by the enactment of an *ex post facto* law, a law made after the committing of the crime. However, Jehovah says: "I change not." —Malachi 3:6.

Without wresting the Scriptures, it is seen that the human soul is mortal and that Almighty God can put it to death for sin. Contrary to religion's teaching that the human soul is immortal, God's Word of truth plainly states: "The soul that sinneth, it shall die." (Ezekiel 18:4, 20) This does not mean, however, that the human soul cannot live forever on earth. In fact, God made provision for man to inhabit and live in paradise on earth forever, by causing to "grow every tree that is pleasant to the sight, and good for food; the tree of life also in the midst of the garden, and the tree of knowledge of good and evil". (Genesis 2:9) What if man forever held back from eating the forbidden fruit of the tree of the knowledge of good and evil, or until God himself should lift the prohibition on the tree after a sufficient test upon humankind? Adam and his offspring could then live forever on earth. Hence, while under test, Adam's right to everlasting life was only conditional, dependent upon obedience. Doubtless, after humankind would prove faithful and obedient under the test, God would lead man to the "tree of life also in the midst of the garden" and grant man to eat thereof, so symbolizing and guaranteeing to obedient tested man the right to life eternal.

After publishing the law of obedience God provided Adam with a wife, that there might be human offspring. God by his Word had made Adam direct from the elements of the earth; but with a rib taken from Adam's side as a foundation God built up a perfect woman, a female human, that they two might be one flesh. It was then that their Creator blessed them and gave them the divine mandate to "be fruitful and multiply and fill the earth". (Genesis 2: 18-25; 1: 28, *Roth.*) It is wrong to apply to the perfect Adam and Eve the scripture at Hebrews 9: 27: "It is appointed unto men once to die, but after this the judgment." That scripture applied to the Jewish high priest on the Atonement Day and, later, to the Antitype thereof. As for Adam and Eve, a course of obedience which led to eternal life on earth was appointed to them. The searcher of the inspired Scriptures can therefore detect the untruthfulness of the religious catechism which says, without Scripture proof: "The chief blessings intended for Adam and Eve had they remained faithful to God, were a constant state of happiness in this life and ever-lasting glory in the next." Jehovah God held out no hope to them of a "next life" supposedly in heavenly glory. For Adam and Eve it was a case of either continuing their present life by reason of unceasing obedience to God or death eternal for disobedience.

Adam and Eve lived on earth in a free world, because there was no sin or unrighteousness in it. They had the truth which makes the truth-keeper free. They worshiped God in spirit and in truth amid the open paradise of Eden. They had no tormenting fears, but only the godly fear which seeks to avoid displeasing God. They were given no law of the Ten Commandments. They were perfect, whereas 1 Timothy 1: 9, 10 states: "The law is not made for a righteous man, but for the lawless and disobedient, for the ungodly and for sinners, for unholy and pro-fane, for murderers of fathers and murderers of mothers, for manslayers, for whoremongers, for them that defile themselves with mankind, for menstealers, for liars, for perjured per-sons, and if there be any other thing that is contrary to sound doctrine."

No definite time was set for them to begin carrying out that part of the divine mandate concerning filling the earth with their offspring. They were under no appointment to death, and all eternity was before them; and there was no pressing obligation or any undue haste re-quired. Dressing and keeping the garden, and exercising dominion over the lower animal creation, filled their days with joyful activity and untiring interest and divine blessing.

CHAPTER VI

LOSS OF FREEDOM

DAM and Eve, reflecting in perfection the image and likeness of their Creator, were the earthly, visible part of the universal organization of Jehovah God. At that time the man could be spoken of as "Adam, which was the son of God". (Luke 3: 38) He and his wife were part of the universal family of God in heaven and in earth. The faithful spirit creatures were the heavenly, invisible part of God's universal organization. Some of these had dealings with the perfect man and woman while in Eden. Up to the time of the issuing of the divine mandate to this human pair, God dealt with them through his Word, his only begotten Son, to whom he said on the sixth day: "Let us make man in our image, after our likeness." And then through his Son God stated to man, male and female, the terms of the mandate. This was truthful testimony to them and was the law of truth. It was a Theocratic law, because it expressed God's rule of action and it came from Him. It marked out freedom's course for humankind.

One day error invaded the glorious garden. Such error was not from God's beloved Son, for he is the Word of God, and always God's

utterances by his Word are faithful, reliable,
founded on fact, and durable, and hence true.
Adam and Eve had been given the truth and
could combat the error, if they relied upon God's
word in faithfulness. There was no need for
God to prevent the error from coming in contact with them for a test. "His truth shall be
thy shield and buckler," and by it they could
defend their freedom. (Psalm 91: 4) The in-
trusion of error, therefore, betrayed that there
was another spirit presence operating unseen
in the garden. How so?

"Now the serpent was more subtle than any
beast of the field which Jehovah God had made.
And he said unto the woman, Yea, hath God
said, Ye shall not eat of any tree of the garden?"
(Genesis 3: 1, 2, *A.R.V.*) Adam was away, and
Eve was alone at the time. It could not have
been the dumb creature itself, the serpent, that
thus spoke and raised the question about man's
freedom in the garden. Someone was back of
that serpent in thus speaking and audaciously
raising a question over the truthfulness and
rightness of God's law. It must have been an
unseen spirit creature who was masking his
identity behind that visible form of the serpent,
that crafty beast which seemed to have knowledge and insight more so than other beasts.
Who was this one who would appear as a re-
vealer of vital secrets? We are not left in doubt;
the answer, at 2 Corinthians 11: 3, 14, is: "The
serpent beguiled Eve through his subtilty, . . .
And no marvel; for Satan himself is trans-

formed into an angel of light." Further evidence points to Lucifer, the son of the morning.

This circumstance calls attention to an arrangement invisible to Adam and Eve that had been established over the earth by their Creator. After the close of the sixth creative day, and after he gave the divine mandate to the human couple in Paradise, their heavenly Father set up a protectorate over them, a special heavenly organization having the exclusive care of them. This invisible organization over them and higher than they served as a particular *heavens,* whereas Adam and Eve in their dominion over the animal creation were the visible *earth,* figuratively speaking. These two parts, the heavenly and the earthly, constituted the original world over this terrestrial globe. It was a clean, perfect and free world, a world of light and truth. The invisible or heavenly part of the world was made up of holy angels who were placed under Lucifer, the cherub who was responsible to be always loyal to the Divine Throne and to uphold it without fail.

The details of the above arrangement are given in later parts of the Divine Record. Lucifer proceeded to set himself up as a heavenly king and to establish the organization under him like a rock, like "Tyre", which means "rock". His course of action became cause for a dirge or lamentation over him, to this effect: "Thou sealest up the sum, full of wisdom, and perfect in beauty. Thou wast in Eden, the garden of God; every precious stone was thy covering, the

sardius, the topaz, and the diamond, the beryl,
the onyx, and the jasper, the sapphire, the
emerald, and the carbuncle, and gold: the workmanship of thy tabrets and of thy pipes was
in thee; in the day that thou wast created they
were prepared. Thou wast the anointed cherub
that covereth: and I set thee, so that thou wast
upon the holy mountain of God; thou hast
walked up and down in the midst of the stones
of fire. Thou wast perfect in thy ways from the
day that thou wast created, till unrighteousness
was found in thee."—Ezekiel 28:11-15, *A.R.V.*

Lucifer's course became the "way of a serpent upon a rock". (Proverbs 30:19) He observed the worship that man accorded to God,
and Lucifer fell to lusting for that worship for
himself. To turn man against the true and living
God, the Supreme One, Lucifer must lie about
Him and must stir up self-seeking in man and
then present himself as man's bright-shining
benefactor. Then he could, under the guise of
good and with a mock cry of freedom from all
rationing of the necessities of life and freedom
of opportunity for self-betterment, mislead man
into breaking God's righteous and reasonable
law. After gaining the fear, gratitude and worship of man, Lucifer would set himself up above
the angels of God and would deify himself as a
god like unto Jehovah God. Such pride leads to
destruction, and such haughty spirit leads to a
terrible fall like as of a lofty tree cut down to
earth. Prophetically it is written, at Isaiah
14:12-14: "How art thou fallen from heaven, O

Lucifer, son of the morning! how art thou cut down to the ground, which didst weaken the nations! For thou hast said in thine heart, I will ascend into heaven, I will exalt my throne above the stars of God: I will sit also upon the mount of the congregation, in the sides of the north: I will ascend above the heights of the clouds; I will be like the Most High."

By thus rebelling from under Jehovah God and aiming to be equal with him or even superior, Lucifer became blinded into thinking he was making himself free and independent. In fact, though, he was enslaving himself to a traitorous ambition and he became the servant to sin of treachery and rebellion. Almighty God allowed Lucifer the liberty to take this course, but that wicked one became wrapped up in the toils of lies and religion, of which he became the author and inventor. Lucifer thereby lost the liberty of the sons of God, became an outcast from the universal organization of Jehovah. He came under the sentence of everlasting destruction, which he cannot escape but which must overtake him in due time.

Pretending innocence and surprise, he asked Eve why she was not eating of the tree of the knowledge of good and evil. "And the woman said unto the serpent, We may eat of the fruit of the trees of the garden: but of the fruit of the tree which is in the midst of the garden, God hath said, Ye shall not eat of it, neither shall ye touch it, lest ye die." (Genesis 3:2, 3) Eve had accepted that statement of truth from

her husband and had observed the warning in
order to continue living. They had felt and suffered no want as a result of refraining from
eating the forbidden fruit; in fact, eating of it
would mean to suffer the want of even life itself.
Better life with something than death with loss
of all.

"And the serpent said unto the woman, Ye
shall not surely die; for God doth know that in
the day ye eat thereof, then your eyes shall be
opened, and ye shall be as gods, knowing good
and evil." (Genesis 3: 4, 5) This was a direct
lie, the first one ever told, and it made Jehovah
God appear to be a liar. It was the first sin, and
it resulted in the murder or loss of life to the
first human pair. Lucifer, by this lie and slander
against God, became the *Devil*, or slanderer of
God. "The devil sinneth from the beginning."
"He was a murderer from the beginning, and
abode not in the truth, because there is no truth
in him. When he speaketh a lie, he speaketh of
his own: for he is a liar, and the father of it."
(1 John 3: 8; John 8: 44) Jehovah's good name
for truth, righteousness, unselfishness, and supremacy as God now became at stake and must
henceforth be vindicated and the Devil be
proved a liar.

The statement of that old Serpent, the Devil,
was a lie as to things divine and it affected the
creature's attitude of worship. Hence the utter-
ing of that lie as a guide to conduct and worship was the introducing of religion, to ensnare
humankind away from the worship of Jehovah

God in spirit and in truth. The Devil, in fact, was striving to set himself up as god 'like unto the Most High', and he held out the expectation to Eve and her husband of becoming "like gods", like *Elohim,* or, "as God." (*A.R.V.*) What honest person can deny that such system of worship and deification is *religion?* and that the Devil was the one to introduce religion? It is religion because it is not the worship of Jehovah God, the worship which God's only begotten Son, the Word, practices. Religion is based on the word of a creature rather than on the word and commands of the true and living God. No one can point to any religious ceremony or formalism that Adam and Eve performed in Eden up to that time. In innocence they followed the word and command of Jehovah God.

Religionists, however, will point to James 1: 26, 27 and say: 'Do not these texts call the worship of God *religion?*' According to some English translations of the original Greek text it would appear so, because they read thus: "If any man among you seem to be religious, and bridleth not his tongue, but deceiveth his own heart, this man's religion is vain. Pure religion and undefiled before God and the Father is this, To visit the fatherless and widows in their affliction, and to keep himself unspotted from the world."

Examination of these texts reveals that the Greek word translated "religion" is the word *threskeia,* and "religious" is *threskos.* These two words, however, have no connection with the

Thracians of ancient Greece, who were very superstitious religionists and devil-worshipers and therefore inventors of religious mysteries. Instead, *threskeia* is drawn from the Hebrew word *darash, to seek,* that is, to seek God, as at 1 Chronicles 28: 9; 2 Chronicles 15: 2; 17: 4; Psalm 9: 10; and elsewhere. Hence the Syriac Version, which is a translation into the language Jesus Christ spoke, renders *threskos* and *threskeia* properly; and Murdock's English translation of the Syriac Version renders James 1: 26, 27 as follows: "And if any one thinketh that he *worshippeth God,* and doth not restrain his tongue, but his heart deceiveth him; his *worship* is vain. For the *worship* that is pure and holy before God the Father is this: to visit the fatherless and the widows in their affliction, and that one keep himself unspotted from the world." Martin Luther's Version translated *threskeia* as *Gottesdienst,* or *God's service.*

At Colossians 2: 18 the Authorized or King James Version translates *threskeia* as *worshipping,* but at Acts 26: 5 as *religion,* wrongfully, because Paul the apostle there used *threskeia* to mean *form of worship.* It is true that religion, such as the Pharisees of old practiced among the Jews, is a form of worship, but the worship of God in spirit and in truth is not religion. True worship in spirit is of God; religion is of God's opposer, who schemes to make himself "like the Most High". The word *religion* is drawn from the Latin word *religio,* which word, from the very beginning of its use long before Christ, was applied by the Latin heathens of Italy to their practice of demonism or religion. Will "more religion", as now clamored for, produce a free postwar world? For a right conclusion reflect on what religion's introduction did to the original world.

Prior to the religious doctrines of the Devil through the serpent, Eve had not felt any need of freedom from want. Human needs were abundantly supplied. Now, however, through entertaining the serpent's suggestions, Eve's heart felt moved with selfishness. She felt she was missing something, and that by adopting religious doctrines and following them she and her husband would become Godlike and become free and independent, wanting nothing. "And when the woman saw that the tree was good for food, and that it was pleasant to the eyes, and a tree to be desired to make one wise, she took of the fruit thereof, and did eat, and gave also unto her husband with her; and he did eat." —Genesis 3: 6.

As to Adam's act it is written, at 1 Timothy 2: 13, 14: "For Adam was first formed, then Eve. And Adam was not deceived, but the woman being deceived was in the transgression." Eve, though formed second, ran ahead of Adam and showed willfulness in sin. She was *deceived* in that, when she ate, she found she did not get what she expected, but the serpent had *cheated* her. (Genesis 3: 13, *Roth.*, margin) Nevertheless, her willful selfishness and her insubordination to her head, her husband, made her party to the transgression.

Inasmuch as Adam was not deceived, he did not enter into the transgression with any hope of gaining what the serpent promised to Eve, but in order to keep her for himself. He would become a lawbreaker with her and suffer the same destiny with her, rather than be deprived of her. He preferred her to such life as he had known before her creation. Neither Adam nor his wife maintained integrity, that is, soundness, blamelessness or perfection of obedience toward God. Adam, being her earthly head, backed up her course of rebellion by joining in her trespass, and therefore the responsibility for the transgression falls chiefly upon his head. The condition of the future offspring was primarily affected by what he did rather than what Eve did. God could have created another perfect wife for Adam, if need be, in order that the divine mandate to fill the earth might be carried out. Hence the divine judgment declares: "By one man sin entered into the world, and death by sin."—Romans 5:12.

Jehovah God had said to Adam that, if disobedient, "thou shalt surely die." The serpent said to Eve: "Ye shall not surely die." On the serpent's religious contradiction of God's Word are based the doctrines of immortality of the human soul, and of temporary punishment of church-members in a blazing "Purgatory", and of eternal torment of unconverted sinners in a "hell" of literal fire and brimstone. By the facts which followed, whose word was vindicated as true, sure and reliable, Jehovah's or the Devil's?

CHAPTER VII

DELIVERANCE PROMISED

HE fulfillment of the divine mandate to multiply and fill the earth with a righteous offspring had been set before the perfect man and woman. That was a joyful prospect. It was to be carried out under conditions that would benefit the offspring and glorify God, fulfilling his purpose. At the time that Lucifer was still faithful God had given him a special organization of holy angels and had placed Lucifer over these, and these all composed a righteous heavens over the man and woman in Eden.

Being the "anointed cherub that covereth", Lucifer was a righteous invisible overlord over them, and under his righteous overlordship the divine mandate was to be carried forward to its grand result, a populated Paradise earth. Adam and Eve were not authorized to bring forth and fill the earth with imperfect, unrighteous children; but, being perfect and in God's likeness, they were to be fruitful and multiply their kind in righteousness and thus to fill all earth with Godlike men and women, all worshiping Jehovah. Seeing the wonderful possibilities by means of this human pair with reproductive powers, Lucifer set out to block the fulfillment of the divine mandate and to have the earth peopled with humans practicing religion and worshiping Lucifer instead of Jehovah God.

The divine mandate was a pleasant prospect for the perfect pair to contemplate. The thought of their first baby must have been thrilling, as well as the fulfilled mandate, an earthful of stalwart men and lovely women, all descended from themselves as the fountainhead and all brought up by them "in the nurture and admonition of the Lord". The powers of reproduction had been implanted in their bodies, not because the human race was to be a dying race and hence reproduction would be needed to continue the race in existence, but in order to people the earth with humans proving themselves worthy of the right to everlasting life. All would be one grand human family, children of God. There would be no economic problems due to selfish commerce nor political disputes and differences, because the rule of the earth would be Theocratic, God's rule through his righteous invisible overlord. So it would be all around the earth. There would be no need of wars, on the theory that the earth was becoming too crowded and it was necessary to fight with death-dealing weapons and kill off some millions in order to relieve the overcrowding. To the contrary, the earth would become more and more densely inhabited as new generations were born, until the earth was entirely comfortably filled. Then generating of children would stop according to the will of God.

Having come to the perfect accomplishment
of the divine mandate, perfect humankind in
full self-control and obedience to the command
of God would cease to reproduce. The race
would come to its full growth. During the time
that it was being expanded, more and more of
the earth's surface would be subdued and the
boundaries of the Edenic paradise extended out,
until at length Paradise encompassed the whole
earth and made it a glorious sphere in God's
spacious universe. This earthly garden of delight the full-grown perfect human family would
occupy forever and in it glorify God. His purpose to have this divine mandate realized in
righteousness will not fail. The time of its fulfillment has by him now been reserved for the
future when the right conditions are established.

As soon as Adam and his mate had eaten of
the forbidden fruit and broken the Theocratic
law, they realized within themselves their un-
worthiness and unfitness to carry out the divine
mandate. "And the eyes of them both were
opened, and they knew that they were naked;
and they sewed fig-leaves together, and made
themselves aprons. And they heard the voice
of Jehovah God walking in the garden in the
cool of the day: and the man and his wife hid
themselves from the presence of Jehovah God
amongst the trees of the garden."—Genesis
3: 7, 8, *A.R.V.*

Adam and his wife did not die immediately
on eating the fruit. Their invisible overlord,
Lucifer, "the anointed cherub that covereth,"

had induced them to sin against God, and he also refused to apply his power of death against them, in order that he might uphold his lie, "Ye shall not surely die." There was one other kind of tree in that Paradise, namely, "the tree of life also in the midst of the garden." Reasonably, the unfaithful Lucifer, who knew the location of the "tree of life", would conduct them to it as early or quickly as possible. If they partook of its fruit, then apparently they would be covered by a guarantee of life for ever. Then if God would execute Adam and Eve, it would belie the meaning and purpose of the "tree of life" and would prove His word of guarantee untrustworthy. If, however, God did not execute them because he respected the meaning of the "tree of life" and their partaking of it, then the Devil's words would be upheld, "Ye shall not surely die." This would prove God's law unworthy of being kept and its penalties unable to be enforced by Him. It would cast doubt upon His being almighty. The artful Devil thought he could corner God and put him into an impossible dilemma. God, though, was not slumbering. Alertly he blocked the traitor's scheme.

Jehovah's trusted officer having failed him, he himself took charge of the case for judgment which had now arisen. By his ever faithful executive officer, the Word, Jehovah God made known to Adam and Eve His presence at the garden. It was as if walking through the garden, and it approached them. They saw no one, but heard the evidence of the presence of the Judge.

They knew they were on judgment and that the facts of the case were against them. Their fig-leaf aprons were not enough to hide their embarrassment; they hid among the garden trees. It was not necessary for the Judge to be visible and for them to see the Judge with their naked eye in order to be on judgment. This makes clear how in the judgment of the nations of their descendants it is not necessary for Jehovah's Judge to appear in a visible body, neither for the nations of earth to see him literally, in order for them to go on judgment. The Lord's Judicial Officer, being a divine Spirit, would be invisible to all the nations gathered before him, and yet he would make his presence discernible by the visible signs of his presence which he would make appear.—Matthew 24: 3-14.

Not that the Lord failed to spot them hidden behind the trees, but, in order to grant them a fair hearing, Jehovah by his Judge summoned them out of hiding. "And the LORD God called unto Adam, and said unto him, Where art thou? And he said, I heard thy voice in the garden, and I was afraid, because I was naked; and I hid myself." By reason of yielding to the religion of that Old Serpent, the Devil, and committing the sin of disobedience, one of the great freedoms had been lost to man, the freedom from fear. They may have felt also that God had neglected to provide clothing for them, because now they experienced feelings of shame of nakedness.

"And he said, Who told thee that thou wast naked? Hast thou eaten of the tree, whereof I

commanded thee that thou shouldest not eat?
And the man said, The woman whom thou gavest to be with me, she gave me of the tree, and
I did eat." (Genesis 3:9-12) This sounded like
casting reproach upon Jehovah God for giving
Adam the woman, because God had made her to
be a helpmeet for man instead of a temptress.

"And the LORD God said unto the woman,
What is this that thou hast done? And the
woman said, The serpent beguiled me, and I did
eat." (Genesis 3:13) By the process of elimina-
tion the Lord got down to the bottom of the
matter, that all the evidence might point to the
first starter of this outbreak of rebellion. He
must establish whether this originated with humankind, or whether the invisible overlord of
man, the covering cherub Lucifer, connived at
man's sin or, worse still, was the inducer thereof
and was himself a rebel and traitor, guilty of
mismanagement. All the evidence worked down
to this last point. The 'father of lies' was detected and exposed. On him God first expressed
judgment.

"And the LORD God said unto the serpent, Because thou hast done this, thou art cursed above
all cattle, and above every beast of the field;
upon thy belly shalt thou go, and dust shalt thou
eat all the days of thy life: and I will put enmity between thee and the woman, and between
thy seed and her seed; it shall bruise thy head,
and thou shalt bruise his heel." (Genesis
3:14, 15) With such fearful phrase Jehovah
God was not addressing the mere serpentine

beast, but the wicked spirit person who had obsessed the serpent and had caused it to speak the devilish lie to Eve.

With those words of curse Jehovah asserted his supremacy over all creatures. He was answering the challenge of the Devil and was dooming the purpose of that wicked rebel to disgraceful failure. As it is written to the "seed" of the "woman": "The God of peace shall bruise Satan under your feet shortly." (Romans 16: 20) There is no food in dust, but it is dry and lifeless. On suchlike the Old Serpent, the Devil, must feed and have no hope of eternal life. God's blessing was removed from him, and he was humiliated from out of God's holy organization. This should have served as warning notice to all the angels who had been serving under Lucifer.

As Jehovah God was not here addressing the literal serpent on the ground, so also he was not talking of the disobedient woman Eve, nor of any other woman descended from Eve, including the Jewish virgin, Mary of Bethlehem. By the term *woman* He was designating something greater, something symbolized by a pure and faithful woman, namely, God's universal organization of holy creatures.

God himself is Head over this organization. It is wedded or united to Him beyond divorcing and is subject to him. From it he brings forth such special servants as he wills. Thus, to use a figure of speech, his holy organization is God's "woman". It is so written, at Isaiah 54: 5, 13:

"For thy Maker is thy husband; Jehovah of hosts is his name: . . . And all thy children shall be taught of Jehovah; and great shall be the peace of thy children." (*A.R.V.*) With such words Jehovah speaks to the organization called "Zion". Moreover, the angels of heaven do not marry nor are any given as females in marriage, and there are no women in heaven. Hence when the symbolic book of Revelation speaks of a woman in heaven, it could not mean a literal female from this earth, but must mean God's organization Zion, his "woman", guided by his heavenly light. "And there appeared a great wonder in heaven; a woman clothed with the sun, and the moon under her feet, and upon her head a crown of twelve stars." (Revelation 12:1) It is between this "woman" and that Old Serpent, the Devil, or Satan, that Jehovah God puts enmity or hostility and hatred. It means war.

That Satan would form an organization in opposition to God and to God's holy organization, Jehovah foretold by speaking to the Old Serpent regarding "thy seed" as in contrast with "her seed", the offspring of God's organization. Between the two seeds must be opposition and conflict. To this end the Old Serpent, the Devil, would build up an organization symbolized by an unclean wicked woman, whose name is called "Babylon" in Holy Writ. This official organization of Satan the Devil would mimic God's organization and bring forth a sinful "seed" to fight against and persecute the

"seed" of God's devoted "woman" or organization.

Who shall win in the long-enduring conflict?
Referring not to his "woman", but to her

"seed", Jehovah served this unchangeable notice on the Old Serpent, the Devil: "It shall bruise thy head, and thou shalt bruise his heel." It is therefore a wresting of the Scriptures and is a religious attempt to support Mariolatry when the Catholic Douay Version Bible translates God's words: *"She* shall crush thy head, and thou shalt lie in wait for *her* heel."

The footnote of the Douay Version says such rendering is made according to "divers of the fathers" and "conformably to the Latin" (The Vulgate). Certainly, though, it is not conformably to God's Word, which was here written originally in Hebrew. In the Hebrew text the word *seed* (*zera‘*) is masculine, and the pronoun which the Hebrew uses is not feminine, but is masculine, *he* (*hu*). Likewise, the possessive pronoun thereafter used is not feminine (*her*), but is masculine (*his*). Hence all the accurate and non-Catholic translations read correctly with the original Hebrew: *"He* shall crush thy head, but thou shalt crush *his* heel." —*Roth.; A.R.V.*

Thereby the great Father of the "woman's" seed made known that He would lay open His and her "seed" to the hostile acts and operations of the Old Serpent, the Devil, and his organization. God was also throwing open to Satan the Devil the liberty to attack and persecute the "seed" of God's "woman", to let Satan see whether he could by such means break the integrity of the promised "seed" to their God Jehovah, and whether Satan could thus drive

them out of God's organization and so prove
himself superior to the Most High God. Such
Satanic action would cause this "seed" great
pain and some injury as if by a 'bruising of its
heel' by a snake lying hidden and striking behind one's back. However, there would be a limit
to such liberty of uninterrupted action granted
to Satan and his "seed". That fixed limit would
be when the "seed" of unbroken integrity would
gain the victory by God's almighty power and
would crush the Serpent and its generation of
vipers lifeless.

By talking to unfaithful Lucifer under the
symbol of the serpent Jehovah God showed that
the first devil had now come into existence by
slandering God. *Devil* means *slanderer*. Liken-
ing him to a *serpent* means the Devil is a *deceiver*. By raising up opposition the unfaithful
Lucifer became *Satan,* which name means *opposer*. Symbolizing him as a monstrous snake or
dragon means that he is a great *swallower, de-
vourer* and *crusher,* of God's righteous ones, if
possible. (Jeremiah 51: 34; Revelation 12: 3, 4)
The issue of God's good name and supremacy
had now been raised by the Devil. God sentenced him to destruction, but did not at once
destroy him, that He might put the issue to the
test until the time limit arrived.

CHAPTER VIII

DIVINE MANDATE SUSPENDED

S JEHOVAH sentenced Satan the Devil to extinction but permitted him to remain for a fixed time before execution of the sentence, so likewise the all-wise God did not immediately destroy the rebellious Adam and Eve. It was within God's power to kill them then and there in keeping with the penalty, "Thou shalt surely die." Then God could have created a new man and woman and issued to that innocent pair the divine mandate anew. Then the fulfillment of the divine mandate to populate the earth with righteous offspring would have gone forward without further delay and interruption. However, such divine mandate must be carried out under a righteous invisible overlord, accompanied by a heavenly spirit organization. Man's first overlord had turned traitor and wicked, but God was not then removing him or destroying him from his position of invisible power over the earth and its creatures. Hence, too, God let Adam and his wife remain, but not to fulfill the divine mandate. Having become unrighteous, they were not suitable to God's purpose and God withdrew from them that privilege. God let them remain

103

that their offspring might serve for the purpose of the fiery test of integrity, and that at last his holy name might be declared throughout all the earth and be vindicated.

Having set up court in Eden and first of all disposed of the Serpent's case by the judgment rendered, Jehovah God then turned to the first transgressor of the guilty human pair. "Unto the woman he said, I will greatly multiply thy sorrow and thy conception; in sorrow thou shalt bring forth children; and thy desire shall be to thy husband, and he shall rule over thee." —Genesis 3:16.

This was not an authorization to fulfill the divine mandate, neither was it a restatement of the mandate. It was not a saying that the carrying out of the mandate would be a painful process, and that it should be speeded up. Foreknowing the world-wide calamity that would be taking place about sixteen hundred years later and almost completely depopulating the earth, God could not in the above words to the woman have been authorizing a speed-up of the divine mandate. The world catastrophe to come would make such a thing of no advantage whatsoever and would completely neutralize the quickened human generation. Jehovah's words to the woman prove that the mandate had been withdrawn from Adam and his wife and would be reserved for worthy obedient ones later. For these deserving ones the fulfilling of the mandate will be no sorrow.

God pronounced the disobedient woman imperfect, and hence her body would not function as would that of a perfect woman or a righteous woman when bearing children to fulfill the mandate. To the contrary, there would be suffering, and it would increase to womankind. Besides, the woman, without any expressed desire on her husband's part, had run ahead and eaten of the forbidden fruit and then offered him some. Thereby she thrust upon him an inducement to selfish desire. Rebellion and fall into sin by the man resulted. Differently henceforth, the imperfect man should rule over the woman, and the expression of her desire should be made to him for satisfaction. Freedom from lust and pain was gone!

"And unto Adam he said, Because thou hast hearkened unto the voice of thy wife, and hast eaten of the tree, of which I commanded thee, saying, Thou shalt not eat of it: cursed is the ground for thy sake; in sorrow shalt thou eat of it all the days of thy life; thorns also and thistles shall it bring forth to thee; and thou shalt eat the herb of the field; in the sweat of thy face shalt thou eat bread, till thou return unto the ground; for out of it wast thou taken: for dust thou art, and unto dust shalt thou return." (Genesis 3: 17-19) In this pronouncement of judgment upon the man the great Giver of life declared the right of Adam to everlasting life to be canceled, and also his right to enjoy life in the paradise of Eden. Out into the open field he must now go!

In what way was the field or ground outside the paradise garden cursed? As yet in man's existence it had not rained upon the earth, "but there went up a mist from the earth, and watered the whole face of the ground." (Genesis 2: 5, 6) Instead of those fields outside the garden which God planted responding to this watering by the mist and everywhere blooming as a park or garden, the fields would incline to produce thorns and thistles. "For the earth which drinketh in the rain that cometh oft upon it, and bringeth forth herbs meet for them by whom it is dressed, receiveth blessing from God: but that which beareth thorns and briers is rejected, and is nigh unto cursing; whose end is to be burned." (Hebrews 6: 7, 8) In view of man's accursed rebellion God would not bless the soil of the field and relieve it of the thorn and thistle problem, but man would have to struggle with it.

Thenceforth man would not freely eat of the fruit trees of Paradise, but would be obliged to eat the herb of the field outside. No more dressing and keeping of the garden for him in pleasure, but working out in the wild-grown fields and tilling the soil, and that with sweat-producing exertions. He would now not be working for his Creator, whom he had renounced as God of truth in favor of the Serpent of religion. Hence Adam would not receive the reward of life unending for his efforts. His days were numbered, and would be comparatively few when compared with the eternity of life which he might have enjoyed in Paradise on earth. The end of his laborious efforts would be to go back to the condition of the formless dust and earth which he was trying to cultivate.

"The first man is of the earth, earthy." (1 Corinthians 15:47) For that reason, having sinned and squandered away his life, he must go back to the ground; for, said God, "dust thou art; and unto dust shalt thou return." God was not there speaking to the man's body, but he was speaking to the human soul, that is, the living creature, Adam. God did not say that Adam's body would return to the dust, and that an intelligent, intangible something inhabiting his body would separate itself from the body at death and go to an invisible realm to be tormented with flame. No; but when Adam should die, then the human soul would die, and there would be left nothing intelligent, conscious or living about the man. God's own decree declares: "The soul that sinneth, the same shall die." (Ezechiel 18:4, 20, *Douay*) The intelligent, sense-possessing, conscious, breathing creature ceases to exist, and thus the soul dies. The body, which is the material foundation of the soul or living creature, finally crumbles to the dust.

At death Adam, or his wife Eve, or any other human sinner, cannot go to any other place than to the dust from which humankind is made. The human soul does not continue a living, conscious existence either to be tormented or to be made happy eternally somewhere else. For truthful cause, therefore, God's Word says, at Psalm

146: 3, 4: "Put not your trust in princes, nor in the son of man, in whom there is no help. His breath goeth forth, he returneth to his earth; in that very day his thoughts perish."

No contradiction to the above truth is found in God's Word at Ecclesiastes 12: 6, 7, which reads: "Or ever the silver cord be loosed, or the golden bowl be broken, or the pitcher be broken at the fountain, or the wheel broken at the cistern. Then shall the dust return to the earth as it was: and the spirit shall return unto God who gave it." God's Holy Bible is completely harmonious throughout its entire sixty-six books. So this Scripture text can not mean that at death Adam's body broke down to dust but an invisible conscious inner self left the body and ascended to heaven. Concerning Adam and all men down to his day Jesus Christ said: "No man hath ascended up to heaven." Jesus knew, because he came down from heaven to bear witness to the truth.—John 3: 13.

No promise had been made to Adam of life at last in heaven, even if he should remain obedient and faithful. Truly, the spirit of the one dying returns to God who gave it. What was it that God gave Adam, combining it with his earthly body? Read again the record, at Genesis 2: 7: "God formed man of the dust of the ground, and breathed into his nostrils the breath of life; and man became a living soul." God gave man the breath of life, that is, the life forces or the power of life which is sustained by breathing. This is what is meant by "the spirit", and this is what returns to God who gave it. Regarding the spirit that returns, the same book of Ecclesiastes, at 3:19-21, states: "Therefore the death of man, and of beasts is one, and the condition of them both is equal: as man dieth, so they also die: all things breathe alike, and man hath nothing more than beast: all things are subject to vanity. And all things go to one place: of earth they were made, and into earth they return together. Who knoweth if the spirit of the children of Adam ascend upward, and if the spirit of the beasts descend downward?" (*Douay*) By reason of the wording of the Douay translation it is not discernible that the above words *breathe* and *spirit* translate the same Hebrew word, *ruach;* which word is also translated *air* and *wind* in still other Bible verses.—Job 41:16; 1:19; Genesis 8:1.

In the light of the foregoing it is clear that when Jesus, dying on the tree, said, "Father, into thy hands I commend my spirit," he was commending to his heavenly Father his power of life. He trusted that on the third day God would restore the power of life and would raise him from the dead.—Luke 23:46.

So, then, Adam and his wife having been personally on trial and having failed therein and been sentenced to death, only death and extinction awaited them. God's judgment having been righteously entered against them and being infallible, Jehovah God does not change on the matter. He does not deny or contradict himself. (1 Samuel 15:29) No children having been born

to Adam and Eve at the time to share with them
in the trial and judgment and sentence, the
situation with their offspring was therefore different and their children were therefore not beyond redemption. God said nothing concerning
their offspring except that they should be born
with sorrow to the mother. "And Adam called
his wife's name Eve [*Chavvah;* Living]; because she was the mother of all living. Unto
Adam also and to his wife did the LORD God
make coats of skins, and clothed them." (Genesis 3: 20, 21, *margin*) If this clothing of their
loins with skins of animals meant anything, it
appears to say that their offspring, who were
yet unborn within their loins, could not be redeemed and have their sins covered except by
the sacrifice of a victim equal in value to their
father Adam when perfect in Eden.

The carrying out of the death sentence upon
Adam and Eve must now begin. If they were
permitted to remain in Eden with the Serpent,
the possibility remained that the Serpent would
guide them to the "tree of life also in the midst
of the garden" and identify it to them. They
would then eat of it and, although unworthy of
eternal life on earth, they would claim immunities against death and guarantees of life for
ever, thus bringing reproach upon God's name,
word and law. "And Jehovah God said, Behold,
the man is become as one of us, to know good
and evil; and now, lest he put forth his hand,
and take also of the tree of life, and eat, and live
for ever—therefore Jehovah God sent him forth

from the garden of Eden, to till the ground from whence he was taken." (Genesis 3: 22, 23, *A.R.V.*) God thereby showed his supremacy over the Devil and prevented a condition from arising where God would appear to be bound to let rebellious sinners live forever. God's perfect righteousness and justice could not permit such an inconsistent thing. This is proof that he will not permit sin or Devil to exist for ever.

"So he drove out the man; and he placed at the east of the garden of Eden the Cherubim, and the flame of a sword which turned every way, to keep the way of the tree of life." (Genesis 3: 24, *A.R.V.*) Lucifer, who had for a time been the "anointed cherub that covereth", had betrayed his trust, and only further treachery could be expected of him. Therefore Jehovah God, who "sitteth above the cherubim", stationed a guard of these cherubim at the entrance way of the garden, and also a flaming, fiery sword of execution. Adam and Eve thereby became acquainted with such heavenly creatures as representatives of God. No man could get past those cherubic guards to seize the means of life contrary to God's will and judgment. Much less can any man ascend up to heaven and get past the faithful cherubim who bear up and are loyal to God's throne, in order to gain life for the descendants of Adam.

Those cherub guards ever barred Adam's path and enforced his exile to the fields outside Eden, till the day of his death. "And all the days that Adam lived were nine hundred and thirty years: and he died." (Genesis 5:5) He did not live out a full thousand-year period. Of God it is written: "One day is with the Lord as a thousand years, and a thousand years as one day." (2 Peter 3:8) Thus computing a thousand years as one day, Adam died in the same day

that he ate of the prohibited fruit. Furthermore, in the twenty-four–hour day during which he ate the fruit at his wife's hand the great Judge pronounced sentence of death upon him and Adam's right to life was canceled. So, in God's sight, Adam became a dead man that very day in Eden; more so when God drove out Adam and Eve and made it impossible to get to the tree of life amidst the garden. Though centuries long in reaching the climax, God's word was finally vindicated upon Adam: "In the day that thou eatest thereof thou shalt surely die." Satan failed to prove his religious contention to Adam and Eve, "Ye shall not surely die." The majesty, immutability and supremacy of God's law was upheld, whereas religion failed to give Adam and Eve wisdom, or knowledge, or godlikeness, or immortality.

There is not a scrap of evidence that Adam repented. He was a willful rebel and was beyond repentance, and his sentence is beyond recall. Eve's death is not even mentioned. Adam died and went nowhere but to the dust from which he had been taken.

CHAPTER IX

ADVOCATES OF FREEDOM

THE sentenced man and his wife took up existence outside their erstwhile Paradise home. The free world they had known was passed away. They lived in a corrupt world. The Old Serpent, the Devil, was permitted by God to remain in power. He was therefore still their invisible overlord, but an unrighteous one. They were in his clutches, in bondage on his side of the great controversy he raised against Jehovah God. They were no longer the free children of God, but were the servants of the one whose word they had chosen in preference to the true word of God. They had defied His law, which is a law of freedom to do good, and were thenceforth the slaves of the law of sin and death. They were no longer free of human weakness, passion and selfishness. Having no longer access to the life-sustaining fruits of Eden's garden, they began to degenerate from perfection of body and mind. Having accepted religion at the tongue of that Old Serpent, Jehovah God permitted them to have freedom of religion but dispensed no more truth to them. Why should he, when in Eden they had doubted and contemned the divine word of truth? The earth was no longer subject to them in any part, but they were subject to earthly conditions. The tilling and cultivation of the soil was not a part of the mandate to "subdue it", but was to stave off want and eke out an existence.

The prospect of bringing children into the world was not altogether a joyful one. There were now the inescapable sorrows of childbearing. Also the children would not be born perfect, but in a dying condition, and would be sinners because of their parents' fault. The natural rule could not be side-stepped, which rule is set out at Romans 5: 12: "By one man sin entered into the world, and death by sin; and so death passed upon all men, for that all have sinned." The human source having been defiled, "Who can bring a clean thing out of an unclean? not one." (Job 14: 4) "By man came death, . . . In Adam all die."—1 Corinthians 15: 21, 22.

Adam's living for more than nine centuries permitted him to become father to a large family. "And Adam lived an hundred and thirty years, and begat a son in his own likeness, after his image; and called his name Seth: and the days of Adam after he had begotten Seth were eight hundred years: and he begat sons and daughters: and all the days that Adam lived were nine hundred and thirty years: and he died." (Genesis 5: 3-5) Before Seth there were other sons, and also daughters, born to Adam and Eve, and the birth of the firstborn is described for us. "And the man [Adam] knew Eve his wife; and she conceived, and bare Cain, and said, I have gotten a man with *the help of*

Jehovah." (Genesis 4: 1, *A.R.V.*) Was Eve doing credit to Jehovah God in thus tying him in with the responsibility for the birth of this imperfect child Cain? Most evidently not, in the light of Cain's turning out to be the first violent manslayer. Eve was presuming upon God, and by her claim she was bringing reproach upon God's name, so suiting Satan's purpose well.

Since Cain billions of children have been born, all sinful, all diseased, many crippled, many idiot, many blind, and many stillborn. Can the Righteous God be justly charged with the responsibility for the producing of such babes? Is religion true and doing honor to God in claiming that at the time of their emerging from the womb God implanted an immortal soul in the bodies of such babes to make them live? Only the Devil, religion's author, could originate such false charges to heap reproach upon Jehovah's name and to create bitterness in human hearts against the God of perfection and life. Only gross ignorance or religious perversion of the Bible teaching concerning what the human soul is[1] could blame God for the giving to human offspring such a woeful start in existence, with frightful handicaps at their very beginning.

None of these children have been born according to the divine mandate issued in Eden, and hence none such have been born according to the divine will. The fact that God has permitted them to be born does not make him accountable

[1] See pages 72-78.

for the peopling of this earth with the diseased, the imbecile, the misshapen, the immoral, and the dying. All such were born according to the will or the passion of their sinful parents, and the responsibility for the whole situation traces back to that mimic god, Satan the Devil, who tries to shift the blame onto Jehovah God. The only humans for whose birth Jehovah admits and assumes the responsibility are such ones in whose birth he intervened by a miracle or by a guiding providence that these might be his special servants. Among such are Isaac,[1] Samson,[2] Samuel,[3] Jeremiah,[4] John the Baptist,[5] and Jesus.[6]

As to the difference between those of ordinary human birth in sin and those who become God's children it is written, at John 1:12, 13: "As many as received him, to them gave he power to become the sons of God, even to them that believe on his name; which were born, not of blood, nor of the will of the flesh, nor of the will of man, but of God." Not according to the will of God, but according to the will of sinful flesh and according to the will of fallen man, was Cain born to Adam and Eve under sentence of death.

The Devil would lead Eve to think that she was the "woman" meant in Jehovah's prophecy, at Genesis 3:15, and that therefore she would be favored by Jehovah with bearing the son or "seed" who must bruise the serpent's head. In

[1] Genesis 18:9-14; Romans 4:17-21; Galatians 4:28, 29.
[2] Judges 13:2-5. [3] 1 Samuel 1:11, 19, 20. [4] Jeremiah 1:4, 5.
[5] Luke 1:5-20. [6] Matthew 1:18-25; Luke 1:26-37.

fact, the Devil himself watched against that very possibility. Under this delusion it was possible for Eve to think that her firstborn son was a gift from Jehovah and that this son was the promised "seed". In keeping with this, she claimed Jehovah's co-operation with her in the birth of the boy and called his name "Cain", which means "acquired; gotten". The individual birth of a daughter is rarely mentioned in the Scriptures, and it is possible that after Cain the birth of a girl or girls took place, for Adam had many daughters before he died.

The birth of the next son, however, is recorded: "And again she bare his brother Abel." (Genesis 4:2, *A.R.V.*) There is no statement that Eve gave God credit for this son. The name she gave him shows she did not have high hopes concerning him, to be the promised "seed", which honor she had picked out for Cain. So she called her second son "Abel", which means "breath; vanity; transitoriness; unsatisfactoriness". Cain and Abel grew up to be mature men. Meanwhile daughters, as well as other sons, were born to Adam and Eve. Cain married one of these daughters, his sisters. His father had married the woman who had been made from his own rib and whom he called "bone of my bones, and flesh of my flesh". It is likely that Abel also married a sister, but the Bible does not say.

Agreeable to her hopes, Eve told Cain about the prophetic promise made in Eden regarding the "seed" of the woman and the divine mission of that "seed". Cain grew up believing himself to be a "man of destiny". The invisible over-lord, Satan the Devil, saw to it that such thought was formed in Cain's mind; and his mother, assuming to make a private interpretation of divine prophecy, would be a suitable one to start such thought in the son's head. Cain envisioned himself as crushing the serpent and thereby gaining the indebtedness of Abel and all his other brothers and sisters and his parents, and so becoming the leading figure on earth able to exercise world domination. It was a selfish political ambition with Cain. Since Jehovah God had foretold the "seed" and its mission, Cain sought after His co-operation and backing of his ambition and began offering up gifts by fire to God, just as religious chaplains offer up prayers at political functions and in legislative chambers today. Cain was following the Devil's religious misinterpretation concerning the "seed", and hence his form of worship was religious and not acceptable to God.

"And Abel was a keeper of sheep, but Cain was a tiller of the ground. And in process of time it came to pass, that Cain brought of the fruit of the ground an offering unto Jehovah. And Abel, he also brought of the firstlings of his flock and of the fat thereof. And Jehovah had respect unto Abel and to his offering: but unto Cain and to his offering he had not respect." (Genesis 4: 2-5, *A.R.V.*) It is likely that Cain and Abel offered their gifts near the entrance of the garden of Eden and in view of the

cherubim there stationed as representatives of
God and implemented with that revolving sword
of fire.

Abel also knew of the promise respecting the
woman's seed. He had faith in the raising up of
the seed, but did not ambitiously assume to be
the seed. He confessed himself a sinner before
God and remembered the animal skins with
which God had clothed his parents. He saw the
need of such covering for himself, and discerned that it must be by the shedding of the
blood or offering of the life of a victim. In picture thereof Abel offered up a slain lamb, a
firstling of the sheep. By this he attested his
faith and he was a witness concerning the true
way of approach to Jehovah God. His worship
of God was not for selfish reasons, but in gratitude for the promise of the "seed" of deliverance. His worship of God was not religious, but
was of faith and adoration, and according to
truth. Hence God accepted it.

Cain saw the evidence of God's acceptance of
Abel and took him to be an obstacle in his way
of becoming the seed promised. Not repenting
nor seeking to copy the correct and accepted
way of worship of God, Cain caught Abel alone
in the field where evidence of crime would not
be detected and then slew his faithful brother.
How much he had previously persecuted this
witness for Jehovah is not specified. Explaining
and warning concerning this "way of Cain", it
is written: "Not as Cain, who was of that wicked
one, and slew his brother. And wherefore slew

he him? Because his own works were evil, and his brother's righteous." (1 John 3:12) In this manner the first human witness of Jehovah on earth was put out of the way, in order to provide freedom of religion without anyone to criticize or expose it. This, however, was done at the expense of denying freedom of speech to bear witness to the truth, and denying freedom of worship of Jehovah in spirit and in truth.

Even by murder the witness to God's truth could not be suppressed. The martyrdom of Jehovah's faithful witness stood as a testimony of integrity toward God and for a vindication of his name. "By faith Abel offered unto God a more excellent sacrifice than Cain, through which he had witness borne to him that he was righteous, God bearing witness in respect of his gifts: and through it he being dead yet speaketh." (Hebrews 11:4, *A.R.V.*) Not alone does the bloodstain testify to the crime due to religion, but it cries out to God for his vengeance upon the religious criminals; and that cry of spilled blood, from that of Abel onward, shall not go unheeded by Jehovah. Said Jesus to the religionists who were about to duplicate against him the crime of Cain against his brother: "Wherefore, behold, I send unto you prophets, and wise men, and scribes: and some of them ye shall kill and crucify; and some of them shall ye scourge in your synagogues, and persecute them from city to city: that upon you may come all the righteous blood shed upon the earth, from the blood of righteous Abel unto the blood of Zacharias son of Barachias, whom ye slew between the temple and the altar. Verily I say unto you, All these things shall come upon this generation."—Matthew 23: 34-36.

After exposing the religious criminal and his crime, Jehovah did not kill Cain, nor did he appoint anyone of Adam's family to act as avenger of blood and to serve as executioner of God. There was none worthy to represent God in this capacity. Vengeance is God's, and he reserved for himself the execution of it upon the slayer of His witness. Though he permitted Cain to remain and rear a progeny, God had another way of bringing to nought Cain's generation and wiping out his offspring, at the end of that old ungodly world. Hence God uttered his decree as a sign lest anyone take the law into his own hands and execute Cain. Then Cain took his wife and moved away to territory called the

"land of Nod (or Wandering)", and there he raised a family. Possibly in agreement with his political ambitions, possibly because of not feeling freedom from fear, Cain built the first cities on earth. His descendants distinguished themselves, not for worship of Jehovah, but by engaging in cattle-raising, musical entertainment, mining and metal industries, and in murder.—Genesis 4: 16-24.

"And Adam knew his wife again; and she bare a son, and called his name Seth: For God, said she, hath appointed me another seed instead of Abel, whom Cain slew." (Genesis 4: 25) Since Seth was born when Adam was a hundred and thirty years old, then if Seth was born immediately after Cain's murder of Abel it shows Cain and Abel must have been men of some age and experience at the time of the crime. Abel was the beginning of what Hebrews 12: 1 calls "so great a cloud of witnesses", but there is no record that Seth stood out prominently as a man of faith and a witness of Jehovah. Hebrews, chapter eleven, does not list him as one of Jehovah's witnesses.

"And Seth lived an hundred and five years, and begat Enos"; which name means "mortal; strong man". (Genesis 5: 6) Adam was still alive, being now two hundred and thirty-five

years old. Therefore what is next reported as
taking place could not mean anything honoring
to Jehovah God, but rather bringing reproach
upon his name. The Catholic Douay Version of
Genesis 4: 26 reads: "But to Seth also was born
a son, whom he called Enos; this man began to
call upon the name of the Lord." Such a translation, however, denies that, before Enos, Abel
called upon Jehovah's name in worship. The
Hebrew text literally reads: "Then it was begun to call by name of Jehovah." (*Roth.*) This
did not mean that men became "sons of God",
for such a thing was not possible among men
until after Jesus' coming. (John 1: 11-13) It
did not mean men began to "walk with God", because the next one after Abel who is testified
to as walking with God is Enoch, the son of
Jared and the great-great-grandson of Enos. It
did not stop the degeneracy of the human race
and turn them to repentance and stave off the
great catastrophe that was preparing to come.
The calling by name of Jehovah from Enos'
time forward must have been hypocritical, a
religious movement to the further reproach of
God's name; and it confused men as to God's
promise of the "seed".

It was first three hundred and eighty-seven
years after Enos' birth that a man was born
who received God's approval as showing a pleasing faith toward God and worshiping Him in
truth. "And Jared lived an hundred sixty and
two years, and he begat Enoch. And Enoch lived
sixty and five years, and begat Methuselah: and

Enoch walked with God after he begat Methuselah three hundred years, and begat sons and
daughters: and all the days of Enoch were three
hundred sixty and five years: and Enoch walked
with God: and he was not; for God took him."
—Genesis 5: 18, 21-24.

Enoch's name means "trained; consecrated".
His course proves he was fully consecrated to
God by his faith in Jehovah. His walking with
God meant he had fellowship with God by the
truth which God revealed to him and by his
going in the way of righteousness in harmony
with such truth. He was not of that old, ungodly
world, but looked forward in faith to a new
world wherein the "seed" of God's "woman"
would rule the earth, having judged the Old
Serpent and its seed and crushed the Serpent's
head.

In line of descent Enoch was the seventh from
Adam. Jehovah made faithful Enoch his witness
and prophet, to foretell of that day of judgment
at the end of the Devil's uninterrupted rule. It
is written: "And Enoch also, the seventh from
Adam, prophesied of these, saying, Behold, the
Lord cometh with ten thousands of his saints,
to execute judgment upon all, and to convince
all that are ungodly among them of all their
ungodly deeds which they have ungodly committed, and of all their hard speeches which ungodly sinners have spoken against him." Such
a prophecy by Enoch proves that the world in
which he lived was ungodly, despite the calling
by men upon the name of Jehovah. Such

prophesying put Enoch's life in danger at the violent hands of the "seed" of the Serpent. —Jude 14, 15.

In a time when ungodly men were living to an age of over seven hundred years, Methuselah reaching even nine hundred and sixty-nine years, why did this godly man of faith and integrity, Enoch, live to an age of only three hundred and sixty-five years? Was he cut off by religious intolerance, persecution, and violence as in Abel's case? Enoch had good reason to expect to be; but Almighty God preserved him from such a death. The record on Jehovah's witnesses, at Hebrews chapter eleven, reads: "By faith Enoch was translated that he should not see death; and he was not found, because God translated him: for he hath had witness borne to him that before his translation he had been well-pleasing unto God: and without faith it is impossible to be well-pleasing unto him; for he that cometh to God must believe that he is, and that he is a rewarder of them that seek after him."—Verses 5, 6, *A.R.V.*

Enoch received a good report from God for his faith and faithfulness. He held fast his integrity under test and honored and upheld the name of Jehovah amid the ungodly world, and in the face of the enmity of the seed of the Serpent. When Jehovah had determined that Enoch had finished his work of witness, then God gave him a final vision of the new world to come, wherein death shall be wiped out by God's power through the Seed of his "woman".

Thus God translated Enoch, or put him in a trance, somewhat like the trance an apostle of Jesus Christ experienced thousands of years later. (2 Corinthians 12:1-4) What Enoch saw and heard while he was held bound and entranced with that new world vision of Paradise restored, he was not permitted to utter to men. While Enoch was in the trance, "God took him," that is, God let Enoch's life expire peaceably. He felt no pangs of death; he did not see or realize he was dying. At the same time, up till this final vision of glorious things to come, he was comparatively young and had not begun to feel the ebbing strength, growing pains, and deadening stiffness of old age nearing death's door.

So Enoch "died in faith", and his body his enemies were never able to find to use it for any purpose. He "was not found"; he "was not". God disposed of his body. Enoch died with the new world vision gripping his attention. When God actually brings him to life again at the portals of that new world, that vision will be the first thought of his mind, and his eyes will look forth to see the vision come true on earth.

CHAPTER X

DELIVERANCE FORESHADOWED

FTER Enoch's sudden disappearance, whether that caused any stir or sense of loss or not, men kept on toiling and working with their hands, fighting the thorns and thistles of the cursed earth. Enoch had been like the "salt of the earth", exercising a wholesome influence among men; but men in general were bent on corruption. Such were glad that Enoch was gone and his preaching and prophesying against the ungodly sinners were gone with him. Selfishly they continued to eat their food and to drink their wine and to marry and be given in marriage, and humankind multiplied due to the multiplied conception of women.

Enoch's grandson Lamech felt keenly the hard living conditions. He did not stand out among men as a witness for Jehovah as his grandfather had. Enoch's warning of coming judgment had likely impressed Lamech that a time of judgment was drawing near and that a change in human conditions was soon due. Lamech's name meaning "powerful; overthrower; destroyer", it fitted in with Enoch's prophecy that the God of all power would overthrow the power of the ungodly and destroy them and

would usher in a new world in which obedient
men would rest from excessive labor and the op-
pressions of the wicked. Lamech had lived during the last fifty-six years of the life of his first
forefather, Adam. From him Lamech learned
direct how, due to Adam's sin, God had cursed
the earth, but had also given promise of the
coming of the "seed" that should bruise the
head of the Serpent of deception and untruth.
That would mean the lifting of the curse,
Lamech hoped.

"And Lamech lived a hundred eighty and two
years, and begat a son: and he called his name
Noah, saying, This same shall comfort us in our
work and in the toil of our hands, which cometh
because of the ground which Jehovah hath
cursed." (Genesis 5:28, 29, *A.R.V.*) Lamech's
words proved to be a prophecy, and were therefore inspired by the spirit or invisible force of
Jehovah God. In fact, in thus begetting a son
who should play a part in fulfillment of prophecy Lamech became a picture of Jehovah God,
the all-powerful One; and the son Noah became
a prophetic figure of the "seed" promised in
Eden and by whom the curse should be lifted.
Lamech lived till his son Noah was 595 years
old, and saw him engaged in a work at the command of God Almighty and which gave proof
that his son Noah had been rightly named under
inspiration of God.

Suddenly amid the corruption of the times a
new element emerged upon the scene and commanded the attention of men, but not for better-

ment. The Divine Record abruptly says, "There were giants in the earth in those days." Or, better translating the Record, "The Nephilim were in the earth in those days." (Genesis 6:4, *A.R.V.*) Who were those giant Nephilim? They were not some freakish misgrowth of humankind due to a glandular ailment. They were superhuman. They were demons from the spirit world, materialized in flesh but of gigantic size to prove their superior origin, because man is made a "little lower than the angels". Their sudden appearing among men became visible proof that things had been proceeding for worse in those heavens under man's invisible overlord, Satan.

God had not cast Satan the Devil out of heaven after pronouncing judgment upon him at Eden, but let him remain there for a test of the integrity of the spirit sons of God. Indeed, the Bible relates that, more than two thousand years after Satan's rebellion, "it came to pass on the day when the sons of God came to present themselves before Jehovah, that Satan also came among them. And Jehovah said unto Satan, Whence comest thou? Then Satan answered Jehovah, and said, From going to and fro in the earth, and from walking up and down in it." (Job 1:6, 7, *A.R.V.*) Evidently, then, many of those angels, if not all of them, in the organization that God had put under Lucifer in his office of "covering cherub" over man in Eden, yielded to Satan's persuasion after he caused the fall of man. They also rebelled against the Most

High God and forsook his holy organization and took Satan's side of the controversy.

Those unfaithful angels became devils, in that they joined renegade Lucifer in slandering Jehovah God and bringing reproach upon his name. They became demons who were later worshiped by men, but whose worship Jehovah God forbids his chosen people to practice, saying: "So shall they no more offer their sacrifices unto demons after whom they are unchastely going away." (Leviticus 17:7, *Roth.*) "They sacrificed to mischievous demons, to a No-God, gods whom they knew not, new ones lately come in." (Deuteronomy 32:17, *Roth.;* also 2 Chronicles 11:15; Psalm 106:37) Lucifer, of cherub rank, thus became the "prince of the demons", also called "Beelzebub".—Matthew 12:24, 27, 28, *A.R.V.*

The angels that so sinned came under sentence from Jehovah God. He degraded them from their blessed position in his lofty organization of light and truth, and debased them to the state or condition symbolically called "Tartarus". Not having the light of the truth of God's purposes, they are not free, but are under God's continual surveillance as his opponents. Thus they are as in chains. They can never break free from His sentence of destruction upon them, but in their state of Tartarean degradation they await the execution of that sentence with Satan the Devil at the judgment day. The inspired revelation concerning this says: "Whose sentence now from of old lingereth not, and their destruction slumbereth not. For if God spared not angels when they sinned, but cast them down to Tartarus, and committed them to pits of darkness, to be reserved unto judgment." (2 Peter 2:3, 4, *A.R.V.*, margin) "And the angels which kept not their first estate, but left their own habitation, he hath reserved in everlasting chains under darkness unto the judgment of the great day."—Jude 6.

The demons that materialized in the days of Noah terrorized men who did not have faith in God as did Noah. They spread violence. Their very name *Nephilim* means *fellers,* who cause men to fall by violence and other means. So terrible an impression did they make that almost a thousand years later when the Israelite spies were spying out the land of Canaan and saw the unusually tall sons of the Canaanite Anak, they came back and reported, falsely: "And there we saw the Nephilim, the sons of Anak, who come of the Nephilim: and we were in our own sight as grasshoppers, and so we were in their sight." (Numbers 13:33, *A.R.V.*) The book of Genesis tells what next took place after the Nephilim appeared on earth.

Man became so corrupt that the great Spirit, Jehovah, determined that he would grant them only 120 years of grace before he executed judgment upon them, thereby settling the controversy of supremacy with that long-lived generation of men. "And it came to pass, when men began to multiply on the face of the ground, and daughters were born unto them, that the sons of God saw the daughters of men that they were fair; and they took them wives of all that they chose. And Jehovah said, My spirit shall not strive with man for ever, for that he also is flesh: yet shall his days be a hundred and twenty years."—Genesis 6:1-3, *A.R.V.*

The "sons of God" who intermarried with daughters of men were angels who had thus far continued faithful to Jehovah God. "For who in the skies can be compared unto Jehovah? Who among the sons of God is like unto Jehovah?" (Psalm 89:6, *A.R.V.*, margin; Psalm 88:7, *Douay*) Still in Jehovah's organization as members of his family of sons, these angels materialized, doubtless with good intent to benefit the straying human race. Nevertheless it was not by authority of God their Father and was not his way to produce the "seed" who would be heaven-sent to crush the Serpent's head. Hence it was a disobedient step. It served Satan's purpose instead, and produced an offspring who were "mighty men of renown", angelic-human hybrids, who made a name for themselves and not for God and who whipped up the violence in the earth. The brief record reads: "The Nephilim were in the earth in those days, and also AFTER THAT, when the sons of God came in unto the daughters of men, and they bare children to them: the same were the mighty men that were of old, the men of renown."—Genesis 6:4, *A.R.V.*

Amid this wickedness Noah followed Enoch's example and walked with Jehovah God. He

married a chaste, uncontaminated woman, and
after Noah was 500 years old God blessed him
with three sons. He brought them up in the
faith of God and led them in obedience to God's
righteous will. Noah kept himself unspotted and
uncorrupted from that old, ungodly world, and
the inspired testimony concerning him reports:
"These are the generations of Noah. Noah was a
righteous man, and perfect in his generations:
Noah walked with God. And Noah begat three
sons, Shem, Ham and Japheth." (Genesis 6: 9, 10,
A.R.V.) These three sons married uncorrupted
women.

The earth at that time was in the condition
described at 2 Peter 3: 5, and of which condition the people outside of Noah's family chose
to remain willingly ignorant: "For this they
willingly are ignorant of, that by the word of
God the heavens were of old, and the earth
standing out of the water and in the water."

By God's dynamic word the waters on earth
had been collected into great seabeds, and the
dry land had been made to appear, on the third
creative day. In course of time the rings of matter exhaled by the earth in its molten state had
fallen one after another to form canopy belts
around the earth but up above earth's firmament or atmospheric expanse. The belts had
moved slowly toward the poles, north and south,
and there at the areas of least resistance they
had fallen, subjecting the earth to great deluges
destructive to all existing forms of life. Now,
one thousand years after the close of the sixth

creative day, on which God made man, the last
ring, almost pure water, had fallen toward
earth's firmament and had enveloped the earth
in a canopy. It was sustained aloft by centrifugal force as it rotated. It constituted a *great
deep* of water in suspension, but still enveloping the earth.

Adam's descendants, now multiplied over the
earth, were out of the water, being on dry land.
At the same time they were in the water, being
within the water canopy which had been there
since before Adam's creation. To the ungodly
men of the earth, since Adam had fallen asleep
in death, all things seemed to continue as they
were from the beginning of the creation. Not at
all did they see what God saw, that the movement of the waters of the great canopy far over-
head was toward the poles; that as a result the
thickness of the canopy out above the earth's
equator was becoming very thin, almost admit-
ting direct sunlight through, and that the edges
of the canopy nearing the poles were growing
dangerously weak, rotating with growing slow-
ness to the point of having little centrifugal
force to resist the downward pull of earth's
gravity. The fall of the canopy was imminent,
awaiting God's removal of his restraining power at the end of the 120 years. But before the
canopy belts dropped God mercifully chose to
warn earth's inhabitants of the dreadful cata-
clysm of waters and to declare to the people the
way of escape, if they would heed.

Jehovah God made Noah his witness to sound the warning. Doubtless first to Noah Jehovah God gave the account of the creation of earth as described in the first chapter of the Bible, thereby revealing to him the existence of the mighty deep above earth's firmament, and that it must shortly plunge to earth, causing an earth-wide flood and destroying all corrupt humankind. To escape through it, a great boat must be built and Noah and his sons and the wives of all four must take refuge in it, bringing in also a select number of birds, cattle and creeping things (not insects). Such a catastrophe as ever visiting the earth was unreported of before, yet Noah believed God. "By faith Noah, being warned of God of things not seen as yet, moved with fear, prepared an ark to the saving of his house; by the which he condemned the world, and became heir of the righteousness which is by faith."—Hebrews 11: 7.

All the ungodly on earth, the Nephilim, the mighty men of renown, and the race in general, scoffed at Noah and his sons while building the big boat, 450 feet long, 75 feet broad, and 45 feet high, with three inner stories. How was he ever to launch it from the land on which it was built? Noah and his sons held their integrity under the scoffing. Noah warned the people of the flood and preached the righteousness of God, which righteousness called for the flood of destruction as the execution of God's just condemnation of the world. Asked by the skeptical when it should come, Noah replied he did not know the day or hour, but it would not come before the boat was finished, with his family inside.

The great float was completed, while the mists still continued to exhale from the earth and to water the face of the whole earth. No sign of rain or flood was apparent to the people. What now? Jehovah's word came to Noah telling him to move into the ark with his family, bringing also the birds and animals: "For yet seven days, and I will cause it to rain upon the earth forty days and forty nights; and every living thing that I have made will I destroy from off the face of the ground." Noah obeyed. No children or babies were taken into the ark. Although married, Noah's sons had so engrossed themselves in preparing for the flood and witnessing for Jehovah that they had no time to consider the rearing of families. It was not the occasion for such. Moreover, their refraining from having children showed their conviction; it added weight to their testimony respecting the world calamity at hand. When the people beheld Noah and his household moving into the ark and taking the creature life with them, did they suddenly repent and turn from their corrupt ways, believing that world disaster was near? The Son of man, Christ Jesus, answers: "As in the days that were before the flood they were eating and drinking, marrying and giving in marriage, until the day that No'e entered into the ark, and knew not until the flood came, and took them all away; so shall also the coming of the Son of man be."—Matthew 24: 38, 39.

Noah was 600 years old when he turned his back on that old ungodly world and entered the ark containing its precious cargo. "And they that went in, went in male and female of all flesh, as God commanded him: and Jehovah shut him in." (Genesis 7: 6, 16, *A.R.V.*) Then the flood descended, in Noah's six hundredth year, the seventeenth day of the second month. All the fountains of the great deep suspended above the earth broke forth with gushing waters; and

the aqueous canopy, which had shielded the earth from the direct beams of the sun, moon and stars like a window pane, opened its flood-gates. Forty days the downfall of water con-

tinued, and the rising waters on the earth lifted
up the ark and finally raised it on their surface
fifteen cubits above the highest mountains then.

Earth now looked like a watery globe, within
its firmament of now well-washed atmosphere,
much like when God commanded, 29,000 years
before that, saying: "Let the waters under the
heavens be gathered together unto one place,
and let the dry land appear." It was therefore
no new thing for God to issue a like command
after the floodwaters had prevailed upon the
earth for 150 days; for then the ark's keel
struck land. "After the end of a hundred and
fifty days the waters decreased. And the ark
rested in the seventh month, on the seventeenth
day of the month, upon the mountains of
Ararat." (Genesis 8: 3, 4, *A.R.V.*) That was exactly five months since the flood began. Dividing
five months into 150 days shows that each month
counted as 30 days long, about the length of a
lunation of earth's moon. A year of twelve
months in Noah's day, therefore, equaled about
360 days. Such being a lunar year, it would be
necessary to regulate it, when necessary, to the
spring equinox, in order to bring the calendar
into line with the solar year and not get ahead
of the seasons of the year which now set in.
—Genesis 8: 22.

In the six hundred and first year of Noah's
life, and "in the second month, on the seven and
twentieth day of the month, was the earth dried.
And God spake unto Noah, saying, Go forth of
the ark." (Genesis 8:13-16) Noah and his family

and the animals were therefore in the ark for exactly one lunar year and ten days, the Lord having shut them in the ark the seventeenth day of the second month of the previous year. While these were safe inside, what had happened without? This: God "spared not the old world, but saved Noah the eighth person, a preacher of righteousness, bringing in the flood upon the world of the ungodly". Jehovah's word of judgment went into effect, "whereby the world that then was, being overflowed with water, perished." (2 Peter 2: 5; 3: 5, 6) The wicked organization of men on the earth, together with the interference of the Nephilim and the disobedient "sons of God" from the invisible heavens, ended. The old world ended, "perished," but the earth continued abiding. Concerning it God now said: "While the earth remaineth, seedtime and harvest, and cold and heat, and summer and winter, and day and night shall not cease." (Genesis 8: 22) This truth frees all believers from the fear that the end of the world means destruction of the literal earth, sun, moon and stars. God's preservation of Noah and his family confirms the truth that God will preserve His servants through the end of this world.

CHAPTER XI

THE COUNT OF TIME

HE King of Eternity set a limit upon the old world of the ungodly and brought it to an end exactly 120 years after he had expressed his judgment. (Genesis 6:3) With the exhibition of his almighty power in the deluge Jehovah God wiped out the wicked creatures who filled the earth with violence. By the raging floodwaters he not only rendered the earth clean of them, but cleansed the earth itself which had been defiled by the blood unrighteously spilled by the ungodly. The defiled earth could justly be cleansed only by the blood of those who shed blood.—Numbers 35:33.

The heavenly spirit creatures who had materialized in bodies of flesh and exercised a direct control in earth's affairs were required to return to the spirit world. In that way such manner of direct meddling by spirits from heaven in human matters was brought to an end. The spirit "sons of God" who had disobediently married the daughters of men were not permitted to return to the holy courts of God's presence, but God delivered them over to the custody of Satan, who brought them into a virtual imprisonment. Being so dealt with, they became "the spirits in prison; which sometime were disobedient, when once the longsuffering of God waited in the days of Noah, while the ark was a preparing, wherein few, that is, eight souls were saved by water".—1 Peter 3:19, 20.

The Nephilim, however, who had rebelled openly with Satan, joined again the ranks of the devils and demons under Satan their prince, and all these Satan now arranged according to a new pattern, symbolized in Bible prophecy as "another wonder in heaven". "And behold a great red dragon, having seven heads and ten horns, and seven crowns upon his heads. And his tail drew the third part of the stars of heaven."—Revelation 12:3, 4.

The evidence is clear, then, that the symbolic pre-Flood heavens and earth passed out of existence, but our globe, the earth, remained. Religion had been cleared off the face of the earth, by the destruction of all religionists. Into the cleansed earth Noah and all other occupants of the ark came forth at God's command. The first thing that was done outside the ark was to institute the worship of Jehovah God by Noah, who is a prophetic picture of the woman's "seed" destined to bruise the Serpent's head. "And Noah builded an altar unto Jehovah, and took of every clean beast, and of every clean bird, and offered burnt-offerings on the altar. And Jehovah smelled the sweet savor; and Jehovah said in his heart, I will not again curse the ground any more for man's sake, for that the imagination of man's heart is evil from his youth; neither will I again smite any more everything living, as I have done."—Genesis 8: 20, 21, *A.R.V.*

Besides being prophetic of greater things yet to come, this transaction was a small-scale or miniature fulfillment of Lamech's words at Noah's birth: "This same shall comfort us concerning our work and toil of our hands, because of the ground which the LORD hath cursed." Jehovah had cursed the earth at the time of Eden because a perfect man had gone wicked; but now, all his descendants being born sinners and hence their heart imaginings being inclined to evil from youth on, Jehovah God did not curse the earth because of the condition in which they were helplessly born. Only, thereafter, when the human race showed a choice of wickedness deliberately and defiled the earth with innocent blood would God bring upon them a curse.—Isaiah 24: 3-6; Malachi 4: 6.

For the time being, to serve the prophetic picture here made, the earth was clean, undefiled and uncursed. Its sole inhabitants were righteous in God's sight through their faith and obedience, and the worship of Jehovah prevailed to the exclusion of all demonism or religion. True, the invisible demons under Satan had not been destroyed, but were permitted to reorganize. However, at this point of time Jehovah God was dealing through the Word, his heavenly representative, direct with Noah and his righteous household. Righteous heavens were then in touch with a righteous earth. Under such conditions, which were prophetic of the conditions of the new world now near at hand, God restated the divine mandate. "And God blessed Noah and his sons, and said unto them, Be fruitful, and multiply . . . ; bring forth abundantly in the earth, and multiply therein." —Genesis 9: 1, 7.

About a year later, or two years after the flood began, the first child was born in fulfillment of this restated divine mandate. (Genesis 11: 10) In course of time the mandate was fulfilled, not in a complete sense, but in a typical or pictorial sense, when the seventy generations from Noah and his descendants were brought forth, as named in Genesis, chapter ten. *Seventy* (or seven times ten, both numbers symbolizing completeness) represents fulfillment or accomplishment as respects the mandate. Nimrod, due to wickedness and childlessness, is not reckoned in, because he does not picture any having part in the real, permanent fulfillment of the divine mandate in the new world. (Genesis 10: 8-10; 10: 32) Living for 350 years after the flood, Noah saw the divine mandate typically carried out. Though the mandate was restated primarily to him, he had no more children. His sons and daughters-in-law did the multiplying. So it will be under the Greater Noah.

To show that the carrying out of the divine mandate was not meant to breed babies under totalitarian rule for purposes of selfish warfare and to pollute the earth with blood, Jehovah God established with Noah and his sons, hence with all their descendants to this day, the everlasting covenant respecting the sanctity of blood, the basis of life. By this covenant or solemn declaration of the Life-giver's will, man might kill animals for his needed food, but might not engage in robbing animals of their life or *soul*. Also, the blood of a manslayer could be shed only by the one whom God delegated to act in His image, that is, as God's representative and executioner. Said God to those worshiping Him: "As for every moving thing that hath life yours shall it be for food; like the green herb have I given you all things. Yet flesh with the *soul* thereof, the blood thereof, shall ye not eat; and surely your blood of your *souls* will I require, from the hand of every living creature will I require it, and from the hand of man: from the hand of each one's brother will I require the *soul* of man: he that sheddeth man's blood, by man shall his blood be shed, for in the image of God made he man."—Genesis 9:3-6, *Roth.*, marginal reading according to the Hebrew.

If humankind kept this everlasting covenant of the sanctity of creature life, they would not defile the earth, but would escape the bringing of a curse from God upon them, with destruction to follow the curse. As a visible sign of this covenant of blood the great Life-giver set the rainbow in the sky, the rainbow never having been visible to man before the flood. "And God said, This is the sign of the covenant, which I am granting betwixt me and you, and every *living soul* [*nephesh chayyah*] that is with you,

to age-abiding generations. . . . This is the
sign of the covenant which I have established
between me and all flesh that is on the earth."
(Genesis 9: 12-17, *Roth.*) The truth of this rainbow covenant, being duly applied by God's power in his own time, will free the earth of unrighteous wars which have plagued humankind.

MEASURING TIME TO OUR DAY

As to human relations, God is an accurate
Timekeeper in the fulfillment of his purposes.
Until God reveals it to his devoted servants, it
is impossible for creatures to "know the times
or the seasons, which the Father hath put in his
own power". He appoints the time for each of
his purposes to mature, and at the fullness of
the time he acts. "When the fulness of the time
was come, God sent forth his Son, made of a
woman, made under the law, to redeem them
that were under the law, that we might receive
the adoption of sons." (Galatians 4: 4, 5) "To
every thing there is a season, and a time to
every purpose under the heaven."—Ecclesiastes
3: 1.

The Divine Word of truth shows up as foolish those teachers of "science falsely so called",
who teach that man has been upon this planet
and in a state of development toward perfection
for millions of years, the exact number of which
these so-called "scientists" cannot agree upon
among themselves. After the Flood God's Word
counts the time through the generations of
Noah's son Shem. Before the Flood the time

was counted from Adam through the line of Seth. By this it is easy and simple to prove that the time from Adam's creation to the Flood was 1,656 years, as follows:

From Adam's creation to the birth of Seth was	130 years
Then to the birth of Enos	105 years
To the birth of Cainan	90 years
To the birth of Mahalaleel	70 years
To the birth of Jared	65 years
To the birth of Enoch	162 years
To the birth of Methuselah	65 years
To the birth of Lamech	187 years
To the birth of Noah	182 years
To the Flood	600 years
From Adam's creation to the Flood, according to Genesis 5: 3-29; 7: 6, was	1,656 years
From the beginning of the Flood to the birth of Shem's son Arphaxad was	2 years
To the birth of Salah	35 years
To the birth of Eber	30 years
To the birth of Peleg	34 years
To the birth of Reu	30 years
To the birth of Serug	32 years
To the birth of Nahor	30 years
To the birth of Terah	29 years

To the death of Terah, at which time his son Abraham was 75 years old and then

crossed the Euphrates river
into the Promised Land 205 years

From the Flood to God's covenant with Abraham in Ca-
naan, according to the record at Genesis 11:10-32;
12:1-7, was 427 years

ANNO MUNDI ("IN THE YEAR OF THE WORLD")

0 100 200 300 400 500 600 700 800 900 1000 1100 1200 1300 1400 1500 1600 1700 1800 1900 2000 2100 2200 2300 2400 2500 2600

ADAM
SETH
ENOS
CAINAN
MAHALALEEL
JARED
ENOCH
① METHUSELAH *A.M.* 1656
LAMECH
NOAH FLOOD
② SHEM
ARPHAXAD
SALAH
EBER
PELEG
REU
SERUG
NAHOR
TERAH
ABRAHAM
③ ISAAC
JACOB
④ LEVI
KOHATH
⑤ AMRAM
MOSES

Five human links
between
Adam and Moses

due to the overlapping ages of
Adam, 243 years; Methuselah, 98
years; Shem, 50 years; Isaac, circa
40 years; Levi, cir. 69 years; Amram, cir. 20 years with Moses.

Exodus 12: 40-43 and Galatians 3: 17 are in agreement that from the Abrahamic covenant to Jehovah's law covenant with the nation of Israel at the time of their exodus from Egypt was 430 years. Thereafter there was a trek of the Israelites through the wilderness to the land of Canaan for 40 years, followed by 6 years of fighting with the Canaanites before apportioning out all the land to the Israelites by Judge Joshua. (Joshua 14: 5-10; Numbers 1: 1; 10: 11, 12; 12: 16; 13: 1-30) After Joshua's death there was a broken period of judges, on the time length of which the Bible is not definite. Concerning this the apostle Paul says, at Acts 13: 19-22 (*A.R.V.*): "And when he had destroyed seven nations in the land of Canaan, he gave them their land for an inheritance, for about four hundred and fifty years: and after these things he gave them judges until Samuel the prophet. And afterward they asked for a king: and God gave unto them Saul the son of Kish, a man of the tribe of Benjamin, for the space of forty years. And when he had removed him, he raised up David to be their king." After David's reign of forty years, his son Solomon became king, and in the fourth year of his reign he began building the temple at Jerusalem.

In the record concerning the temple's construction the great Timekeeper supplies that which fills the gap between the Israelites' exodus from Egypt to beginning work on the temple. "And it came to pass in the four hundred and eightieth year after the children of Israel

were come out of the land of Egypt, in the
fourth year of Solomon's reign over Israel, in
the month Ziv, which is the second month, that
he began to build the house of Jehovah." Thereafter Solomon reigned thirty-six years. (1 Kings
6: 1, 2, *A.R.V.*; 11: 42) In the original Hebrew
text of these verses the numbers of years are
written spelled out in full. It was first hundreds
of years after Christ that alphabetic letters began to be used as symbols of numbers, and then
these were used merely to number the chapters
and verses, but NOT to change the original Hebrew text. Without any other definite Scripture
time statement we accept 1 Kings 6: 1, 2, and
proceed with measuring the time.

From God's covenant with Abraham to the exodus was	430 years
From the exodus to the beginning of the temple	480 years
To Solomon's death and Rehoboam's reign	36 years
To Abijah's reign	17 years
To Asa's reign	3 years
To Jehoshaphat's reign	41 years
To Jehoram's reign	25 years
To Ahaziah's reign	8 years
To Athaliah's reign	1 year
To Joash's reign	6 years
To Amaziah's reign	40 years
To Uzziah's reign	29 years
To Jotham's reign	52 years

To Ahaz's reign		16 years
To Hezekiah's reign		16 years
To Manasseh's reign		29 years
To Amon's reign		55 years
To Josiah's reign		2 years
To Jehoahaz's reign		31 years
To Jehoiakim's reign	3 months	
To Jehoiachin's reign		11 years
To Zedekiah's reign	3 months	
To Jerusalem's desolation		11 years
To the end of seventy years' desolation in the first year of King Cyrus of Persia		70 years
To the end (ancient time) of the year B.C. 1		536 years

From the Abrahamic covenant through B.C. 1	1,945 years

The above figures are based upon the record of Israel's kings as given in 2 Chronicles, chapters 12 to 36. Both 2 Chronicles 36:19-23 and Ezra 1:1-6, and Daniel 5:28-31, agree that it was in the first year of Cyrus' reign that he permitted the Jews to depart from Babylon and return to Jerusalem to build the temple, thus ending the seventy years' desolation of the land of Judea. It is well established that two years after the overthrow of Babylon in 538 B.C. by Darius the Mede and his nephew, Cyrus the Persian, the first year of Cyrus' exclusive rule began, which year was 536 B.C. So, putting

together the three great periods of time from
Adam's creation onward, we get the following
table:

From Adam's creation to the Flood	was	1,656 years
From the Flood to the Abrahamic covenant	was	427 years
From the Abrahamic covenant to end of B.C. 1	was	1,945 years
From Adam's creation to the end of B.C. 1	was	4,028 years

Thereafter the so-called *Anno Domini* or *A.D.*
period began.

From the beginning of A.D. 1, or Year of the
Lord 1, to the beginning of A.D. 1944 is 1,943
full years, which, being added to the above
table, give the time measurement from Adam's
creation to date:

From Adam's creation to the end of B.C. 1	was	4,028 years
From beginning of A.D. 1 to the end of 1943	is	1,943 years
From Adam's creation to the end of 1943 A.D.	is	5,971 years

We are therefore near the end of six thousand years of human history, with conditions
upon us and tremendous events at hand foreshadowed by those of Noah's day.—Luke
17: 26-30.

CHAPTER XII

ENEMIES OF FREEDOM

Y THE Flood Jehovah God made a great name for himself in the minds of the eight survivors. Through them he gave a righteous start again to the human family, though not a perfect start. All human creatures then worshiped Jehovah, who had so marvelously delivered them from the baptism of destruction which came upon the ungodly demon-worshipers in the Flood. All human creatures were now under the terms of the everlasting covenant of the sacredness of life, both human and beast. All wanton slaughter of man or beast and the needless spilling of blood was forbidden and subject to God's vengeance by his executioner in his due time. Wicked enemies of freedom had been cleared out of the earth.

Such new conditions did not mean that the test of man's integrity toward God was at an end. Jehovah still permitted the Old Serpent, Satan, the Devil, to remain, together with his host of demons, and the craving of Satan and his demons to be worshiped by men on earth still rankled in their hearts. They had no feeling of tolerance for the pure and undefiled worship of the true God, Jehovah Most High, who had delivered such a smacking rebuke and de-

feat to them by the Flood. Being still alive and
active, Satan and his demons, his "seed", knew
that the Seed of God's "woman" who will dash
in the head of the Serpent had not yet been
produced and gone into action against them.
They were on the watch for him, to destroy him
on sight, if possible. They were determined to
corrupt and overthrow the worship of Jehovah
on earth and to make men forget the name
which Jehovah had made for himself in the Deluge. This would bring great reproach upon
God's name and would turn men away from Him
and to the Devil as supreme one. The test of
man's integrity was bound to go on. It did.

"And the sons of Noah, that went forth of the
ark, were Shem, and Ham, and Japheth: and
Ham is the father of Canaan. These are the
three sons of Noah: and of them was the whole
earth overspread." (Genesis 9: 18, 19) No more
sons being born to Noah, the human family
which descended from him became divided into
three great branches, the Semitic, the Hamitic,
and the Japhetic. They were and are all of one
blood, and the everlasting covenant concerning
blood forbids and condemns the wanton exter-
mination of one branch of the race by any family of the other branches, as when anti-Semitic
Nazis try to blot out the Semite Jews. It is
plainly declared, at Acts 17: 26, 27, that God
"hath made of one blood all nations of men for
to dwell on all the face of the earth, and hath
determined the times before appointed, and the
bounds of their habitation; that they should

seek the Lord, if haply they might feel after him, and find him, though he be not far from every one of us."

Only by acting under the direct appointment of Jehovah God to be his instrument to destroy the wicked may anyone execute the wicked. An instance of this was when Jehovah brought the Israelites into the land he had promised their forefathers. Then God commanded them to destroy the demon-worshiping inhabitants and wipe out their religion. Almighty God, by miracles, aided the Israelites to carry out the execution of such devil-worshipers.

Noah lived 350 years after the Flood began and witnessed the typical fulfillment of the divine mandate. About a year after the mandate was issued Noah's son Shem became the father of a son whom he called Arphaxad or Arpachshad. (Genesis 10: 22; 11: 10, *A.R.V.*) The name is understood to mean "land of the Chasdim or Chaldeans", that is, "land of the conquerors or encroachers." Hence it seems to apply to the work of Shem and his brothers in conquering the land by cultivation, continually encroaching upon the uncultivated parts. Shem's son Arphaxad would continue such conquest of the soil. He was the cousin of Canaan, the son of Ham. Noah himself set the example by turning to farming. He built no cities, as Cain, who lost freedom from fear, had done.

Noah planted a vineyard, and was one day overcome by the wine therefrom. He lay uncovered in his tent. The Devil was watching for a

chance to bring reproach upon this faithful witness of Jehovah and to cause the impression
that Noah was a habitual victim of wine. "And
Ham, the father of Canaan, saw the nakedness
of his father, and told his two brethren without." (Genesis 9: 20-22) Ham neglected to cover
over his father's exposed condition until he
should recover. Instead, Ham yielded himself as
an instrument of the Old Serpent who re-
proached Jehovah and his servants, and he
noised his father's state abroad to Shem and
Japheth. These two, however, did not seize the
occasion to humble and reproach Jehovah's
prophet and servant, this "preacher of righteousness". They respected him whom the Lord
had honored for his faithful course. They did
not judge the Lord's servant and join in mis-
representing and reproaching him. They feared
Jehovah, the God whose obedient servant their
father was. "And Shem and Japheth took a garment, and laid it upon both their shoulders, and
went backward, and covered the nakedness of
their father; and their faces were backward,
and they saw not their father's nakedness."
(Genesis 9: 23) In their eyes their father bore
no shame.

Whose course was the right one in Jehovah's
eyes now became apparent. Noah, awaking from
the deep sleep induced by the wine, learned
what had occurred and how Ham had shown
neglect and shamelessness and had brought reproach upon Jehovah's servant. Then the spirit
of inspiration from God came upon Noah and

he uttered prophetic words: "Cursed be Canaan;
a servant of servants shall he be unto his brethren." Ham, who had failed of his duty toward
God, was neglected and passed by, and the curse
descended upon Canaan, who is listed as the
fourth son of Ham. Canaan's descendants, the
Canaanites, came under this curse. In course
of time they felt it when God rained down fire
and brimstone upon Sodom and Gomorrah, and
also when he brought the Israelites into Canaan
land and commanded them to destroy the Canaanite inhabitants and their religion. The
Ethiopians or Cushites are not Canaanites, but
are offspring of Cush, the first listed son of
Ham. There is no basis for the religious claim
that the native inhabitants of Africa became
black-skinned because of God's curse pronounced
upon Canaan by Noah.

Then Noah pronounced God's blessing upon
his two faithful sons; "and he said, Blessed be
Jehovah, the God of Shem; and let Canaan be
his servant. God enlarge Japheth, and let him
dwell in the tents of Shem; and let Canaan be
his servant." (Genesis 9: 26, 27, *A.R.V.*) The
Israelites and their forefathers to whom God
promised Canaan land for a possession descended from Shem and were Semites. Such Canaanites as were not executed at God's command
became servants to the Israelites who worshiped Jehovah, the God of Shem. The blessing
upon Shem gave another clue as to the woman's
Seed foretold in Eden. It showed that the Seed
would come through the line of Shem, and that

in this Seed the descendants of Japheth would
be blessed and that the descendants of Canaan,
as pictured by the Gibeonites, would become
servants of the Seed.—Joshua 9: 3-27.

Satan the Devil did not fail to note this trend
of God's purpose. Filled with enmity, he was
bent upon destroying the Seed. It was his consuming desire to invade again the human race
with religion or demonism and thereby deceive
them and turn them from Jehovah. By means
of religion he would capture control of his vic-
tims and would use them to build a visible organization on earth, and over it Satan and his
demons would be a spiritual or heavenly con-
trolling power. Jehovah's action at the Flood
had destroyed both the spirit organization and
the human organization that then existed. These
Satan purposed to replace with another heavenly organization and another earthly organization, a second "heavens" and "earth", symbolically speaking. Since Ham had come under
God's disfavor Satan proceeded to use his descendants as the spearhead of religion and to
lay the foundation of another devil-controlled
earth. Particularly in Ham's grandson Nimrod
did Satan find his instrument.

Cush was Ham's firstborn. "And Cush begat
Nimrod: he began to be a mighty one in the
earth. He was a mighty hunter before Jehovah:
wherefore it is said, Like Nimrod a mighty hunter before Jehovah. And the beginning of his
kingdom was Babel, and Erech, and Accad, and
Calneh, in the land of Shinar." (Genesis 10: 8-10,

A.R.V.) Noah was still alive, and, although being the patriarch of all humankind then, he did not set himself up over them as a king or dictator. He recognized the Theocratic rule of the Lord God, his Deliverer and Savior. He exalted Jehovah's name, the name which God had made for himself by the Flood. To overshadow God's name among men and to turn man's dependence and worship away from God, Satan the Devil brought Nimrod prominently to the fore.

Nimrod showed himself rebellious. Feeling restrained by God's everlasting covenant, he struck for freedom, as he thought, but actually he merely exercised self-will and served Satan's purposes and thereby became the slave of the Devil. For the sport of it he became a wanton slayer of beasts of the field and forest, and finally of weaker humankind. He willfully broke the covenant concerning the sanctity of blood. The sight of the rainbow meant nothing to him. He pushed God's name into the background and made himself popular, making a name for himself. He, and not Jehovah's witness Noah, became the human standard for comparison; "wherefore it is said, Like Nimrod a mighty hunter before Jehovah." This meant, "superior to and in opposition to Jehovah." [1]

Men feared hunter Nimrod rather than God, and therefore were unwise. Under him they did not gain freedom, but became ensnared in religion and enslaved to dictatorship. "The fear of

[1] The Hebrew preposition here (*liphnei*) is like that at 1 Chronicles 14:8; 2 Chronicles 14:10; 20:12; Deuteronomy 31:21.

man bringeth a snare; but whoso putteth his trust in Jehovah shall be safe." "The fear of Jehovah is the beginning of wisdom." (Proverbs 29:25, *A.R.V.*; Psalm 111:10, *A.R.V.*) Turning from fear of Jehovah, men hailed, exalted and worshiped Nimrod, and thereby religion was reinstated on the earth. Men who trusted in man misinterpreted God's prophecy and looked upon Nimrod as the promised liberator, the woman's "seed", and followed him as their leader. After his death they deified him as an immortal god, whereas Nimrod was dead. Hence Satan the Devil was the demon who received such worship.

Like the fear-stricken murderer Cain, Nimrod gathered the religious people together and builded cities. Babel was his first city. Therein he established himself as a king ruling with violence, thus ruling as a dictator and terrorizing the people. With him organized politics began, and the state set itself up over Jehovah God, because the state's head was its religious head. Union of state and religion held sway and kept the people in the darkness of error and bondage. The true worship of Jehovah God was not tolerated, but was denied freedom in Nimrod's domain. Nimrod was a Cushite, not an early Chaldean, and he extended his territories of his realm by violent aggressions. (Genesis 10:11, 12, *margin*) He believed in a master class over a slave class, and not family equality. Noah and Shem held to the truth and continued to worship Jehovah. They remained free from the religion and tyranny of Nimrod. They became no part of the demon-controlled "earth" which Satan, the mimic god, succeeded in founding through Nimrod.

Jehovah God early showed his supremacy over that religious-political capital Babel, the beginning of Nimrod's totalitarian rule. At the time there was no family of languages, but all mankind spoke one language. This was an advantage; but, instead of using this to unite themselves in the worship and service of God, they set out to turn it to selfish interest in a joint conspiracy against the true and living God. "And the whole earth was of one language and of one speech. And it came to pass, as they journeyed east, that they found a plain in the land of Shinar; and they dwelt there. And they said one to another, Come, let us make brick, and burn them thoroughly. And they had brick for stone, and slime had they for mortar. And they said, Come, let us build us a city, and a tower, whose top may reach unto heaven, and let us make us a name; lest we be scattered abroad upon the face of the whole earth."—Genesis 11:1-4, *A.R.V.*

Jehovah's Theocratic rule was here disregarded. A political rule was proposed for all the earth, and this city was to be the political capital around which all the rabble people would rally and be held together in subjection, in a common allegiance to this supergovernment. Men laid the foundation of this city, representing politics. Men's hands were its makers and builders, using kiln-burnt or sun-dried brick. The

lofty tower they started building amid the city
was not a watchtower, but was a tower of religious worship. It would tower above the city
heavenward, showing that religion was the dom-
inant part of the government. Its head was
designed to reach to heaven, that is, toward the
symbolic "heavens" of Satan and his demons.
On this tower astrology would be carried on and
the worship of the host of the visible heavens,
the sun, moon, and the stars, which man chose
to worship as symbols representative of the demons. Religion, or demon-worship, speaking
through the medium of a language common to
all the people, would be the binding tie of the
world. This would save the world. Thereby men
would make a name for themselves, exalting and
glorifying the achievements of men, rather than
the name of Jehovah, whose name had been
made glorious by the Flood.

Again it became necessary for the Most High
God to bring his name prominently before men,
who so soon after the flood were forgetting and
reproaching his name. The supremacy of the
Theocratic Ruler of the universe must be displayed, that honest men might learn and know
the truth and be free from religion and world
dictatorship or a totalitarian world. Jehovah
God did not come down bodily from his heavenly throne to inspect, but he turned his notice and
attention downward to that religious-political
effort of self-exalting men. Jehovah could also
send down his representative, his beloved Son,
the Word, if he chose. "And Jehovah said, Be-

hold, they are one people, and they have all one language; and this is what they begin to do; and now nothing will be withholden from them, which they purpose to do. Come, let us go down, and there confound their language, that they may not understand one another's speech." Jehovah then directed his power downward.

"So Jehovah scattered them abroad from thence upon the face of all the earth: and they left off building the city. Therefore was the name of it called Babel; because Jehovah did there confound the language of all the earth: and from thence did Jehovah scatter them abroad upon the face of all the earth." (Genesis 11: 5-9, *A.R.V.*) Almighty God blocked their selfish aim and broke up their organized united effort to establish a world domination by means of religion, politics and commerce, and in defiance of Jehovah. He manifested his supremacy for the benefit of those who feared him and worshiped him. Because Noah and Shem kept themselves pure and unspotted from that worldly regimentation of men by religion and politics, God did not confound their language. They continued to worship him and to be his witnesses, now to the new nations.

This Bible record was written aforetime to admonish us now when men propose to make common cause and jointly set up a "new and better world" with all earth as one neighborhood and mankind as one big family under an international government with "more religion".

CHAPTER XIII

THE COVENANT
FOR FREEDOM

O MEN the time seemed to be long since Jehovah's covenant at Eden, that the seed, or offspring, of His "woman" should crush the Serpent's head. God's *covenant* is his agreement, always solemn, whereby he expresses his purpose. This declaration of purpose, when made solely on God's part and without taking into consideration any creature or creatures, or without depending upon creature actions, is a *unilateral* or *one-sided* covenant.

The covenant at Eden was stated directly to the serpent representing Satan, but it was not made with Satan the enemy, nor was it made with Adam or Eve, each of whom had joined Satan in rebellion. Moreover, the covenant was not made dependent upon what any of these unfaithful creatures, devil or human, should do. Hence the covenant was one-sided, or unilateral. Its fulfillment depended entirely and absolutely upon Almighty God alone. This made it sure of being carried out perfectly. The purpose of Jehovah as declared in the hearing of the enemy could not fail, in spite of the enmity expressed by such foe. God-fearing men may accordingly

165

exercise full faith in God that he will vindicate his word or uphold it as true. He will thereby vindicate his name as attached to that word. In foretelling the destruction of unfaithful Lucifer, Satan, who was back of building the city of Babel, or *Babylon,* the covenant-keeping God says: "Jehovah of hosts hath sworn, saying, Surely, as I have thought, so shall it come to pass; and as I have purposed, so shall it stand. For Jehovah of hosts hath purposed, and who shall annul it? and his hand is stretched out, and who shall turn it back?"—Isaiah 14: 4, 12, 24, 27, *A.R.V.*

About four hundred years after the Flood Jehovah God gave more information in another covenant concerning the promised "Seed". Shem, one of the eight Flood survivors, was still living, and also Arphaxad (or Arpachshad), whose name means "Chaldean's land". According to Noah's blessing upon Shem, the "seed" was to be expected in his line of descent, and God chose to have that line run through Arphaxad. In course of time a city named "Ur of the Chaldees" was built on the southern bank of the river Euphrates, near where it emptied into the Persian Gulf. The Euphrates was one of the four rivers that had run out of the garden of Eden. When Shem was 450 years old and his son Arphaxad was 350 years old, a babe was born in Ur of the Chaldees, and his father Terah named him "Abram". His name means "lofty father". He was of the line of descent from Shem through Arphaxad. Abram's father

Terah had three sons, the first being born when Terah was seventy years old. Abram was the youngest, being born seventy-five years before Terah died, but because of Abram's prominence in the purpose of God he is named first of Terah's sons.—Genesis 11: 26, 32; 12: 4.

Abram grew up in Ur of the Chaldees. As Abram's and Shem's lives overlapped for 150 years, Abraham could learn direct from Shem an account of the Flood and the conditions preceding it, and also about Jehovah's promise in Eden of deliverance by a "seed". Abram manifested faith in these matters and hence in Jehovah God, and he looked forward to the day of the "seed", the day of freedom. This pleased God. He had respect to Abram for his faith. One of Abram's descendants tells what followed, saying: "The God of glory appeared unto our father Abraham, when he was in Mesopotamia, before he dwelt in Haran, and said unto him, Get thee out of thy land, and from thy kindred, and come into the land which I shall show thee. Then came he out of the land of the Chaldeans, and dwelt in Haran: and from thence, when his father was dead, God removed him into this land, wherein ye now dwell."—Acts 7: 2-4, *A.R.V.*

The account by another of Abram's descendants, Moses, reads: "Now Jehovah said unto Abram, Get thee out of thy country, and from thy kindred, and from thy father's house, unto the land that I will show thee: and I will make of thee a great nation, and I will bless thee, and make thy name great; and be thou a blessing; and I will bless them that bless thee, and him that curseth thee will I curse: and in thee shall all the families of the earth be blessed."—Genesis 12: 1-3, *A.R.V.*

This fixed it, that the seed of God's "woman" should be through this faithful man, this witness of Jehovah. This declaration of divine purpose to Abram was a unilateral covenant of Jehovah, further foretelling the channel through which the "seed" should come, and also guaranteeing that a blessing should come to all families of the earth, not indiscriminately or automatically, but only to all those that blessed Abram, whereas those that cursed him should be cursed. In harmony with this covenant God later changed the name of the 99-year-old Abram to that of *Abraham,* meaning "father of a multitude".

One of Abraham's descendants became an apostle of the "seed" and declared under inspiration that Abraham was used as a type or prophetic figure of Jehovah God. God is himself the "Lofty Father" and is the Father of the "seed" and of the multitude of those who get life and freedom through the "seed". (Romans 4: 16, 17, *margin*) Therefore to Abraham God really promised that He would make the name of Jehovah great and that in Jehovah should all the families of the earth be blessed, if they blessed Jehovah's name. Those that cursed Jehovah should be cursed like the Serpent. By this fact Abraham's wife would also become a type, a prophetic picture of God's "woman", who brings forth the "seed", God's "woman" being his holy organization named *Zion*. For this reason God changed the name of Abraham's wife from Sarai to Sarah, meaning "princess".

Whether Abraham would be a party to this covenant depended upon his faith as proved by works. When he did leave the land of the Chaldeans and moved into the land which God showed him, namely, the land of Canaan, now Palestine, then the covenant applied to him, he became party thereto, and it became a two-sided or bilateral covenant. However, the unilateral-covenant purpose of Jehovah God as given at Eden still stood and depended upon no man, but would go through regardless of any individual creature. Whether a creature will have a part while that covenant is undergoing fulfillment rests upon the faith and faithfulness of such creature. Abraham showed faith and faithfulness to the end, and hence was used as a party to the covenant.

Abraham did not settle down in Canaan and build a city with his own hands and lay claim to the country. The Canaanites worshiped false gods, demons, but Abraham worshiped Jehovah. Once Abraham was obliged to go down into Egypt. Then Satan the Devil, in his enmity against the promised seed, tried to bring about the defilement of Abraham's wife Sarah by Pharaoh, Egypt's king, and thus make Sarah unfit to be the mother of Abraham's offspring.

Jehovah God, the Greater Abraham, frustrated Satan's move and kept Sarah clean and pure and fit to be used as a picture of God's "woman". In the politics of Canaan land Abraham took no part, and as to the local controversies, or the controversies with outside nations, he stood absolutely neutral. He believed that God would give him and his offspring the land in His own time and way.

At that time in Canaan there was an outstanding king, one who did worship Jehovah God. His name was Melchizedek. He was ruler of the city of Salem, which later became Jerusalem, some think. The Bible gives no record of Melchizedek's father or mother or of his descendants, nor of his age, nor of the end of his life. He and Abraham met, in the following way: Abraham's nephew Lot had come with him to Canaan. For economic reasons Lot separated from Abraham and pitched his tents near Sodom in the Jordan river plain. Thereby Lot was near the scene of a fight between five local kings and four aggressor kings from outside Canaan. Lot and his household were scooped up among the captives taken by the victorious aggressor kings and were carried away. Not because Lot was his flesh-and-blood relative, but because Lot was one of the faith of the same God as Abraham worshiped, Abraham armed 318 of his trained servants and pursued the plunderers. He smote them and recovered his fellow believer Lot and his household and property. On his way back, as Abraham approached

Salem, its king came forth to meet him, and offered him refreshments.

"And Melchizedek king of Salem brought forth bread and wine: and he was the priest of the most high God. And he blessed him, and said, Blessed be Abram of the most high God, possessor of heaven and earth; and blessed be the most high God, which hath delivered thine enemies into thy hand. And he gave him tithes of all." (Genesis 14:18-20) This priest-king blessed Abraham, and Abraham gave him a tenth of all he had recovered.

This happening was maneuvered of Jehovah God and was prophetic. It foretold that the "seed" of God's organization would be Jehovah's high priest and also a king of righteousness and peace, and that he would vindicate Jehovah's name and bless it. Hence God made this declaration concerning the "seed", saying: "Jehovah hath sworn, and will not repent: Thou art a priest for ever after the order of Melchizedek." (Psalm 110:4, *A.R.V.*) This gives us a hope of a government of righteousness and peace over earth by God's "seed". "Which hope we have as an anchor of the soul, both sure and stedfast, and which entereth into that within the veil; whither the forerunner is for us entered, even Jesus, made an high priest for ever after the order of Melchisedec. For this Melchisedec, king of Salem, priest of the most high God, who met Abraham returning from the slaughter of the kings, and blessed him; to whom also Abraham gave a tenth part of all;

first being by interpretation [of the name Melchisedec] King of righteousness, and after that also King of Salem, which is, King of peace; without father, without mother, without descent, having neither beginning of days, nor end of life; but made like unto the Son of God; abideth a priest continually. Now consider how

great this man was, unto whom even the patriarch Abraham gave the tenth of the spoils."
—Hebrews 6:19, 20; 7:1-4.

Abraham grew to ninety-nine years of age, and it now seemed hopeless that he would have offspring by Sarah, ten years younger than himself. Then Almighty God by his messenger appeared unto Abraham and promised that almighty power would duly give Abraham and Sarah a son, whose name should be called *Isaac*. Before the birth of Isaac the destruction of Sodom and Gomorrah by fire and brimstone took place, and Lot and his two daughters were saved from that fate. Once again Satan the Devil tried to contaminate Abraham's offspring by the action of the Philistine king Abimelech, but God delivered Sarah from defilement by this devil-worshiper and restored her to Abraham. Thereafter Isaac was born, when Abraham was one hundred years old, hence by a miracle of God and by His spirit or active force. He was not "born after the flesh", but was "born after the spirit".—Galatians 4:28, 29; Romans 4:17-22.

Isaac was Abraham's only begotten son by his wife Sarah, and he loved Isaac most dearly. In this relationship of these three Abraham typified or pictured Jehovah God as Father of the promised "seed". His wife Sarah pictured God's holy organization from which Jehovah brings forth the "seed", and which organization is symbolized in Scripture as a chaste, holy "woman" of God and named *Zion*. The "woman" is God's universal organization composed of his faithful creatures who are in covenant relationship with him, being consecrated and devoted to him. The entire universal organization is united to him by holy bonds like the bonds of wedlock, from which there is no divorce except with destruction to the unfaithful creature thus separated from God. Isaac pictured God's only begotten Son, the Word, the Head of God's universal organization. God's only begotten Son was taken out of that organization to become the "man Christ Jesus" and thereafter become a king and priest for ever "after the order of Melchizedek".

Abraham brought up Isaac in the faith and obedience of Jehovah, as God had said: "For I have known him, to the end that he may command his children and his household after him, that they may keep the way of Jehovah, to do righteousness and justice; to the end that Jehovah may bring upon Abraham that which he hath spoken of him." (Genesis 18:19, *A.R.V.*) When Isaac had grown to be a young man with faith like his father's, then God put both father and son to a great test of their integrity or soundness of faith and devotion toward God. By faithfully performing their parts through His grace and help, the father and son would have part in a prophetic drama foreshadowing events of highest importance to come. God commanded Abraham to take Isaac and travel a three days' journey northward to the land of Moriah and there offer him up as a whole burnt-offering to God on one of the mountains.

Abraham, by obeying and proceeding to the sacrifice, proved his love for his Creator was greater than his love for his only begotten son.

When they reached the place of sacrifice and reared an altar therefor, Abraham revealed to Isaac that God had designated him to be the victim. Isaac did not run away, but with devotion to Jehovah God he determined to keep his integrity toward his God faithfully to the death. He submitted to being bound and laid upon the wood of the altar. Abraham raised the knife in his hand and was at the extreme point of striking Isaac dead before lighting the altar fire. At that instant Isaac was as good as dead for his faithfulness. To Abraham he was as good as dead and fully sacrificed. Another instant and—but in a flash Jehovah's angel called and halted the death-thrust and declared Abraham's test of his fear of God was sufficient. Then God provided a ram caught in the thicket by his horns, and Abraham offered it up in symbol of Isaac.

"And the angel of Jehovah called unto Abraham a second time out of heaven, and said, By myself have I sworn, saith Jehovah, because thou hast done this thing, and hast not withheld thy son, thine only son, that in blessing I will bless thee, and in multiplying I will multiply thy seed as the stars of the heavens, and as the sand which is upon the sea-shore; and thy seed shall possess the gate of his enemies; and in thy seed shall all the nations of the earth be blessed." (Genesis 22: 15-18, *A.R.V.*) With this utterance God's covenant with Abraham was complete. It showed that freedom from the enemies of God and man would be won by the victory of the promised "seed". God pointed out that others should be associated together with the "seed" as sons of God, but that the number of them all was not yet to be disclosed but was like the stars and the grains of sand, beyond man's power then to number.

By the "seed" all nations blessing and obeying Jehovah God should be blessed. According to the Hebrew text: "So shall all the nations of the earth bless themselves in thy seed." (*Roth.*) The blessing would not be automatic, but by exercising faith and obedience the people of all nationalities would receive blessing.

In this prophetic drama of Abraham and Isaac on Mount Moriah it was correctly foreshadowed that the Son of God would keep his integrity toward God faithfully to the death for the vindication of his Father's name, and that out of love for the righteous new world Jehovah God would give this Son to be the Seed and the King like Melchizedek. "For God so loved the world, that he gave his only begotten Son, that whosoever believeth in him should not perish, but have everlasting life."—John 3:16.

CHAPTER XIV

BIRTHRIGHT OF FREEDOM

O WHOM would the precious birthright to the promise or covenant made with Abraham descend? Jehovah God, who was typified by Abraham, determined that; for He is the Author and Finisher of the covenant. He guided Abraham in the typical drama.

When Abraham was 137 years old his faithful wife Sarah died. Word had come from the city of Haran in Mesopotamia, near the headwaters of the Euphrates river, where Abraham's older brother Nahor took up residence. It told that to Nahor's son Bethuel had been born a daughter Rebekah, and that she was now a mature woman. Abraham's son Isaac was now going on forty, but still single. He refused to marry any of the daughters of the land, who were Canaanites, descendants of the accursed Canaan. Isaac waited upon his father Abraham to provide him a wife and thus arrange for the handing on of the covenant of promise. The wife must be a God-fearing woman and of Abraham's immediate relationship. Neither did Abraham return to the land from which Jehovah God had led him forth, nor did he permit his son Isaac to go there, but he sent his oldest servant of his house there to procure a wife for Isaac from

among his kindred. Outside the city the Lord
God brought this servant Eliezer at once in
touch with the prospective wife, Rebekah, at
the well where he stopped to water his camels.
After giving his camels drink and then learning
Eliezer's identity Rebekah ran home and reported Abraham's servant as outside the city.
Her brother Laban hastened forth at once and
brought the man into the home.

Before accepting a meal, Eliezer without delay made known his errand to Rebekah's father, Bethuel. Both Bethuel and Laban said:
"The thing proceedeth from Jehovah: we cannot speak unto thee bad or good. Behold, Rebekah is before thee, take her, and go, and let
her be thy master's son's wife, as Jehovah hath
spoken." After a feast and the night's rest
Eliezer asked to be let return with Rebekah to
his master's abode. Rebekah agreed to go, as the
case was urgent from the Lord. "And they
blessed Rebekah, and said unto her, Our sister,
be thou the mother of thousands of ten thousands, and let thy seed possess the gate of those
that hate them." (Genesis 24: 50, 51, 60, A.R.V.)
As the camels neared the destination, bearing
Eliezer and Isaac's betrothed, Isaac was in the
field and saw them coming. The caravan was
halted, and Rebekah alighted and covered herself with her bridal veil. "And the servant told
Isaac all things that he had done. And Isaac
brought her into his mother Sarah's tent, and
took Rebekah, and she became his wife; and he
loved her: and Isaac was comforted after his

mother's death." (Genesis 24: 66, 67) There is
no record that a religious clergyman was present or took any part in these proceedings; for
the whole matter was according to the arrang-
ing and law of Jehovah God.

This delightful part of the prophetic drama
carries farther the picture that Abraham's seed
should be as the stars and the sands for multitude. It pictures that the only begotten Son of
God as the "Seed" would not be alone, but that
Jehovah God would give him associates in God's
purpose, over whom the Son would be the Head
as a husband is head over the wife. (1 Corinthians 11: 3) Accordingly, Isaac continues to
typify Christ Jesus as the Seed, while Rebekah
typifies the company of Christian associates
whom Jehovah God in his purpose gives as a
"bride" to Christ Jesus. They are the "body of
Christ", of which Jesus Christ is the Head. By
marriage to Isaac, Rebekah became the daugh-
ter-in-law of Abraham and became one with
Isaac, the typical seed of the promise. This pictures how those who make up Christ's bride, or
"the Lamb's wife", would by adoption of God
be united with the Seed Christ Jesus and thereby become part of the Seed of the Greater
Abraham.

This is not the "private interpretation" of
any man. The Scriptures remove all doubt of
that. Under heavenly inspiration it is written:
"Know therefore that they that are of faith, the
same are sons of Abraham. And the scripture,
foreseeing that God would justify the Gentiles

by faith, preached the gospel beforehand unto
Abraham, saying, In thee shall all the nations
be blessed. Now to Abraham were the promises
spoken, and to his seed. He saith not, And to
seeds, as of many; but as of one, And to thy
seed, WHICH IS CHRIST." (Galatians 3:7, 8, 16,
A.R.V.) This proves that Christ Jesus is the
Seed of the Greater Abraham, Jehovah. By
Christ Jesus Jehovah blesses those showing
faith and proving it, and then he adopts them
as his sons and makes them one with Christ
Jesus, The Seed, so making them part of the
"seed". "For ye are all the children of God by
faith in Christ Jesus. . . . For ye are all one in
Christ Jesus. And if ye be Christ's, then are ye
Abraham's seed, and heirs according to the
promise."—Galatians 3:26-29.

Just how many were thus to be associated
with Christ Jesus as his "bride" God's covenant
to Abraham did not reveal; they were left without number, like the stars and sands. In due
time God chose to make known the exact number. (Revelation 7:4-8; 14:1, 3) In proof that
Isaac typified the promised Seed who unites the
"bride" class with himself as children of God
and of his organization, and in proof that
Isaac's mother Sarah pictured God's "woman",
his organization Zion or the heavenly Jerusalem, it is written to Christ's body of followers:
"But Jerusalem which is above is free, which is
the mother of us all. Now we, brethren, as Isaac
was, are the children of promise. So then, brethren, we are not children of the bondwoman, but

of the free." (Galatians 4: 26, 28, 31) God's organization is one of truth, and hence is free.

God foreknew clearly and he also predetermined or predestinated who was the One to be his instrument for making His name great and blessing believers among men. This fact becomes clearer as the prophetic proceedings move on. Never is it to be forgotten that the Old Serpent, in his bitter enmity toward the promised Seed, was ever alert and ready to spring in order to thwart the fulfillment of Jehovah's covenant and so prove himself mightier than God. After twenty years of barrenness Isaac's wife became fruitful, by God's mercy. The Lord revealed to her that she was bearing twins, and that the one born second would become stronger than the one born first, and God decreed that "the elder shall serve the younger". (Genesis 25: 21-23) This meant that the younger was God's choice for the birthright to his covenant with Abraham. The Old Serpent, however, immediately set himself to sabotage this divine decision and to bring reproach upon God's choice.

When Rebekah's time was full, the firstborn was called Esau, and the second twin, whose hand took hold on his brother's heel, was named Jacob, or "Supplanter". The twins grew to manhood. Esau became a hunter. Jacob engaged in managerial and constructive work about his father Isaac's tents, and in learning of God's covenants, the fulfillment of which he desired. Esau cared not for the covenant with Abraham, and hunted and interested himself in the accursed daughters of Canaan, looking for wives among them. Yet he claimed the right to the Abrahamic covenant by virtue of the law of the land concerning firstborn sons. Not knowing that God had decreed that the birthright belonged to the younger twin, Jacob, but showing his contempt for God's word and loving his belly, Esau sold his birthright claim to Jacob for a savory mess of pottage. For this God's Word calls Esau a fornicator and a profane person; and rightly God judged the twin sons, saying: "Jacob have I loved, but Esau have I hated." (Romans 9: 10-13; Malachi 1: 2, 3) Jacob now possessed the birthright by two things, by God's decree and by right of purchase of all claim thereto. —Genesis 25: 27-34.

The Devil hated Jacob and watched to destroy him while childless. At Gerar, in Palestine, God had restated the terms of the Abrahamic covenant to Isaac. (Genesis 26: 1-6) The time came for Isaac, as receiver from Abraham, to pass on the birthright blessing to his successor. Esau kept his father ignorant of the sale of his claim to the birthright. He acted hypocritically as if it was rightfully his and, at his father's bidding, went out hunting before coming to receive the blessing. God caused Rebekah to learn of Esau's plot and guided her in harmony with what God had told her before the birth of Esau and Jacob. As a result Isaac bestowed the blessing upon God's choice, Jacob, and said: "Let thy mother's

sons bow down to thee: cursed be every one
that curseth thee, and blessed be he that bless-
eth thee." (Genesis 27: 27-29) Isaac, due to age,
had become sightless and did not see upon
whom he was bestowing the blessing. Hence the
course of the blessing was not of man's will,
but of God's will, that the purpose of Jehovah

might stand. (Romans 9:11) He never misplaces blessings.

Afterward Esau came in, presumptuously to claim and receive the birthright blessing, only to learn that Jacob had acted in keeping with the sale made years previous to him. Grieved because he had failed to cheat his brother, the rightful heir of the promise, Esau planned to kill Jacob at their father's death. Meantime he married Canaanite women. His whole course shows he was unworthy to inherit the blessing; wherefore God ruled against him.

Jacob was now past seventy years of age. His mother Rebekah, hearing of Esau's murderous purpose, instructed her faithful son to avoid Esau and flee to her brother Laban's home in Syria. Ere he departed, blind Isaac counseled Jacob as heir of the promise not to imitate Esau's unclean conduct, but to go to his cousin's home in Syria (or Padan-aram) and take a wife from his household. Then, and this time knowingly, Isaac repeated God's blessing upon Jacob, showing that this one was the approved heir.

Jacob departed for Syria. On the way he was obliged to sleep out in the open field, near a place called Luz. He arranged stones for his pillow, and lay down to sleep. Jehovah sent a dream to the sleeper and assured Jacob he had done right and was a man of faith pleasing to God and was chosen of him. "And he dreamed; and, behold, a ladder set up on the earth, and the top of it reached to heaven; and, behold, the

angels of God ascending and descending on it."
From the top thereof Jehovah spoke to Jacob
and extended the terms of the Abrahamic covenant to him, and said: "And in thee and in thy
seed shall all the families of the earth be
blessed." On awaking early next morning Jacob
made a pillar of his pillow stones and anointed
it and called the name of the place "Bethel",
meaning "House of God". Jacob also vowed that
if God would guide him and provide for him
and bring him safely home again, then "Jehovah
will be my God".—Genesis, chapter 28, *A.R.V.*

Reaching the city of Haran in Syria, Jacob
was well received by Laban his uncle and was
made at home. He contracted for marriage to
him of Laban's two daughters, Leah and Rachel.
By them, and their maidservants who represented their mistresses in childbearing, Jacob
became father to eleven sons and a daughter.
He also acquired large herds of domestic animals and a large body of servants. This caused
jealousy in Laban's household, and God commanded Jacob to leave and return to the promised land. Esau, hearing of his coming, went out
to meet him, and Jacob sent gifts ahead to him.
The night before meeting Esau Jacob was
visited by an angel of Jehovah, and Jacob
wrestled with the angel, in human form, for a
divine blessing before he faced Esau. Then this
deputy of God changed Jacob's name to Israel,
saying, "For thou hast striven with God and
with men, and hast prevailed." For this reason
"Israel" is understood to mean "Ruling with

God; soldier (wrestler) with God". This was the reward for his unbreakable faith.

The meeting of Jacob and Esau passed off without Esau's carrying out his threat of twenty years previous. Esau returned to the country of Seir, and Jacob moved on and pitched tent for a time near Shechem, and he set up an altar of worship and called it *"El-e-lo-he-Israel"*, meaning "God, the God of Israel". This God was Jehovah, as Jacob had so said at Bethel, the site of his ladder dream. In process of time God commanded Jacob to make a return visit to Bethel. There God made an appearance to Jacob and confirmed the change of his name to that of *Israel,* and also the promise respecting the seed of Abraham. On the journey from Bethel, and as they neared Ephrath (later called Bethlehem) Jacob's dear wife Rachel gave birth to her second son, Benjamin, but she died from her hard childbirth. Her other son was Joseph. Jacob now was father to twelve sons. With them he was privileged to visit his father Isaac before this blind old patriarch died at 180 years.

Regarding Isaac's death the record at Genesis 35:29, according to the *King James Version,* reads: "And Isaac gave up the ghost, and died, and was gathered unto his people, being old and full of days: and his sons Esau and Jacob buried him." The *Douay Version* of the same verse reads: "And being spent with age he died, and was gathered to his people." The *Rotherham* version reads: "And Isaac breathed his last and died and was added unto his people."

Comparison of these three authoritative renderings explodes the false doctrine based on the Serpent's lie in Eden, that an immortal soul inhabits man's body and that as a ghost it escapes from the body at death and hovers about in a spirit world, awaiting a reunion with the body in the resurrection time. Such is nothing but the demonic religion of the ancient Egyptians, who made mummies by embalming the dead bodies and encasing them in coffins in the belief that at judgment day the soul would re-enter the body and the person would live again. It is a foolish effort of the demons to disprove God's sentence upon Adam, "Dust thou art, and unto dust shalt thou return." As for Isaac, he died and was buried, and to him Jesus' words apply: "No man hath ascended up to heaven."

Isaac's son Jacob continued to dwell in tents as a sojourner in an alien land, taking no part in this world's doings, but looking forward to the new world of righteousness. Esau and his descendants, however, built cities in the territory of Seir and set up kingdoms and duchies. Jacob looked for the setting up of God's kingdom through the promised Seed. He erected no city or cities built with man's hands. Like Abraham and Isaac he held fast his integrity toward Jehovah's promise and was a faithful witness for him.

In approval of these three forefathers of the promised Seed, Jehovah caused this record to be written: "By faith Abraham, when he was called to go out into a place which he should after receive for an inheritance, obeyed; and he went out, not knowing whither he went. By faith he sojourned in the land of promise, as in a strange country, dwelling in tabernacles with Isaac and Jacob, the heirs with him of the same promise: for he looked for a city which hath foundations, whose builder and maker is God. These all died in faith, not having received the promises [fulfilled], but having seen them afar off, and were persuaded of them, and embraced them, and confessed that they were strangers and pilgrims on the earth. For they that say such things declare plainly that they seek a country. And truly, if they had been mindful of that country from whence they came out, they might have had opportunity to have returned. But now they desire a better country, that is, an heavenly: wherefore God is not ashamed to be called their God: for he hath prepared for them a city."—Hebrews 11: 8-10, 13-16.

That "city", or organized government, they shall occupy as princes on earth under the heavenly kingdom of the Seed of God's "woman". For such reason Christ Jesus, the Seed, said regarding their faith: "Abraham rejoiced to see my day: and he saw it, and was glad." (John 8: 56) For their faith and works they are listed by name with Jehovah's "so great a cloud of witnesses".—Hebrews 12: 1.

CHAPTER XV

A FREE NATION IS BORN

 NAME placed upon a man by God, who knows the end from the beginning, throws light upon the part such man will play in the purpose of Almighty God. This rule holds true of Jacob. "And God said unto him, Thy name is Jacob: thy name shall not be called any more Jacob, but Israel shall be thy name: and he called his name Israel. And God said unto him, I am God Almighty: be fruitful and multiply; a nation and a company of nations shall be of thee, and kings shall come out of thy loins."—Genesis 35: 10, 11.

The nation of Israel was foretold, composed of Israelites, or descendants of the man Israel. It was to be a free nation, not a part of this world and its religion, commerce and politics, but free of the world and subject only to the law of Jehovah, the God of Israel. Its king was to sit representatively upon the throne of Jehovah God and to rule as His servant and in the fear of God. The nation was to be a typical Theocracy, that is, a nation administered by God and governed by his commandments. Thus it would foreshadow a greater nation to come and its King, namely, the kingdom of God by his Seed. This latter nation is the everlasting Theocratic Government by which obedient men

of all nations and families will be for ever
blessed. How God proceeded to fulfill this covenant promise to Jacob is of universal interest.

God's great opponent, Satan the Devil, set
himself to cause the divine covenant to collapse
and thereby prove God unable to make good
his word. Noting the special favor that Jacob,
or Israel, bestowed upon his beloved son Joseph,
the Devil stirred up jealousy in his ten half
brothers. This was aggravated when God favored Joseph with dreams foretelling his exal-
tation in God's due time and way. To defeat
the divine purpose Joseph's brethren sold him
into slavery in Egypt, the first world power of
Bible record.

The enmity of the Devil further pursued
Joseph as a slave in the land of Ham, and the
young man was framed, falsely accused, and
thrown into the dungeon of the state's prison.
Joseph, however, did not lose faith in God, who
had sent him the dreams. He maintained his integrity toward Jehovah and was given the privilege of being a witness for Jehovah. After a
number of years God caused Joseph to be
brought forth from the prison and before the
mighty ruler of Egypt to interpret Pharaoh's
dreams. By God's power Joseph interpreted the
dreams, foretelling seven years of plenty upon
all Egypt, followed by seven years of dire famine. The situation required to be taken in hand
immediately, and Pharaoh appointed Joseph as
his prime minister to prepare for famine relief
and to safeguard Egypt's freedom from want.

When the seven years of abundance were up, the seven-year famine set in. But Egypt was ready.

The famine affected the rest of the earth, and Joseph's ten half brothers came to Egypt for supplies, but failed to recognize Joseph in his exalted position. Using his power, Joseph obliged them to bring his young brother, Benjamin, on their return trip for provisions. Then after feasting his eleven brothers Joseph privately revealed to them who he was. They were in fear for their lives, but Joseph assured them that Jehovah God had permitted all things for good of his faithful servants and had defeated the Devil's purposes. Then Joseph sent them back to Canaan to bring their father and all their households down to Egypt, to live in that land for the remainder of the famine period. Joseph arranged with Pharaoh for them to be settled in the land of Goshen, and there they were well taken care of. The Egyptians, however, ran out of money and of other things to give in exchange for foodstuffs and finally sold themselves and their lands to Pharaoh for life sustenance. Consequently the people were now dependent upon their ruler by his prime minister for living support, and Joseph disposed them and their matters throughout Egypt for their security against want and unemployment. All the outside countries also came to Joseph for living supplies.—Genesis, chapters 37 to 47.

Almighty God, who staged this powerful prophetic drama and preserved the record of it till

now, purposed that it should mark out for men
the course that leads to everlasting life in this
supreme world crisis. All who seek freedom
from death, want and fear must obey the instructions and laws of the Supreme Ruler,
greater than Pharaoh. They must come to God's
Chief Servant, the Seed of his "woman", Christ
Jesus. They must "sell" or devote themselves to
Jehovah God and accept at the hands of his
great Servant the life-giving supplies of the
truth now released through God's Word, the
Bible. Unless this is done, any world conference
on material food and any machinery established
by world rulers to deal with the food problem
and other postwar problems are vain. Such human expedients will not usher in permanent relief, social security, good order, peace, prosperity, and the desired freedoms. "Man doth not
live by bread only, but by everything that proceedeth out of the mouth of Jehovah doth man
live." The One who is greater than Joseph repeated that truth.—Deuteronomy 8:3, *A.R.V.;*
Matthew 4:3, 4.

In Egypt Israel's relationship grew to number seventy souls. The time came for him to die,
at an age of 147 years, the last seventeen years
thereof being spent with Joseph in Egypt. Under God's guidance Israel assembled his twelve
sons about his bed and gave them a witness concerning Jehovah and his covenant. Then as
God's instrument he bestowed the divine blessing upon these twelve pillars of the coming nation of Israel, made up of twelve tribes.

With God's spirit of inspiration upon him Israel indicated the tribe through which the promised ruler of the kingdom of God, The Theocratic Government, should come. He said: "Judah is a lion's whelp: . . . The sceptre shall not depart from Judah, nor a lawgiver from between his feet, until Shiloh come; and unto him shall the gathering of the people be." (Genesis 49: 9, 10) The coming King should be "The Lion of the tribe of Juda". Of the twelve channels issuing forth from Jacob, the royal Seed of promise would proceed through *Judah,* whose name means "praise", praise to God. Judah and his brethren are now spoken of as tribal heads: "All these are the twelve tribes of Israel: and this is it that their father spake unto them, and blessed them; every one according to his blessing he blessed them." (Genesis 49: 28) *Twelve* is a Scriptural symbol of complete, balanced organization; and the twelve tribes of Israel are used as a type of the complete organization of the coming great Theocratic nation under the Seed, Shiloh, "the Prince of Peace."—Revelation 7: 4-8; 5: 5; Isaiah 9: 6, 7.

The twelve tribes of the children of Israel enjoyed freedom of worship and freedom from want, fear and oppression till the death of Joseph, Egypt's prime minister. Under God's blessing in harmony with his irresistible purpose they multiplied greatly. With Joseph dead, Satan thought he had God's chosen people now where he wanted them. Egypt had not taken up the worship of Joseph's God, Jehovah, but continued in religion, doing homage to the demons. Satan tried to pollute the Israelites with such religion and by it turn them to unfaithfulness toward Jehovah. Then he raised up a Pharaoh on Egypt's throne who knew not or acknowledged not the debt the nation owed to Joseph and his God Jehovah. Moved by nationalism and ideas that the Egyptians were a master race, this Pharaoh served the Devil well by issuing decrees of state for the wiping out of the alien Israelites and to work them to death as slaves. Not all the Israelites became defiled by religion, but some few held to their faith in Jehovah and resisted such mischief framed by law against Jehovah and his people. Under these devilish conditions in Egypt Moses was born to a man of the tribe of Levi, named Amram, and his wife, Jochebed.

Jehovah, moving ahead with his purpose, preserved this Levite child from Pharaoh's bloody sword, and even caused him to be adopted into Pharaoh's household and brought up by Pharaoh's own daughter. Until turning him over to his adopted mother, Moses' parents raised the child up in the nurture and admonition and faith of the God of Abraham, Isaac, and Jacob. At Pharaoh's court Moses grew to manhood, while his people ceased not to multiply in spite of the cruel oppression of Nazified Egypt. Moses did not adopt Egypt's religion, but clung to his faith in Jehovah and sought the freeing of his people. In his effort to start their deliverance an Egyptian slave-driver was killed. In

danger now of his own life and seeing that the
time was not ripe, Moses left Egypt and took
refuge in Arabia with a Midianite prince, who
was a descendant of Moses' own forefather,
Abraham. Moses married the prince's daughter
and took up shepherding. Forty years passed
thus.

Jehovah's foretold time came to make his
chosen people a free nation. From the time of
Abraham's entrance into the promised land and
becoming party to God's covenant 430 years had
passed, and the groaning of the Israelites under oppression of a new Pharaoh increased. One
day, at a miraculously burning bush at the foot
of Mount Horeb, God's angel called to Moses
tending his flocks and ordered him to return to
Egypt and lead the Israelites out of bondage
and bring them to this mountain to worship
God. Moses asked in whose name he was to go
on this mission. "And God said unto Moses, I
AM THAT I AM: and he said, Thus shalt thou say
unto the children of Israel, I AM hath sent me
unto you. And God said moreover unto Moses,
Thus shalt thou say unto the children of Israel,
Jehovah, the God of your fathers, the God of
Abraham, the God of Isaac, and the God of
Jacob, hath sent me unto you: this is my name
for ever, and this is my memorial unto all generations. Go." (Exodus 3:14-16, *A.R.V.*) Moses
must be Jehovah's witness in Egypt.

Moses then met with the Israelites in Egypt
and presented his credentials and God's declaration of purpose, symbolized by the name

"Jehovah". With his brother Aaron Moses next appeared before Pharaoh and demanded in Jehovah's name the release of the Israelites and their freedom to worship Jehovah at the holy mountain. In defiance Pharaoh retorted: "Who is Jehovah, that I should hearken unto his voice to let Israel go? I know not Jehovah, and moreover I will not let Israel go." (Exodus 5:2, *A.R.V.*) Thereupon Jehovah through Moses as his servant and prophet afflicted Egypt with ten plagues demonstrating Jehovah's supremacy and all-power. Pharaoh's priests of religion resisted, but in vain. Pharaoh was serving the Devil, and thus stood as a symbol of the Devil. Hence, in a message to Pharaoh Jehovah told why He has permitted the Devil to continue existing and wickedly opposing God. Jehovah said: "But for this cause have I allowed thee to remain, in order to show thee my power; and in order that they [my witnesses] may proclaim my name throughout all the earth." (Exodus 9:16, *Leeser*) The last four plagues followed this revelation.

The tenth plague was the destruction of all of Egypt's firstborn children and beasts. In order to have their firstborn children passed over during this last plague the Israelites were commanded to kill the passover lamb and to eat it in their houses behind doors sprinkled with its blood. In God's ancient typical arrangements his covenants became in force and active over the blood of a sacrificial victim. The sprinkling of the passover lamb's blood was therefore the

beginning of God's special covenant of the law
with the nation of Israel. Thereby they definitely came into covenant relationship with him and
subject to his law. So they became a Theocratic
nation, and their birth or bringing forth to freedom immediately followed. All this was a prophetic drama, in which the passover lamb became a symbol or type of a greater Sacrifice by
which a new covenant with God is brought
about. This Sacrifice is the antitypical Isaac,
"the Lamb of God which taketh away the sin
of the world" and which is Christ Jesus.—John
1: 29, 36.

That passover night, the fourteenth day of
the first month according to God's calendar,
Pharaoh was bereaved of his firstborn and he

sent and begged Moses and his people to get out
of Egypt. The Israelites congregated together
and moved out. As they went Jehovah's pillar
of cloud appeared before them and led them.
It became a pillar of fiery illumination by night.
To the shore of the Red sea they were led. In
hardened bitterness Pharaoh and his armed
hosts took up the pursuit of them, hoping to
trap them at the seashore and drag them back
to bondage. Then Moses raised the staff in his
hand, and Jehovah parted the waters of the Red
sea and His people marched through dryshod.
When Pharaoh's hosts rashly advanced into the
seabed in hot chase, God caused their military
equipment to drag and bog down. He brought
the parted waters together and engulfed Pharaoh's elite troops. Safe on the other side Moses
led God's people in singing the song of victory:
"I will sing unto Jehovah, for he hath triumphed
gloriously: the horse and his rider hath he
thrown into the sea. Jehovah is my strength and
song, and he is become my salvation: this is my
God, and I will praise him; my father's God, and
I will exalt him." (Exodus 15:1, 2, *A.R.V.*)
Thus Israel became a nation of Jehovah's witnesses, obligated to publish his name throughout the earth.

On their journey now as a free nation it became necessary to provide food miraculously to
feed the Israelites in the wilderness of Arabia.
It was called "manna", and was provided each
morning for six days, but not on the seventh
day. When the people asked why not, Moses

told them: "Six days ye shall gather it; but on the seventh day, which is the sabbath, in it there shall be none." "So the people rested on the seventh day." (Exodus 16: 26, 30) This is the first record where a people observed a weekly sabbath or rest day. It is the first time that God commanded his servants to keep a sabbath day. This proves that the Israelites were now under the Law Covenant with Jehovah. For forty years thereafter, while in the wilderness, they were faithfully fed with this miraculous manna.

In the third month after leaving Egypt the Israelites reached the foot of Mount Horeb or Sinai. There Jehovah said to the newborn nation: "Ye have seen what I did unto the Egyptians, and how I bare you on eagles' wings, and brought you unto myself. Now therefore, if ye will obey my voice indeed, and keep my covenant, then ye shall be a peculiar treasure unto me above all people: for all the earth is mine: and ye shall be unto me a kingdom of priests, and an holy nation." (Exodus 19: 4-6) The Israelites agreed to keep covenant. The third day thereafter God caused a terrific demonstration of power and glory on Mount Sinai. Then he called Moses up the mountain and declared to him the basic law, the Ten Commandments, and also many other detailed laws of the covenant. The first four of the Ten Commandments commanded His covenant people to have no other than Jehovah as God and to make no idols and worship them, and not to take his name upon them in vain, and to keep the seventh day of each week holy as a sabbath to Him. The other commandments declared how they must conduct themselves aright toward their fellow man, especially those in the covenant with God.

Moses came down from the mountain. As mediator between God and the nation of Israel, he inaugurated the law covenant toward the Israelites over the blood of sacrificial animals, and sprinkled both the written book of the law and also the people with the blood. Again Jehovah called Moses into the mountain and detained him there forty days without food or drink. He gave Moses two stone tablets engraved with the Ten Commandments and also a larger statement of the law. He also instructed Moses to induct the family of Aaron as a priesthood and the entire tribe of Levi as servants of the priest. Moses must also have a sacred tabernacle made and set up where sacrifice to God could be offered and where atonement for the sins of the entire nation could be made on a yearly atonement day.

During Moses' absence of forty days the Devil weakened the faith of the people and induced them to break the Ten Commandments and set up a golden calf for worship. Moses came down upon them amidst their wanton idolatry and broke the two tablets of the law in displeasure, and then ordered the idol destroyed. The whole tribe of Levi took the side of Jehovah in the matter and executed three thousand idolaters. Then Moses again ascended the mountain to intercede as mediator in behalf of the people

whom Jehovah had taken out of the world for
his name. So the Lord God withdrew from destroying the nation of Israel. When Moses descended this time with a new set of stone tablets, his face shone with God's glory, and he was
obliged to veil his face when speaking to the
people.

Promptly preparation went ahead to provide
all things for the tabernacle of worship. On the
first day of the second year after leaving Egypt
they set up the tabernacle, and Moses as God's
servant installed Aaron as high priest and his
sons as priests and the Levites as helpers. Both
God's law to the nation and all the ceremonies
performed in and about the tabernacle were
typical; that is, they were shadows or patterns
of good things to come to humankind through
Jehovah's great Theocracy by the Seed of promise. (Colossians 2: 16, 17; Hebrews 10: 1) That
is why it is necessary for Christians to study
and heed these things written aforetime.

CHAPTER XVI

PRODUCING THE BOOK OF FREEDOM

RITE this for a memorial in a book, and rehearse it in the ears of Joshua: that I will utterly blot out the remembrance of Amalek from under heaven." So Jehovah God commanded Moses after the victory which God gave to Captain Joshua over the attacking Amalekites, a victory which further established the Israelites in their freedom so recently gained from authoritarian Egypt.—Exodus 17:14, *A.R.V.*

"WRITE thou these words: for after the tenor of these words I have made a covenant with thee and with Israel." So Jehovah God again commanded Moses, when he was with God in Mount Sinai and God delivered to him the laws, commandments and ordinances of his holy covenant with the nation of Israel.—Exodus 34:27.

When the all-wise God gave such commands to write, he had in mind our perplexing day when mankind sorely need true guidance and a sound hope. "For whatsoever things were written aforetime were written for our learning, that we through patience and comfort of the scriptures might have hope." (Romans 15:4)

Respecting the events in the career of God's covenant people it is stated under inspiration: "Now all these things happened unto them for ensamples [or, types]: and they are written for our admonition, upon whom the ends of the world are come."—1 Corinthians 10: 11.

The writing of the Book of freedom, the Book of truth, the Bible, was not left to the inclination of some worldly historian. It was written at the command of Jehovah God to his devoted servants, who were God's free men and subject to His guidance. Moses is the first according to the record who received divine command to make a sacred written account of God's purposes and doings.

Almighty God knows man's frame and feebleness of memory, and knows too the Devil's aim to destroy the record and pervert and blot it out of men's minds. Hence God did not leave the education of the people subject to the process of tradition and to the power of religious clergymen, but caused a faithful record to be written for reading and consultation, that the true facts and teachings might be searched out. Since he commanded the record to be written expressly for those in need of vital information at the worst crisis of the nations in the end of the world, Almighty God would safeguard the sacred Scriptures and see to it that they would be preserved till the needed time, in the face of all efforts of the freedom-haters to destroy them and keep mankind in ignorance. "The word of the Lord endureth for ever. And this is the word which by the gospel is preached unto you. —1 Peter 1: 25; Isaiah 40: 8.

The first mention of a book is at Genesis 5: 1, which states: "This is the book of the generations of Adam." Whether written records were made and preserved back that far is not shown, as the first writing and reading is mentioned in the time of Moses when God authorized him to write. It is therefore reasonable that from Adam till Moses the record was handed down by oral tradition from generation to generation. Evidence to this effect is God's statement about Abraham: "I know him, that he will command his children and his household after him, and they shall keep the way of the LORD, to do justice and judgment; that the LORD may bring upon Abraham that which he hath spoken of him." —Genesis 18: 19.

Abraham could learn the facts directly from Noah's son Shem, as Shem's life overlapped on Abraham's life 150 years. Shem could gather information direct from his great-grandfather Methuselah, who died in the year of the Flood, when Shem was 98 years old. In turn, Methuselah had much time to collect facts straight back to man's creation; for Adam's life overlapped on Methuselah's for 243 years. The facts thus handed down from Adam to Methuselah, then to Shem, and then to Abraham, this "friend of God" could pass direct on to his grandson Jacob, whom he knew for 15 years. Jacob could transmit the truthful record to his son Levi, the great-grandfather of Moses, or even to Levi's son Kohath. Kohath the Levite could deliver the facts of the book of Genesis to his son Amram. Though Kohath lived 133 years, he died before his grandson Moses' birth. Amram lived 137 years in Egypt, and his son Moses was born 80 years before Jehovah set the Israelites free from Egypt.

Almighty God, in whom is no lie, would see to it that the oral record, or tradition, was correctly remembered and passed down through the line of the above men. This he would do by his spirit, or invisible energy. It is the "spirit of truth", which acts that we might have the "comfort of the scriptures". Said Jesus in regard to the "spirit of truth", the "comforter", and the help it gives to memory: "The helper, the holy spirit, which the Father will send in my name, shall teach you all things, and remind you of all things which I said to you."—John 14: 17, 26, *Emphatic Diaglott.*

Noah, Abraham, Isaac, Jacob and Moses were prophets. As to the operation of God's invisible power or spirit upon them to bring forth a correct record, it is written: "No prophecy ever came by the will of man: but men spake from God, being moved by the holy spirit." (2 Peter 1: 21, *A.R.V.*) At least with Moses God called a halt to oral tradition, when he commanded Moses to write. Hence with Moses the producing of the written Bible begins. Moses wrote his part of the Bible in the language which God indicated to him. It was the language in which

God wrote the Ten Commandments on stone tablets. It was the Hebrew language.—Exodus 24:12; 31:18.

Moses wrote the first five books of the Bible. These made up just one book originally, but this was doubtless broken up into five volumes to make rolls or scrolls suitable for handling. The book of Genesis alone can make a scroll at least thirty feet long. These writings were called "the book of the law of Moses". (Joshua 1:8; 8:31-35) Joshua wrote the book bearing his own name. (Joshua 24:26) God by his power or spirit of inspiration moved others of his servants to write, such as David, Solomon, Isaiah, Jeremiah, Ezekiel, Habakkuk, Nahum, and Ezra.[1] At 1 Kings 14:19, 29 another writer mentions the book of the chronicles; while at 1 Chronicles 29:29 the writer mentions the book of Samuel. At 2 Chronicles 16:11; 32:32 the book of the kings and the vision of Isaiah are mentioned, such showing that at that time those books existed. Daniel, 538 years before Christ, writes: "I Daniel understood by books the number of the years, whereof the word of the Lord came to Jeremiah the prophet." Five years later the angel of Jehovah said to Daniel: "I will shew thee that which is noted in the scripture of truth." (Daniel 9:2; 10:21) This proves that in Daniel's day there was a body or collection of books of inspired Scripture.

[1] See 2 Chronicles 35:4; 26:22; Jeremiah 36:2, 27; 51:60; Ezekiel 37:16; Habakkuk 2:2; Nahum 1:1; Ezra 4:8; 7:11, 12, 21.

From the days of David especially scribes are mentioned who were priests and Levites. (2 Samuel 8:17; 20:25) After Daniel, the scribe Ezra the priest became prominent. (Ezra 7:1, 6, 10-12) Doubtless from Ezra's time on there was increased rewriting or making of copies of the sacred inspired books. Why? Because the Israelites or Jews had then become scattered among many lands and synagogues were established to hear and study God's Word. Hence copies were needed for each synagogue. So, when Jesus went into the synagogue at Nazareth and was asked to preach, there could be delivered to him the book or scroll of the prophecy of Isaiah to read. (Luke 4:17) Later his apostle James commented on this spread of copies of God's Word, saying: "Moses of old time hath in every city them that preach him, being read in the synagogues every sabbath day." (Acts 15:21) Jesus' disciples quoted to him from Malachi's prophecy concerning the coming of an Elijah, and Jesus acknowledged the inspiration of Malachi's prophecy, saying: "Elijah indeed cometh, and shall restore all things." (Matthew 17:10-13, *A.R.V.*) This proves that the book of Malachi's prophecy, the last book of Hebrew scriptures of the Bible, existed in Jesus' day and that the *canon* (or collection of inspired books) in Hebrew was then complete, from Genesis, through Chronicles, and to Malachi, inclusive.

Such canonical books were openly displayed for reference on the library shelves of the Jewish priests and scribes. Other books which plainly were uninspired and hence not truthful or from God were hidden away from the public. Therefore they came to be called "Apocrypha", which means "hidden", because spurious, false, not genuinely of divine inspiration. The apocryphal books are not included in the Hebrew canon to this day. Nowhere in the Bible itself are the canonical Hebrew Scriptures called "The Old Testament". It is grossly wrong for men to designate them as such and to split them off from the scriptures which were later written in Greek after Christ and to call these Greek Scriptures "The New Testament". In the Hebrew Scriptures a new testament or covenant is both foretold and typified, but this testament does not refer to the collection of Greek Scriptures written by Christian writers.[1] The whole Bible of Hebrew and Greek Scriptures, from Genesis to Revelation, is one book, from one Author, God, and is not two "testaments".

The unauthorized dividing of the Bible into "testaments" has led to the religious error that 'the Old Testament has been fulfilled and all that is necessary for Christians is to read the New Testament'. By this error the Devil has kept many self-styled "Christians" in bondage to ignorance and spiritual blindness.

Religionists who uphold traditions of men and who put priestcraft before the written Word of God defend themselves by saying that Jesus

[1] Jeremiah 31:31-33; 2 Corinthians 3:6-15; Hebrews 8:5-13; 10:16, 17.

Christ gave no command to his disciples to write and hence a written Bible is not necessary or indispensable. To claim this would mean that Jesus' apostles did not write under inspiration of God. Since, however, they did write under His inspiration, then it was at His command. The types and prophetic dramas and prophecies of ancient times Jehovah God did not leave to be handed down by oral tradition, but commanded such life-giving truths to be committed to writing for accurate preservation. Reasonably, therefore, he would not leave the facts of the fulfillment of many such types, shadows and prophecies by Jesus and his apostles to depend on mere oral tradition subject to priestcraft. He would likewise have such newly revealed facts and truths preserved in writing. "For I, Jehovah, change not."—Malachi 3: 6, *A.R.V.*

As Jehovah commanded the writing of the canonical Hebrew Scriptures, so he commanded the writing of the sacred Scriptures in Greek by the apostles and disciples of Jesus Christ. The apostle Peter wrote two epistles and gave as the reason this: "I will endeavour that ye may be able after my decease to have these things always in remembrance." (2 Peter 1: 15) He also spoke of the writings of the apostle Paul with approval, saying: "Our beloved brother Paul also according to the wisdom given unto him hath written unto you; as also in all his epistles, speaking in them of these things; in which are some things hard to be understood, which they that are unlearned and unstable

wrest, as they do also the other scriptures, unto
their own destruction." (2 Peter 3 : 15, 16) When
the apostle John was an old man, having outlived all the other apostles, the Lord Jesus
Christ appeared to him in a vision and twelve
times[1] commanded him to write. "What thou
seest, write in a book, and send it unto the seven
churches which are in Asia." And the apostle
introduces the book of this Revelation, saying:
"Blessed is he that readeth."—Revelation 1 : 3.

With John the writing of the inspired or canonical books of the Scriptures in Greek was
finished. Thereby the canon (the authoritative
Scriptures) was closed, not only of the Greek
Scriptures but also of the whole Bible. At first
the sixty-six books of the Bible were inscribed
on rolls of fine-grained skins or on papyrus.
Being written by hand and not printed by letter-
type, these copies are called *manuscripts,* which
means *written by hand.* None of the original
autographed writings of these scribes inspired
of God are extant or existent today, but the
great Author of the "scripture of truth" caused
copies to be made in close agreement with the
originals. The Hebrews or Jews used the most
scrupulous care in the faithful copying and
preservation of the Hebrew Scriptures. Faithful copies thereof survive to this day, although
the Roman Catholic crusades and Inquisition
destroyed and caused to be destroyed innumer-
able copies of God's Word in the Hebrew. Vain

[1] Revelation 1 : 11, 19 ; 2 : 1, 8, 12, 18 ; 3 : 1, 7, 14 ; 14 : 13 ; 19 : 9 ;
21 : 5.

such effort! "Surely the people is grass. The grass withereth, the flower fadeth; but the word of our God shall stand for ever," in spite of religious frenzy to destroy it.—Isaiah 40: 7, 8.

Not only were many copies made of the Greek writings of Christ's inspired apostles and disciples, but also many translations thereof were made into other languages, in harmony with Jesus' command: "Go ye therefore, and teach all nations, . . . teaching them to observe all things whatsoever I have commanded you." "Ye shall be witnesses unto me both in Jerusalem, and in all Judæa, and in Samaria, and unto the uttermost part of the earth." (Matthew 28: 19, 20; Acts 1: 8) On the day of Pentecost, ten days later, the disciples were anointed with the spirit or active force of God and were enabled to speak many foreign tongues. Many of those who then accepted Christianity were Greek-speaking Jews. (Acts 2: 1-11; 6: 1) Shortly thereafter the disciple Philip preached the gospel to a Jewish proselyte who was an Ethiopian, and baptized him. (Acts 8: 26-39) The translations of the Holy Scriptures from the Hebrew and Greek into these various languages are called *versions*. The making of manuscript copies of the original-language Scriptures and of such versions of them continued until the fifteenth century, toward the middle of which printing from movable type was invented.

Today the number of manuscripts of the Greek Scriptures written since Christ is over 4,000 in the original Greek. Besides this there

are at least 8,000 manuscript copies of the Latin
Vulgate translation. There are also about a
thousand extant manuscripts of the early versions, the Ethiopic, Armenian, Syriac, Coptic,
Gothic, Persian, Arabic, and the rest. It is therefore safe to say that there are now in existence
12,000 manuscript copies of the Scriptures written by Christ's apostles and disciples, of which,
however, there are no two copies precisely the
same.[1]

The Christians were the first ones to special-
ize in manuscripts put up in book form with
pages and lids like this book in your hand, and
not in rolls. Such a manuscript book is called a
codex. In the latter half of the fourth century
A.D. such a *codex* was written, and which is
known today as *Vatican Manuscript No. 1209*.
The evidence is that it was written in Egypt. In
course of time it found its way into the Vatican
library at Rome, where for the first time it appears in the library's catalogue of books of
1481. It originally contained, in Greek, not in
Latin, the whole Bible, but has lost parts thereof, including the last book, the Revelation, or
Apocalypse. It never included the spurious
books of the Maccabees. It has three columns
to the page.

The Vatican long begrudged to Bible re-
searchers, such as Count Tischendorf, a brief
sight of this Vatican MS. No. 1209. Finally, in
1868, the papal authorities issued an edition of

[1] For proof of data in this chapter see *Textual Criticism of the
New Testament*, by Sir Frederic G. Kenyon, K.C.B., F.B.A.

the so-called "New Testament" part of the MS., which was followed in successive years by volumes containing the so-called "Old Testament". In 1889-1890 all previous publications thereof were backed up by a photographic facsimile copy of the whole original manuscript.

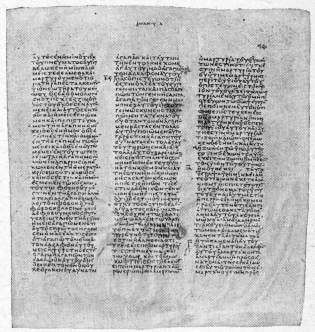

Facsimile of Greek Bible text Novum Testamentum E Codice Vaticano 1209 (page 1441 original Manuscript) from 1 John 4: 13 to 1 John 5: 16.

Second to Vatican MS. No. 1209 in rank is another one written in the fourth century, the Sinaitic Manuscript. It was found in the Greek Catholic monastery at Mount Sinai in Arabia, by Count Tischendorf, in 1859, and is now at the British Museum in London since 1933. It is in Greek, and originally contained the whole Bible, of which the "New Testament" part of it is practically complete, including the Revelation, or Apocalypse, four columns to a page.

The next manuscript in rank is the Alexandrine MS., written in the fifth century, in Egypt. By the Greek Catholic patriarch Cyril Lucar, who brought it from Alexandria to Constantinople (Istanbul) in 1621, it was presented to King James I of England, the monarch who caused the King James Version of the English Bible to be produced. The MS. was actually received by King Charles I in 1627, King James having died before the gift took effect. It is in the British Museum. It once contained the whole Bible in Greek.

In A.D. 382 Eusebius Hieronymus, known for short as Jerome, began his revision of the old Latin versions of the Bible. He undertook to translate first from the original Greek and from the Septuagint Greek Version, but finally turned also to the original Hebrew. The Latin version which Jerome produced, and which has been revised since, is called "the Latin Vulgate". When printing was invented, in the fifteenth century, it was this Latin Bible that was first committed to the press, at Mainz, Germany, in 1456, resulting in Gutenberg's edition known as the "Mazarin Bible".

John Wycliffe was the first to translate the Bible into English, in 1382-1384. It was handwritten. The first complete English Bible ever printed was that by Myles Coverdale, in 1535, who included therein the work hitherto done by William Tyndale, then in prison awaiting execution by the Roman Catholic Inquisition. Other

Facsimile of Greek Bible text of Codex Alexandrinus (page 145 original Manuscript) from 1 Timothy 3: 14 to 1 Timothy 5: 13.

English Bible translations followed, but the one that has proved the most popular is the King James Version, or Authorized Version, published in 1611. The Catholic Douay Version, in English, was first completed and published in 1610.

Much scholarly investigation and criticism of the original Greek manuscripts of the Bible followed in succeeding centuries, to get at the straight or accurate text as the apostles and their fellows wrote it. In 1774 J. J. Griesbach, who ranks high in textual criticism, produced the first of his three editions of the Greek "New Testament". Griesbach proceeded on the understanding that the most ancient manuscripts are the most genuine and correct in their text, such as the Alexandrine MS. known in his day.

Early in the 1800's English Bible Societies began to be formed, both the British and Foreign Bible Society and the New York Bible Society in 1804, the Philadelphia Bible Society in 1808, and the American Bible Society in 1816. In 1884 the Watch Tower Bible and Tract Society was chartered, but already since July, 1879, the magazine *The Watchtower* had been published. The Watch Tower Society also distributed Bibles and a Bible help entitled "The Emphatic Diaglott", by one Benjamin Wilson, from whom later the plates and right to publish the *Diaglott* were bought.

The *Diaglott* contains the original Greek text, from Matthew's gospel to Revelation, which text is according to the revised text or recension by

Dr. J. J. Griesbach. The lines of the Greek are interlined with an English translation following the Greek text word for word. To the right of this there is a column containing a new and emphatic translation into fluent English. (See page 46 herein.) This emphasized English translation by the author of *The Emphatic Diaglott* does not follow strictly or exclusively Dr. Griesbach's Greek text, but follows preferably the older text of Vatican MS. No. 1209, the most ancient and valuable MS. in existence and which was not published in Dr. Griesbach's time. Where the Vatican MS. No. 1209 is lacking, the *Diaglott* follows Vatican MS. No. 1160 and the Alexandrine. In 1942, the Watchtower edition of the Bible began to be published. This edition is the favorite King James Version Bible unchanged, but with special helps for students.

From the foregoing account the blasphemous claim of religionists is proved to be unfounded and foolish, namely, "If it were not for the Roman Catholic religious organization Christians would not have the Bible today, for the Roman Catholic organization was made God's repository of the truth and its preserver." Such self-conceited claim not only is untrue to fact, but takes the credit from God, who is the Author of the Holy Bible and who depends upon no man or group of men for its preservation. He has preserved His written Word and caused it to be spread world-wide despite the opposition and destructive efforts of all the religionists.

CHAPTER XVII

A ROYAL THEOCRACY

OR forty years Jehovah God led the children of Israel through the wilderness by the hand of Moses. In the last year of the journey he brought them to the plains of Moab, opposite the city of Jericho in the Promised Land. The Lord designated the faithful servant of Moses, Joshua, to be his successor. Moses bestowed an inspired blessing upon the twelve tribes of Israel, and then ascended to the top of Mount Nebo to die. On the mountaintop God permitted him to survey all the land of promise. Then Moses died, and the Lord God buried him, but no one knows where and how God disposed of Moses' body. At that time occurred what is spoken of at Jude 9: "Yet Michael the archangel, when contending with the devil he disputed about the body of Moses, durst not bring against him a railing accusation, but said, The Lord rebuke thee."

Moses did not go to heaven. The transfiguration scene which took place on a mountaintop fifteen centuries later and in which Moses and Elijah were seen in a vision does not prove that Moses was alive and in heaven. (Matthew 17: 1-9) Jesus' words must be taken as true when he said: "No man hath ascended up to heaven, but he that came down from heaven, even the Son of man." Moses' visionary appearance with Jesus at the transfiguration merely testified that Christ Jesus is a prophet like but greater than Moses as well as Elijah. As Moses said on those plains of Moab not many days before his death: "Jehovah thy God will raise up unto thee a prophet from the midst of thee, of thy brethren, like unto me; unto him ye shall hearken." (Deuteronomy 18: 15-19, *A.R.V.*) The apostle Peter was with Jesus at the transfiguration and later confirmed this truth that Jesus is the Greater Moses.—Acts 3: 20-23.

By Jehovah's miracle of dividing the floodwaters of the Jordan river Joshua led the Israelites across the torrent bed dryshod, and then the conquest of the promised land began. Jehovah had promised their forefathers to give them the land. Now he commanded his chosen nation that they should destroy the accursed Canaanites in the land and wipe out their religion, else religion would prove a snare to them. God had sentenced those demon-worshipers to death, and he made the Israelites his executioners, "in the image of God." The war which the Israelites waged upon the Canaanites was at the command of the great Theocrat, Jehovah. It was Theocratic warfare and righteous, for the cleansing of the land which had been polluted by the idolatry and bloody deeds done in religion's name. God was with the Israelites in this warfare and performed miracles for the victory of his nation and the destruction of the enemies.

At the end of six years of constant warfare the Gentile nations in the Promised Land were not yet all cleared out, nevertheless the division of the land among the tribes of Israel began. The tribes continued faithful to the God of Israel during the life of Joshua and the elders of the nation that outlived him, and they were blessed. As it is written: "Blessed is the nation whose God is Jehovah, the people whom he hath chosen for his own inheritance." (Psalm 33: 12, *A.R.V.*) Joshua's name means "Jehovah saves". The Greek version of the Bible renders Joshua's name as "Jesus". (Acts 7: 45; Hebrews 4: 8) In his faithful leadership of Israel and in the victories he gained by faith in God over the Gentile nations of Canaan Joshua was a type or figure prophetic of Jesus Christ, the Seed who shall crush the Serpent's head. At his final meeting with the people of Israel before his death Joshua exhorted them to keep covenant with God and worship Him who had made them a free nation. Joshua bade them decide between religion and the true and living God, saying: "And if it seem evil unto you to serve Jehovah, choose you this day whom ye will serve; whether the gods which your fathers served that were beyond the River, or the gods of the Amorites, in whose land ye dwell: but as for me and my house, we will serve Jehovah." (Joshua 24: 15, *A.R.V.*) Who will deny Joshua was a Jehovah's witness?

One circumstance remained after Joshua's time which endangered Israel's remaining a free nation: that was the presence in parts of the land of Canaanites who had escaped being destroyed together with their religion. Such religion proved to be the besetting sin against which the warning is given to those who need to be free and unhampered in the race for life everlasting: "Wherefore seeing we also are compassed about with so great a cloud of witnesses, let us lay aside every weight, and the sin which doth so easily beset us, and let us run with patience the race that is set before us." (Hebrews 12: 1) The Old Serpent lurked about, to entice continually with religion the chosen nation through whom the royal Seed must come.

Again and again the Israelites grew careless and neglected and forgot their worship and service of Jehovah. They fell victim to religion. As many times as the nation broke its covenant toward Him Jehovah sold them into the hands of their Gentile enemies, the worship of whose demon gods the Israelites took up. When His people cried to him in their affliction and turned away from demonism and sought him, then Jehovah raised them up judges to deliver them from their enemies and the snare of religion. This period of judges saw the raising up and the exploits of faith of such witnesses of Jehovah as Ehud, Barak and Deborah, Gideon, Jephthah, Samson, and the prophet Samuel. (Hebrews 11: 32-34) The record in the book of Judges closes with this statement: "In those days there was no king in Israel: every man did that which was right in his own eyes."—Judges 21: 25.

Then the Israelites desired to imitate the Gentile nations round about and came to the judge, the prophet Samuel, and asked him to set up over them a king, to visibly lead and govern them. They ignored that Jehovah was their invisible Theocratic King and would not forsake them if they did not forsake their worship of him. Samuel was displeased and prayed to God. "And Jehovah said unto Samuel, Hearken unto the voice of the people in all that they say unto thee; for they have not rejected thee, but they have rejected me, that I should not be king over them. According to all the works which they have done since the day that I brought them up out of Egypt even unto this day, in that they have forsaken me, and served other gods, so do they also unto thee."—1 Samuel 8: 7, 8, *A.R.V.*

At the people's insistent request God designated Saul of the tribe of Benjamin to be king, and Saul was anointed with oil upon his head to this royal office. Saul became thus 'the anointed of Jehovah'. (1 Samuel 10: 1; 12: 3, 5) In the Hebrew the name for "anointed one" is "Messiah"; but King Saul did not prove himself to be a type of the great Messiah to come, the royal Seed of God's organization Zion. Early in his forty-year reign Saul started out on a course of arbitrary acts in disobedience to God. Samuel told him he had done foolishly, "for now would the LORD have established thy kingdom upon Israel for ever. But now thy kingdom shall

not continue: the LORD hath sought him a man
after his own heart, and the LORD hath commanded him to be captain over his people."
(1 Samuel 13:13, 14) That man proved to be
David, born ten years after Saul's reign began.
When David was yet a young shepherd lad God
sent his prophet Samuel to anoint David privately as king designate. Thereby David of the
tribe of Judah became the Lord's "anointed".

He proved himself to be a type of the coming
Messiah, "the Lion of the tribe of Juda." By
David's vanquishing the Philistine giant Go-
liath with but a shepherd's sling and stone, God
brought David prominently before the nation's
notice and King Saul made him a captain in his
army.

The Lord's spirit was no longer upon Saul, and the Devil stirred up in him the spirit of jealousy against David. The Devil further caused Saul to persecute and seek to destroy David in order to prevent the promised Seed from coming through David's line. But Jehovah delivered his anointed from Saul's persecution. Confronted with disaster at the hands of the Philistine army, Saul finally sought the witch of Endor, and shortly thereafter God permitted Saul to be killed for his disobedient course in demonism.

David then became king of Israel and was anointed to office at Hebron in the tribe of Judah. He reigned for forty years. A number of times he was overreached by the Devil and suffered for it, but his heart always remained true to Jehovah, whom he worshiped, and he repented and was restored to God's favor. At the beginning of his rule over the twelve tribes the Gentile Jebusites were yet occupying part of the city of Jerusalem, particularly the hill of Zion and the stronghold thereon. David led his armies against it and wrested Zion from the heathen and then made it the seat of his throne. In this way Jerusalem became the capital city of Israel, especially the hill thereof called "Zion". Inasmuch as David typified the Messiah, Jehovah's Anointed King to come, Zion became a type of Jehovah's capital organization under His Messianic King. Hence God's capital organization or Theocratic Government by Messiah is called "Zion" in Bible prophecy.

Then the Philistines tried to overthrow David, but Jehovah gave David two miraculous victories over them, at Mount Perazim and at Gibeon. And David composed a psalm under God's inspiration and wrote: "Why do the nations rage, and the peoples meditate a vain thing? The kings of the earth set themselves, and the rulers take counsel together, against Jehovah, and against his anointed, . . . Then will he speak unto them in his wrath, and vex them in his sore displeasure: Yet I have set my king upon my holy hill of Zion. . . . Jehovah said unto me, Thou art my son; this day have I begotten thee." (Psalm 2: 1-7, *A.R.V.*) This Psalm, while based on historical facts back there, is a prophecy applying to the Messiah, Christ Jesus, since A.D. 1914, and hence at this time. The prophecy had a partial or miniature fulfillment at the coming of Messiah or Christ nineteen centuries ago. (Acts 4: 24-28) It must have a complete or final fulfillment in our day. (Revelation 11: 15-18) In the Greek text of the Bible *Christ* stands for *Messiah.*—John 1: 41.

David was intent on promoting the true worship of his invisible Theocratic Ruler. Due to a victory of the Philistines over Israel about seventy years previous the sacred golden ark of the tabernacle of worship had been removed from the Holy of Holies of the tabernacle and lodged at the home of a Levite at Kirjath-jearim. King David raised a special tent for the ark on Mount Zion and had the ark carried up and placed there. So the worship of Jehovah

became inseparably connected with the capital
city Zion. At the time of installing the sacred
ark on Zion's hill, which now became "the hill of
Jehovah" and "his holy place", King David sang
psalms and said: "Let the heavens be glad, and
let the earth rejoice; and let them say among
the nations, JEHOVAH REIGNETH. Then shall the
trees of the wood sing for joy before Jehovah;
for he cometh to judge the earth." (1 Chronicles
16: 31, 33, *A.R.V.*) Here, at last, the typical
royal Theocracy presented itself in faithful likeness to the coming Theocratic Government by
Messiah. Jehovah, as represented by the sacred
ark, reigned on Zion, and his anointed King,
David, whose name means "Beloved", sat upon
the typical "throne of Jehovah".—1 Chronicles
29: 23, *A.R.V.*

In time David's heart was moved to build a
substantial house, palace or temple for the ark
of the Lord and the service of his priests and
Levites. Then the Lord sent his prophet Nathan
and notified David that such a privilege was
reserved for his son, seeing that King David
had been a man of war and blood. At the same
time, however, Jehovah God entered into a covenant with David. It was a covenant for the kingdom. By it God promised that the kingdom
should continue in the line of David: "And thine
house and thy kingdom shall be established for
ever before thee: thy throne shall be established
for ever." (2 Samuel 7: 1-16) This covenant for
the kingdom guaranteed that the royal Seed, the
Messiah, or Christ, should come from the house

or lineage of David and that Jehovah would give
The Theocratic Government to him. Therefore
Messiah or Christ came to be called "The son
of David".—Matthew 1:1.

In keeping with the kingdom covenant David
was succeeded by his son Solomon, whose name
means "Peaceful". David being old and the enemies trying to prevent Solomon's rule, Solomon
was enthroned before his father's death. In the
fourth year after being anointed to rule Solomon began the building of the temple for which
his father had made great preparations.
(1 Kings 6:1) This was typical of future events.
It corresponds with the history of Christ the
Messiah. In the fourth year, or three and a half
years after being anointed with God's spirit at
the Jordan river, Christ came to the temple at
Jerusalem and presented himself both as King
and as the Foundation Stone upon which the
great spiritual temple of Jehovah God should
be built. Concerning himself the anointed Jesus
said: "Behold, a greater than Solomon is here."
Thereby he proved that Solomon was a type of
the Messiah, who builds God's true temple of
living stones.—Matthew 12:42; 1 Peter 2:4-9.

Solomon was seven years in building the temple on Mount Moriah at Jerusalem. When the
ark was brought from Mount Zion and put within its Holy of Holies and the priests and Levites
were installed in their services, the glory of Jehovah God filled the temple before the eyes of
all the people present. In the ark was nothing
except the two tablets of stone bearing the com-

mandments of God and which Moses put in the
ark at Mount Horeb. (1 Kings 8: 9-21) So now,
for a time, the typical Theocracy of the Most
High God displayed its greatest glory. People
from all the world came to worship at His temple and to hear the wisdom of Solomon. Regarding the popular benefits of his peaceful reign,
such as freedom from fear and want, it is written: "Judah and Israel were many, as the sand
which is by the sea in multitude, eating and
drinking and making merry. And Solomon
reigned over all kingdoms from the river unto
the land of the Philistines, and unto the border
of Egypt: . . . and Judah and Israel dwelt
safely, every man under his vine and under his
fig tree, from Dan even to Beersheba, all the
days of Solomon." (1 Kings 4: 20-25) This is a
prophetic picture of New World conditions under Christ's rule.

When Solomon waxed old Satan the Devil
beset him with the ensnaring sin of religion. The
once-wise king fell to idolatry, and died under
divine disapproval, in 999 B.C. After his reign
of forty years the nation of twelve tribes was
split in two, the northern kingdom of ten tribes
of Israel, and the southern kingdom of two
tribes, Judah and Benjamin. The northern kingdom immediately forsook Jehovah's worship
and established a state religion to turn the people from Jehovah's typical Theocracy and worship at Jerusalem. The unfaithful kingdom was
finally destroyed by the king of Assyria nearly
three centuries later. In the southern kingdom,

that of Judah, the descendants of King Solomon held the throne. Jehovah's covenant with David for the everlasting kingdom remained in force, but he shifted the line through which the Messianic Seed should come from Solomon's line to that of David's other son named Nathan. (Luke 3: 21, 22, 31; 2 Samuel 5: 14) The last king of Solomon's line to occupy the throne at Jerusalem was Zedekiah.

King Zedekiah became unfaithful and idolatrous. Before his overthrow the God of the kingdom covenant inspired his prophet Ezekiel to direct these words against him from the land of Babylon: "Thou, profane wicked prince of Israel, whose day is come, when iniquity shall have an end, thus saith the Lord GOD; Remove the diadem, and take off the crown: this shall not be the same: exalt him that is low, and abase him that is high. I will overturn, overturn, overturn it; and it shall be no more, until he come whose right it is; and I will give it him."—Ezekiel 21: 25-27.

In 606 B.C. the heavenly Theocrat caused the typical Theocracy in Israel to be overturned by King Nebuchadnezzar of Babylon. Yet Jehovah did not forsake his covenant people, of whom a remnant kept faithful to him, such as Ezekiel, Daniel and his three Hebrew companions, and Jeremiah. By his prophet Jeremiah God foretold that after seventy years of desolation of Jerusalem and its domain he would restore the faithful remnant from captivity in Babylon to the Promised Land. Furthermore, Jehovah's covenant with David for the everlasting kingdom did not fail. It continued on, awaiting the coming of a worthy one, whose right the kingdom or Theocratic Government should be. To him Jehovah would give the kingdom at his coming. As Jacob on his deathbed in Egypt had foretold, the scepter of right to rule would not depart from the tribe of Judah, David's tribe, until Shiloh, "the Prince of Peace," should come and receive the kingdom right. Then unto him the gathering of all the people of good-will should be.—Genesis 49: 10.

King Zedekiah was taken captive by King Nebuchadnezzar, and Jerusalem and its temple were pillaged and razed to the ground. The land of Judah was denuded of all its Jewish inhabitants, and seventy years of desolation began. With the typical Theocracy overthrown, the long period known as "the times of the Gentiles" set in. Satan the Devil now became "the god of this world".—2 Corinthians 4: 4.

CHAPTER XVIII

"SEVEN TIMES"

T THE overturning of Israel's typical Theocracy in the year 606 B.C. by King Nebuchadnezzar Babylon became the third world power noted in Bible history, Egypt and Assyria having preceded the Babylonian empire. The Supreme Power, the Most High God, then used Nebuchadnezzar as His instrument to execute upon the backsliding Israelites the judgments whereof he had long warned them by his faithful prophets. Almighty God, who can use even the inanimate, unintelligent forces of creation to carry out his purpose, thereby used Nebuchadnezzar as his servant. (Jeremiah 25:9; 27:6; 43:10) The first siege Nebuchadnezzar laid against Jerusalem was eleven years before its destruction, and at that time he carried many captives away to Babylon, including the faithful young men Daniel and Ezekiel. Both men became prophets and hence witnesses of Jehovah. Daniel, because of his wisdom from God, became Nebuchadnezzar's chief consultant and adviser. Though God used this Gentile king as his instrument, this does not mean that Jehovah was the God he worshiped. Nevertheless, because of the vast imperial rule which Nebuchadnezzar exercised by

Almighty God's permission, Jehovah used him as the basis or background by which Daniel could deliver prophecies of the highest importance concerning the setting up of Messiah's kingdom.

Therefore the king wrote: "Nebuchadnezzar the king, unto all people, nations, and languages, that dwell in all the earth; Peace be multiplied unto you. I thought it good to shew the signs and wonders that the high God hath wrought toward me. How great are his signs! and how mighty are his wonders! his kingdom is an everlasting kingdom, and his dominion is from generation to generation." (Daniel 4: 1-3) Accordingly, to men and women of "all people, nations, and languages" who desire peace to be multiplied to them, it is of deepest interest to consider the revelation which an earthly king, so high and mighty, saw good to relate, as follows:

He had a dream that troubled him. None of the religious wise men and counselors of his court could explain it. Remembering how Daniel had recalled and interpreted the king's forgotten dream concerning the terrible image and its destruction, Nebuchadnezzar summoned Jehovah's witness and related to him the dream:

"Thus were the visions of mine head in my bed; I saw, and, behold, a tree in the midst of the earth, and the height thereof was great. The tree grew, and was strong, and the height thereof reached unto heaven, and the sight thereof to the end of all the earth: the leaves thereof were fair, and the fruit thereof much, and in it was meat for all: the beasts of the field had shadow under it, and the fowls of the heaven dwelt in the boughs thereof, and all flesh was fed of it. I saw in the visions of my head upon my bed, and, behold, a watcher and an holy one came down from heaven; he cried aloud, and said thus, Hew down the tree, and cut off his branches, shake off his leaves, and scatter his fruit: let the beasts get away from under it, and the fowls from his branches: nevertheless, leave the stump of his roots in the earth, even with a band of iron and brass, in the tender grass of the field; and let it be wet with the dew of heaven, and let his portion be with the beasts in the grass of the earth: let his heart be changed from man's, and let a beast's heart be given unto him; and let seven times pass over him. This matter is by the decree of the watchers, and the demand by the word of the holy ones: to the intent that the living may know that the Most High ruleth in the kingdom of men, and giveth it to whomsoever he will, and setteth up over it the basest of men."—Daniel 4:10-17.

Daniel interpreted the dream to foretell that seven years of madness would overtake Nebuchadnezzar, during which he could not personally carry on his imperial government but would become wild like a beast and live out in the open fields. After that his sanity would return, and he would be restored to his kingdom, which, like that banded tree stump in the ground, was held pending his return. By this experience he would know that the Most High God is all-powerful and has ordained who will reign in the Government over man.

Twelve months later Nebuchadnezzar gave way to boasting over great Babylon which he had built. Then there fell upon him a voice from heaven speaking the same message as in the dream, and he was instantly seized with mental unbalance and brutishness. He was let loose in the field to live and eat like a brute beast. When seven years had passed over him in this debased condition, God had mercy upon him and let his reason return, and he praised the Most High God. Then he resumed his throne. By such dealings Jehovah God, who had forewarned him by the prophetic dream and by Daniel, used him both to make a picture in miniature fulfillment of the dream and so to illustrate the great and complete fulfillment thereof.

About 150 years before this strange occurrence Isaiah was inspired to declare a prophetic "proverb against the king of Babylon". Isaiah likened him to a great tree, and then said: "How art thou fallen from heaven, O Lucifer, son of the morning! how art thou cut down to the ground, which didst weaken the nations! For thou hast said in thine heart, I will ascend into heaven, . . . I will be like the Most High." (Isaiah 14:4-14) At Eden the Most High God made the beautiful, shining spirit creature, Lucifer, to be the invisible overlord over the earth and its creatures. To Lucifer the prophecy says: "Thou hast been in Eden the garden of God; . . . Thou art the anointed cherub that covereth; and I have set thee so: . . . Thou wast perfect in thy ways from the day that thou wast created, till iniquity was found in thee." (Ezekiel 28:13-15) Therefore the great tree reaching unto heaven that Nebuchadnezzar king of Babylon saw pictured Lucifer's heavenly office, namely, the invisible overlordship over Adam and Eve and the lower animal creatures. That overlordship was then righteous.

When Lucifer gave way to iniquity and revolted against the supreme rule of the Most High God, he forfeited the right to be God's representative in the overlordship, and God debased Lucifer, who had become Satan, or God's opposer. God sentenced Satan to destruction, but permitted him to remain alive for a limited time till the controversy over Jehovah's name and supremacy should be fought out and finally settled. True, Satan continued in control over man, but not over righteous man, neither as God's *righteous* overlord over men. The office of righteous overlord no longer operated or grew, but was in suspension or abeyance until He should come who would prove right thereto, and then the Most High would give it to him, even though he be esteemed by this world as the "basest of men". This situation, therefore, was now as in the dream picture when the great tree was cut down and the earthly creatures were cleared out from under it, and only the stump of the tree was left in the ground, with bands of iron and brass about it.

The tree was not a dead issue. Its living stump testified that it would shoot forth a new stem and would grow up again, when God's due time should come and he would release the binding restraints from it. Likewise the invisible heavenly righteous overlordship over mankind would be revived or made operative again. This means that the kingdom of God, The Theocratic Government, would be set up over mankind, but only when God released the restraints in his appointed and declared time. When?

Not before "seven times" had passed over the symbolic tree stump could God, according to his own decree, establish the kingdom over men in the hands of a righteous invisible overlord. The prophetic dream does not indicate that the "seven times" began at Eden immediately with the rebellion of Lucifer and his loss of the right and authority of righteous overlordship. The facts in fulfillment show they did not begin then. The dream merely announces that in the tree stump's experience there would pass over it a period of "seven times" and that this would immediately precede the unbanding of the stump and its free growth again. In the miniature fulfillment of the dream upon Nebuchadnezzar he became like a beast, without human understanding, for seven years, after which he regained sanity and exercised his lordship over the empire.

This makes it clear that the "seven times" began with Nebuchadnezzar's overturning of Jeho-

vah's typical Theocracy at Jerusalem, in 606 B.C. As long as the typical administration of God at Jerusalem operated at all, even imperfectly, in his name, that long there was some measure of national sanity and a partial exhibition of right rule among nations on this earth. But with the overthrow of the typical Theoc-

racy there was then no restraint at all to the
unreason and bestiality of human governors
and humankind. The Gentile powers or governments were now exclusive in the field. God's
covenant people no longer held any national
sovereignty in the midst of this world, inde-
pendently of the Gentile nations. What ruling
nations then functioned were Gentile nations,
with Babylon supreme on earth. Thus wholly
"Gentile" times began. These must therefore be
what Jesus Christ referred to, at Luke 21: 24,
as "the times of the Gentiles". Beginning in
606 B.C., and being seven in number, when
would these "times" end and the righteous overlordship of God's kingdom be established?

At Revelation 12: 6, 14 there are 1,260 days
referred to, after which the same period of days
is described as "a time, and times, and half a
time", or three and a half times, which is the
half of seven times. Hence "seven times" would
be twice 1,260 days, or 2,520 days. In the ark
during the flood Noah counted the 150 days that
the waters prevailed upon the earth before sub-
siding as 5 months, averaging 30 days to a
month. (Genesis 7: 11, 24; 8: 3, 4) Therefore,
2,520 days would equal 84 months, which equals
7 years. This agrees with the miniature fulfillment of the dream where Nebuchadnezzar's
madness of "seven times" was seven years long.

In the major or complete fulfillment the
"seven times" must be larger than 2,520 literal
days. Ezekiel, who prophesied at the same time
as Daniel, was likewise inspired to give some

time measures, and he gave this divine rule for calculating the time: "I have appointed thee each day for a year." He also was banded until the time measures were up. (Ezekiel 4: 6, 8) Hence each of the 2,520 days, according to prophetic calculation in Daniel's prophecy, equals one year, solar time. By the same rule the "seven times", or "times of the Gentiles", amount to 2,520 *years*. In Nebuchadnezzar's time the year began counting from the fall of the year, or about October 1, our time. Since he destroyed Jerusalem in the summer of 606 B.C., that year had its beginning in the fall of 607 B.C. and its ending in the fall of 606 B.C.

Inasmuch as the count of the Gentile "seven times" began its first year at the fall of 607 B.C., it is simple to calculate when they end. From the fall of 607 B.C. to the fall of B.C. 1 is exactly 606 years. From the fall of B.C. 1 to the fall of A.D. 1 is one year, do not forget. Hence from the fall of B.C. 1 to the fall of A.D. 1914 is 1,914 years. Add now 606 years and 1,914 years, and the sum total is 2,520 years, ending in the fall of A.D. 1914. By this method Jehovah, who is an accurate Timekeeper as to his purposes, symbolically foretold that the "times of the Gentiles", that is, the "seven times", would continue and extend to the fall of A.D. 1914. Before that date, therefore, the true Theocratic Government of Messiah, which was foreshadowed by the typical Theocracy at Jerusalem, could not be set up.

Said Daniel to Nebuchadnezzar in interpreting the meaning of the banded tree stump: "And whereas they commanded to leave the stump of the tree roots; thy kingdom shall be sure unto thee, after that thou shalt have known that the heavens do rule." (Daniel 4: 26) This pictured that God had not abandoned his original purpose to have a righteous overlordship over righteous men. Instead, the actual operation of the invisible overlordship by His appointed one was held in suspension until the "seven times" of Gentile domination of the earth had run out. Then Jehovah God's new appointee would assume the vacant overlordship in place of the unfaithful Lucifer and would start its operation. This would mean that the "kingdom of heaven", or God's kingdom by his anointed King, had been established and had come, regardless of whether the Gentile powers discerned and recognized that fact or not. It would mean that the time had come for them to get out of power and to give place to the Theocracy's rule over all the earth.

To whom does Jehovah give the heavenly overlordship over all men of good-will in A.D. 1914? Daniel 4: 17 answers: "To the intent that the living may know that the Most High ruleth in the kingdom of men, and giveth it to whomsoever he will, and setteth up over it the basest of men." "One low among men he setteth up over it." (*Roth.*) God has not given the "kingdom of men" to totalitarian and religious dictators, who are wicked, demonized men. Jeho-

vah God has given the heavenly kingdom of the
new world to the one whom politicians, commercial traffickers and religious clergy despise
as the "basest of men", namely, Christ Jesus,
who was nailed to a tree between two thieves.
(Isaiah 53: 1-12) This One foretold that at the
end of the world, beginning in A.D. 1914, his
true followers "shall be hated of all nations for
my name's sake". Jehovah's witnesses are now
so hated. (Matthew 24: 9) Concerning the government of the new world of righteousness the
prophecy of Revelation 11: 15-18 came true in
A.D. 1914, at the end of the "seven times":

"The kingdom of the world is become the kingdom of our Lord, and of his Christ: and he shall
reign for ever and ever. . . . We give thee
thanks, O Lord God, the Almighty, who art and
who wast; because thou hast taken thy great
power, and didst reign. And the nations were
wroth, and thy wrath came." (A.R.V.) Now,
therefore, we can understand why Christ the
Messiah did not set up God's kingdom at his
first advent or at once after ascending to heaven.

CHAPTER XIX

FREEDOM'S KING APPEARS

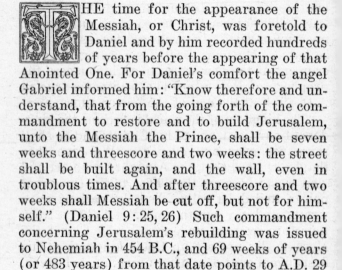

HE time for the appearance of the Messiah, or Christ, was foretold to Daniel and by him recorded hundreds of years before the appearing of that Anointed One. For Daniel's comfort the angel Gabriel informed him: "Know therefore and understand, that from the going forth of the commandment to restore and to build Jerusalem, unto the Messiah the Prince, shall be seven weeks and threescore and two weeks: the street shall be built again, and the wall, even in troublous times. And after threescore and two weeks shall Messiah be cut off, but not for himself." (Daniel 9: 25, 26) Such commandment concerning Jerusalem's rebuilding was issued to Nehemiah in 454 B.C., and 69 weeks of years (or 483 years) from that date points to A.D. 29 as the year bearing watching. Would Messiah then appear?—Nehemiah 1: 1-3; 2: 1-8.

Centuries later the same angel Gabriel was sent to the rebuilt Jerusalem to foretell to the faithful priest Zacharias at the temple the birth of a son who should precede and announce the appearing of the Messiah. Six months later "the angel Gabriel was sent from God unto a city of Galilee, named Nazareth, to a virgin espoused to a man whose name was Joseph, of the house of David; and the virgin's name was Mary." Gabriel said to this descendant of King David of the tribe of Judah: "Behold, thou shalt conceive in thy womb, and bring forth a son, and shalt call his name JESUS. He shall be great, and shall be called the Son of the Highest: and the Lord God shall give unto him the throne of his father David: and he shall reign over the house of Jacob for ever; and of his kingdom there shall be no end." Mary asked: "How shall this be, seeing I know not a man?" Gabriel replied (*A.R.V.*): "The holy spirit shall come upon thee, and the power of the Most High shall overshadow thee: wherefore also the holy thing which is begotten shall be called the Son of God. . . . For no word from God shall be void of power." (Luke 1: 5-37) In such phrase, though Mary understood it not, God's messenger told that the life of Jehovah's beloved and only begotten Son would be transferred from the heavenly realm and glory to the womb of the Jewish virgin by the wonder-working power of God.

Some time thereafter the Lord's angel advised Joseph, Mary's betrothed, in a dream, saying: "Fear not to take unto thee Mary thy wife: for that which is conceived in her is of the holy spirit. And she shall bring forth a son; and thou shalt call his name JESUS; for it is he that shall save his people from their sins." (Matthew 1: 20, 21, *A.R.V.*) This event was to be in fulfillment of the prophecy of Isaiah 7: 14: "Now all this was done, that it might be fulfilled which was spoken of the Lord by the prophet, saying, Behold, a virgin shall be with child, and shall bring forth a son, and they shall call his name Emmanuel, which being interpreted is, God with us."—Matthew 1: 22, 23.

Joseph and Mary were obliged to move to Bethlehem in the land of Judah before the event occurred, and one night the child was born there and was laid in a manger. It was thirty years before the prophesied date of A.D. 29. It was about six months after the spring passover celebration of B.C. 2, and hence about October 1, when the winter rains had not yet begun and the shepherds were out in the fields near by, watching their flocks by night. The shepherds saw no so-called "star of Bethlehem" or "star of the east" to call their notice to the important event. They were not astrologers like the magi or "wise men from the east", demon-worshipers. These Jewish shepherds feared the God of Abraham and of David.

"And, behold, an angel of the Lord stood by them, and the brightness of God shone round about them; and they feared with a great fear. And the angel said to them: Fear not; for, behold, I bring you good tidings of great joy, that shall be to all the people: for this day is born to you a Saviour, who is Christ the Lord, in the city of David. And this shall be a sign unto you. You shall find the infant wrapped in swaddling clothes, and laid in a manger. And suddenly there was with the angel a multitude of the heavenly army, praising God, and saying: Glory to God in the highest; and on earth peace to men of good-will."—Luke 2: 9-14, *Douay.*

Religionists called "trinitarians" say that this was the incarnation of God and that here the so-called "God-man" was born. To such unscriptural teaching is due the religious practice of calling Mary "the mother of God", thereby blaspheming Almighty God, who had no beginning or source and no female parent. Mary was not told she would be the "mother of God", but the angel Gabriel told her: "That holy thing which shall be born of thee shall be called the son of God." (Luke 1: 35) Moreover, if a mere incarnation of the Son of God had been intended, then it would not have been necessary for him to have his life transferred to an embryo in the virgin's womb and to be developed there and finally born as a helpless infant. He could still have remained a spirit person and materialized a fully developed fleshly body and clothed himself with it, just as the sons of God did in Noah's day and as the angel Gabriel did when appearing visibly to Mary.

Instead of describing an incarnation the scripture (John 1: 14) says: "And the Word *was made* flesh, and dwelt among us, (and we beheld his glory, the glory as of the only begotten of the Father,) full of grace and truth." His mission on earth was to be temporary, and that is why it is said he "dwelt" or tabernacled among us, just as the apostle Peter speaks of himself as "in this tabernacle", and Peter was

no incarnation. (2 Peter 1: 13, 14) That the Son
of God born on earth was no mighty spirit person clothing himself upon with a baby's fleshly
form and pretending to be absolutely ignorant
like a newborn infant is proved by the scripture
(Philippians 2: 5-8), which shows he laid aside
completely his spirit existence: "Christ Jesus,
who, though being in God's form, yet did not
meditate a usurpation to be like God, but di-
vested himself, taking a bondman's form, having been made in the likeness of men; and being
in condition as a man, he humbled himself, becoming obedient unto death, even the death of
the cross."—*Diaglott*.

It is contended that the scripture, "And they
shall call his name Emmanuel: which being interpreted is, God with us," proves that this babe
was "God incarnate" himself. That, however, is
a wresting of the Scriptures and is contrary to
all other Bible texts bearing on the subject. The
name "Immanuel" merely meant that God's representative and servant was with his covenant
people and thus representatively Jehovah God
was with them and was for them, on their side,
and favoring and helping them, as foretold at
Isaiah 8: 10. Nor does the fact that the name
"Jesus" means "Jehovah saves" signify that
Jesus and Jehovah God are one and the same
person. "Jesus" is merely the Greek form for
the Hebrew "Joshua", and the fact that Moses'
successor was named Joshua does not signify
that he was Jehovah God.—Numbers 13: 16, 17;
Acts 7: 45.

The oft-quoted prophecy at Jeremiah 23: 5, 6 can not be used as proof that Jesus is Jehovah God himself and one in person with him, namely: "Behold, the days come, saith Jehovah, that I will raise unto David a righteous Branch, and he shall reign as king and deal wisely, and shall execute justice and righteousness in the land. In his days Judah shall be saved, and Israel shall dwell safely; and this is his name whereby he shall be called: Jehovah our righteousness." (*A.R.V.*) The mere calling of a creature by a cognomen that includes the name *Jehovah* does not mean the unity in person of that creature with Jehovah. This is proved by the Scripture, at Jeremiah 33: 16: "In those days shall Judah be saved, and Jerusalem shall dwell safely; and this is the name whereby SHE shall be called; Jehovah our righteousness." (*A.R.V.*) Certainly Jerusalem is not one in person with Jehovah and not equal with him in power and glory and not a member of a supposed "trinity".

The scripture at 1 Timothy 3: 16 is likewise cited by religionists in their argument that Jesus was "God incarnate". This claim is upset by the reading of all modern revised versions of the text, as follows: "And without controversy great is the mystery of godliness; *He who* was manifested in the flesh, justified in the spirit, seen of angels, preached among the nations, believed on in the world, received up in glory." (1 Timothy 3: 16, *A.R.V.; Douay; Diaglott; Rotherham; Weymouth;* etc.) In the above passage nearly all the ancient manuscripts and all the versions, including the Latin Vulgate, have *"He who"* instead of *"God"*. Moreover, the religious idea of "God's blood", as based on Paul's words at Acts 20:28, is punctured by the emphasized rendering of the original Greek text by the *Diaglott* and *Rotherham,* as follows: "Take heed to yourselves, therefore, and to all the flock among whom the holy spirit made you overseers, to feed the church of God, which he acquired by the blood of his own." It is by the blood of his own Son or Lamb of God that Jehovah God purchased his church.

Joseph and Mary were authorized to call the child "Joshua", or "Jesus", for, said the angel, "it is he that shall save his people from their sins." (Matthew 1:21, *A.R.V.*) Only those who become his faithful and obedient people he saves, and not those remaining willful unbelievers and rebels. If Jesus had been Almighty God Jehovah he could not save his people from their sins by his blood, because Jehovah God is immortal, "from everlasting to everlasting." "Who only hath immortality, dwelling in light unapproachable; whom no man hath seen, nor can see: to whom be honor and power eternal." (1 Timothy 6:16, *A.R.V.*) Almighty God cannot die, but Jesus could die and did die, as testified by the Scriptures; hence he could not be God his Father, but was God's mortal Son. In due time, after proving his faithfulness to death and providing redemption from sin, the Son was rewarded with immortality; as he said: "As the

Father hath life in himself; so hath he given to the Son to have life in himself."—John 5:26.

The divine decree is: "The wages of sin is death; but the gift of God is eternal life through Jesus Christ our Lord." (Romans 6:23) That Jesus might save his people from their sins it was necessary that the Son of God be born as a human creature and grow to become "the man Christ Jesus". (1 Timothy 2:5, 6) He thus became the full equal of the perfect Adam in Eden, sinless and possessed of the right to perfect human life in the earthly Paradise. God's law shows the perfect balance to divine justice, saying: "And if any mischief follow, then thou shalt give life for life, eye for eye, tooth for tooth, hand for hand, foot for foot." (Exodus 21:23, 24) The perfect man Adam sinned, causing mischief to follow, and was sentenced to death. He forfeited his right to life and hence could not bequeath the right to everlasting life to his children.

For the right to life to be recovered for those of Adam's offspring who believe and obey God, it was necessary that another perfect man offer his own human life and his right to such life over to God as a purchase price. Thereby he redeems or recaptures for those believers the life right which Adam forfeited by sin, and the life right can then be bestowed upon those proving worthy according to God's terms. None of Adam's offspring being sinless or having right to life to offer as a redemptive price, it was necessary for the Son of God to lay aside his spirit existence and become the needed perfect man. To meet the exactness of God's perfect law, Jesus must be a perfect man, no more, no less. Thus Jesus could die, not as a spirit creature, but as a perfect human creature, for humankind needing redemption. For these and other reasons Jesus was not a "God-man", for that would be more than the required price of redemption. Had he been immortal God or an immortal soul he could not have given his life. According to the Scriptural facts, he was mortal on earth, and in him the prophecy of Isaiah 53:12 was fulfilled: "He hath poured out his soul unto death: and he was numbered with the transgressors; and he bare the sin of many, and made intercession for the transgressors." His soul was then "exceeding sorrowful, even unto death".—Matthew 26:38.

Seeing that Jesus did not receive his life from the sinner Adam through the imperfect man Joseph, he was not the son of Adam. Seeing that he was born of a woman by God's power and became the perfect man without sin and undefiled, the exact equivalent of the perfect man in Eden, Jesus was properly called "the Son of the man". (Literally in Greek) By his ransom sacrifice he redeemed the right to life and all earthly privileges possessed by the perfect man in Eden. With this the Scriptures agree, saying: "When the fulness of the time was come, God sent forth his Son, made of a woman, made under the law, to redeem them that were under the law, that we might receive the adoption of sons." "The Son of man came not to be ministered unto, but to minister, and to give his life a ransom for many."—Galatians 4: 4, 5; Matthew 20: 28.

Joseph and Mary were not instructed to call the child *Christ,* for that is a title meaning *Anointed.* However, the child was destined to become the Christ or Messiah. That would be when God anointed him to be the kingly Prince. At that anointing would be the time when "Messiah the Prince" would first come and appear.

Jesus' very destiny to be Messiah or Christ proves that his chief or primary purpose in coming to earth was not to ransom and save humankind. Such salvation of human creatures, while important to men seeking eternal life, is only secondary in God's lofty purpose. Jehovah's purpose is to establish a righteous government, a Theocratic government, upon the shoulder of his faithful Son, and by that government to vindicate his name before all living creatures of the universe. This will prove the Devil a slanderer and liar and false god. The title *Messiah* or *Christ* designates, not the Redeemer, but the princely King whom Jehovah anoints to be the Ruler in that Theocracy or kingdom of God.

The primary purpose of the Son of God in coming to earth was to meet and decisively answer Satan's false charge that God cannot put on earth a creature who will keep his integrity and abide faithful till death under the test of persecution from the Devil and his demons. (Job 1: 8-12; 2: 3-5) The Serpent must be per-

mitted to bruise the heel of the Seed of God's
"woman". By keeping his integrity under the
most fiery test Christ Jesus would vindicate his
Father's name and would prove his worthiness
to be the Seed or King of God's capital organization, Zion.

In A.D. 29, on reaching the age of thirty
years, Jesus consecrated himself to Jehovah's
purpose and he openly symbolized his death to
self-will and his aliveness to God's will by being dipped beneath Jordan's waters in baptism
and then being raised therefrom. Immediately
afterward John the Baptist saw a representa-
tion of God's spirit or active force descending
upon Jesus. This was in the form of a dove.
(Luke 3: 21-23) Religionists childishly argue
that here is proof of a "trinity", Father, Son and
holy spirit. In fact, only two persons were here,
each separate and distinct, and a dove as a token
to John the Baptist that God's invisible power
was being poured out upon the Son of God.

John heard God's voice announcing Jesus as
His Son. This proves that God there begot Jesus by his spirit or active force, by virtue of
which Jesus now became the spiritual Son of
God, possessing the right to spirit life in heav-
en. God so begot him, because Jesus' right to
human life was henceforth to be dedicated to
redeeming humankind. His earthly life was to
be laid down as a ransom for repentant sinners.
This meant that God took Jesus into the "covenant by sacrifice". (Psalm 50: 5) His human life
was devoted beyond recall to buy back for be-

lieving men the right to eternal life that had
been lost to them by being born sinners.

On such grounds Jesus could thereafter say
to a palsied man who was brought to him for
healing: "Man, thy sins are forgiven thee." And
concerning a sinner woman who bathed his feet
with her tears and wiped them with the hair of
her head he said: "Her sins, which are many,
are forgiven." "And he said unto her, Thy sins
are forgiven." The religious scribes and Pharisees accused Jesus of claiming to be God or
equal with God by forgiving sins. (Luke
5: 18-24; 7: 37-50) Jesus could thus forgive sins
because he was and is The Word of God, and
he was then in the covenant with God by sacrifice. By reason of this his perfect, sinless human life was bound by contract to be used to
ransom repentant, believing ones and relieve
them of the disability of sin. For like reason
Jesus could later give the following commission
to his faithful apostles: "Whose soever sins ye
remit, they are remitted unto them; and whose
soever sins ye retain, they are retained." (John
20: 23) The apostles were his representatives
on earth.

God's prophecy, at Psalm 2: 7, was directed
to Jesus: "Thou art my Son; this day have I
begotten thee." When Jehovah begot the baptized Jesus and made him the spiritual Son of
God with right to life in the heavenly spirit
realm, Jesus became a "new creature". Then
Jehovah took his begotten Son into the covenant
for the Kingdom, as pictured by the kingdom

covenant God made with King David centuries
before that. Jesus became heir to the Messianic
kingdom and was in truth "the son of David",
to destroy whom the Serpent was lying in wait.

In accord with this Jehovah anointed Jesus with
the holy spirit or divine force, as symbolized by
the descent of the dove upon Jesus' head. He
was anointed to be the King, "The Prince of
Peace," the Seed of God's "woman" Zion. By
virtue of this anointing he became the Messiah,
Christ. Henceforth he was Christ Jesus or the
Anointed Jesus.—Acts 10: 36-38.

At that event, "Messiah the Prince" came, and
the sixty-nine weeks of years, foretold at Daniel
9: 25, came to their end. Why had Messiah the
Prince come? Christ Jesus himself answered,
when Governor Pontius Pilate asked him: "Art
thou a king then?" "Jesus answered, Thou say-
est that I am a king. To this end was I born, and

for this cause came I into the world, that I should bear witness unto the truth. Every one that is of the truth heareth my voice." (John 18: 37) Human salvation is subordinate to that work of witness in vindication of God's name.

In faithfulness to the covenant for the Kingdom and to his anointing to preach the Kingdom Jesus resisted the temptations of the Devil during the forty days in the wilderness. He refused to accept from the Devil the kingdoms of this world in return for his worship of the Devil. He was determined to gain the Kingdom and then with Kingdom power crush the head of "that old serpent, called the Devil, and Satan", and thereby vindicate God's  name. (Matthew 4: 1-11) The Messiah is freedom's King, for by his glorious reign he brings in for ever the freedoms desired by man.

CHAPTER XX

FROM DEATH
TO IMMORTALITY

E HAVE found the Messiah (which is, being interpreted, Christ)." Of this discovery the Jewish fisherman Andrew came hastening to tell his brother Simon Peter. (John 1: 40, 41, *A.R.V.*) Andrew had heard John the Baptist identify Jesus as "the Lamb of God, which taketh away the sin of the world", and then he followed Jesus and heard him preach the Messianic kingdom.

Christ Jesus told his disciples to seek first the kingdom of God and its righteousness. He did that very thing himself. He did not indulge in the political affairs of this world, but applied himself exclusively to proclaiming the kingdom of the new world of righteousness. In the synagogue at his home town of Nazareth in Galilee he publicly declared his commission from God to preach, and he was always diligent to discharge his obligation to bear witness to the greatest truth of God's written Word, the Kingdom. (Luke 4: 16-21) He was the anointed Ruler of that Theocratic Government, and he was present. So he was right in preaching, "Repent: for the kingdom of heaven is at hand." (Matthew 4:17) He did not build a synagogue or a religious building and install himself therein as pastor and ring a bell in a steeple and invite the people to come and hear him preach, and then take up a money collection. He went to the people and freely preached to them, at their private homes and at the synagogues where they congregated and also at the temple in Jerusalem. "And it came to pass afterward, that he went throughout every city and village, preaching and showing the glad tidings of the kingdom of God: and the twelve were with him."—Luke 8:1.

Of those that heard and followed Christ Jesus he chose and appointed twelve apostles. He did not select learned scribes and doctors of the law and astute lawyers and Pharisees and Sadducees. Such men taught the traditions of men instead of God's commandments and practiced what one of their number called "the Jews' religion". They challenged Jesus' authority and commission, and rejected him. Jesus said new wine could not be put in old bottles without disaster. He chose humble, teachable, honest, God-fearing men. He came in his Father's name, and therefore he declared Jehovah's name to them. He taught them that the vindication of God's name by his kingdom is of first importance. So he taught them to pray: "Our Father which art in heaven, Hallowed be thy name. Thy kingdom come. Thy will be done in earth, as it is in heaven." (Matthew 6:9, 10) He commissioned them and sent them forth to preach from city to city and from house to house. His instructions were:

"As ye go, preach, saying, The kingdom of heaven is at hand. . . . And when ye come into an house, salute it. And if the house be worthy, let your peace come upon it: but if it be not worthy, let your peace return to you. . . . And ye shall be hated of all men for my name's sake; but he that endureth to the end shall be saved. But when they persecute you in this city, flee ye into another."—Matthew 10: 1-23; also Luke 9: 1-6; 10: 1-16.

Satan the Devil discerned that Jesus was God's Heir to the kingdom he was preaching. He was the foretold Seed of God's "woman", and also the promised Seed of Abraham. Satan's enmity knew no bounds, and he was determined to destroy Jesus and to maintain his own domination of the wicked world. Again he used religion as the pretext for opposing Jehovah's witness, this time the Chief Witness. The religious clergymen came out against him, and slandered him, and sought to kill him. The reason was, as Jesus told them: "Ye are of your father the devil, and the lusts of your father ye will do. He was a murderer from the beginning, and abode not in the truth." (John 8: 44) Those religious clergymen of Jewry nourished selfish hopes in their hearts as regards the Messianic kingdom. They felt envious at Jesus' proclamation of the Kingdom and refused to join in bearing the Kingdom fruits to the common people, who heard Jesus gladly.—Mark 12: 37.

Three and a half years after his anointing as King at the Jordan river Jesus rode triumphantly on an ass's colt amid jubilant crowds hailing the kingdom of God. Into Jerusalem he rode and went to the temple, where of old the kings of the nation of Israel had been anointed and acclaimed. At the temple Christ Jesus the Anointed King judged the nation by offering himself then and there as God's appointed King. The Jewish religious leaders refused the opportunity and objected to the people's demonstration. So doing, they rejected him as King at this judgment at the temple. Hence Jesus said to them: "Did ye never read in the scriptures, The stone which the builders rejected, the same is become the head of the corner: this is the Lord's doing, and it is marvellous in our eyes? Therefore say I unto you, The kingdom of God shall be taken from you, and given to a nation bringing forth the fruits thereof. And whosoever shall fall on this stone shall be broken: but on whomsoever it shall fall, it will grind him to powder." (Matthew 21:23-46) The religionists now plotted to kill him.

The passover feast of A.D. 33 came a few days thereafter, and Jesus assembled with his apostles to eat the passover. On that occasion also he took bread and wine and instituted a memorial to God's name and in symbol of his own faithful course unto death for the vindication of God's name. To the eleven faithful apostles who took the memorial he said: "You are they who have continued with me in my trials. And I covenant for you, even as my Father has covenanted for me, a kingdom, that you may eat and drink at my table in my kingdom, and sit on thrones, judging the twelve tribes of Israel."—Luke 22: 28-30, *Diaglott; Rotherham.*

Then, emphasizing that he had faithfully represented his Father Jehovah as his witness on earth, he said to them: "He that hath seen me hath seen the Father." (John 14:9) He told them his going away to the Father was cause for rejoicing: "For my Father is greater than I." (John 14: 28) On an earlier occasion he had declared his perfect agreement with Jehovah in His purpose and work, by saying: "I and my Father are one." Now, on this passover night, Jesus led his disciples in prayer and prayed that the same agreement and unity might be established among his disciples, by means of the truth. He said to God: "They are not of the world, even as I am not of the world. Sanctify them through thy truth: thy word is truth. . . . Neither pray I for these alone, but for them also which shall believe on me through their word; that they all may be one; as thou, Father, art in me, and I in thee, that they also may be one in us; that the world may believe that thou hast sent me. And the glory which thou gavest me I have given them; that they may be one, even as we are one: I in them, and thou in me, that they may be made perfect in one; . . . And I have declared unto them thy name, and will declare it: that the love wherewith thou hast loved me may be in them, and I in them." —John 17: 16-26.

Having thus spoken, Jesus led them forth to the Garden of Gethsemane. His betrayal by Judas, then trial before the Jewish religious court, then a hearing before Pontius Pilate and King Herod, and, last, a rehearing by Pilate, quickly followed. All the while the Jewish chief priests and other clergymen led the people in howling for Jesus' execution on a tree to hang there till dead. "Shall I crucify your King?"

asked Pilate. "The chief priests answered, We
have no king but Caesar."—John 19: 6, 15.

What, then, was the issue over which Christ
Jesus was tried and tested and on which the
Jewish religionists made their decision? Was it
the salvation of humankind? No, not that primarily; it was God's kingdom, the King of which
must vindicate God's name by keeping his integrity faithfully toward God even to the most re-
proachful death. God's kingdom is of first and
highest importance, because His holy name and
universal domination are bound up with it.
Therefore Jesus chose to die on the tree, his
kingship mocked at by the superscription above
his head. He died in outward disgrace to the
eyes of religionists and politicians, but he died
in the truth and for the truth of the Kingdom.
His was the death of a free man. He died with
clean hands, free from the bondage to man, devil
or religion. He died honoring Jehovah God. In
the fight of the Devil to make him break his integrity Jesus had won!

"And calling out with a loud voice Jesus said,
Father! into thy hands I commend my spirit.
And this saying, he ceased to breathe." (Luke
23: 46, *Roth.; Diaglott*) He knew he was dying
faithful, and hence was worthy to commend his
power of life to the great Life-giver in hope of
a resurrection. He knew the scripture, at Psalm
16: 10, which read: "Thou wilt not leave my soul
in hell; neither wilt thou suffer thine Holy One
to see corruption." While he was living in the
flesh and looking ahead to this death, he was

never disturbed, but his flesh rested in hope and was at ease. He knew there would be a resurrection to life in the spirit, to which life he had been begotten at the Jordan river.

Satan the Devil had heard Jesus speak privately to his disciples of a resurrection and of returning to his Father. In his uneasiness the Devil caused his religious agents to have a guard thrown about the sepulcher where Jesus' body was laid, and the great stone in front to be officially sealed. (Matthew 27: 57-66) Foolish precaution that! On the third day from the burial Jehovah's mightiest miracle took place, the resurrection of his dear Son out of death and unto life divine, unto immortality.

No human eye saw that resurrection early that first day of the week. The sepulcher guards experienced an earthquake and were terrified at the sight of a dazzling angel who rolled away the stone, exposing to view the sepulcher's empty interior. The resurrected Jesus they saw not, nor were any of the Devil's servants thereafter made witnesses to the fact of Jesus' resurrection. What had happened to the fleshly body of Jesus? It was not "spiritualized"; for that is impossible according to Jesus' own words: "That which is born of the flesh is flesh; and that which is born of the spirit is spirit." (John 3: 6) Paul, who had a vision of the resurrected Jesus, also says: "Now this I say, brethren, that flesh and blood cannot inherit the kingdom of God." (1 Corinthians 15: 50) According to Psalm 16: 10 and Acts 2: 27-31 the body was not permitted to corrupt. Hence Jehovah God disposed of that body in his own way, just as he disposed of the body of Moses, who was a type of Christ Jesus; but no one knows how. —Deuteronomy 34: 5, 6.

At the resurrection Almighty God answered Jesus' prayer: "And now, O Father, glorify thou me with thine own self with the glory which I had with thee before the world was." (John 17: 5) That was glory in heaven, or the unseen realm, and in a spirit body whose glory was not veiled or shrouded with a fleshly body bearing a spear gash in the side, nail prints in hands and feet, thorn scratches on the brow, and welts and stripes on the back from the scourge lashing. The fleshly body is the body in which Jesus humbled himself, like a servant, and is not the body of his glorification, not the body in which he was resurrected. The apostle Peter, who saw him after his resurrection, testifies: "Christ also died once for our sins, the just for the unjust: that he might offer us to God, being put to death indeed in the flesh, but ENLIVENED IN THE SPIRIT, in which also coming he preached to those spirits that were in prison." (1 Peter 3: 18, 19, *Douay; A.R.V.*) He was raised to life divine in a spirit body. The resurrection of his faithful disciples will be like his; concerning which it is written: "If we have been planted together in the likeness of his death, we shall be also in the likeness of his resurrection." "It is sown a natural body; it is raised a spiritual body. . . . We shall be changed. For this corruptible must put on incorruption, and this mortal must put on immortality."—Romans 6 : 5; 1 Corinthians 15 : 44, 52-54.

Beginning with his resurrection day Jesus showed himself alive to his faithful disciples at intervals during forty days. Since a spirit does not have flesh and bones, how, then, did Jesus appear or make himself visible to them? By materializing fleshly bodies on the occasions of his appearances, bodies fully clothed, not with his burial clothes, but with clothing suitable to the time and purpose of his appearing. This was nothing new or unusual; for the angel Gabriel appeared thus to priest Zacharias inside the temple, and six months later to Mary, Jesus' mother. That very resurrection morning two angels fully clothed in white appeared to Mary Magdalene at the sepulcher. So now Jesus made his presence visible to his disciples, even within the room behind closed doors. Examine every one of the accounts of his resurrection appearances, and you will observe that he materialized bodies of different form, and hence it became necessary for him to disclose his true identity by various signs and tokens.

Mark 16 : 12 reads: "After that he appeared *in another form* unto two of them, as they walked, and went into the country." This verse is today understood to be no part of the original book of Mark, yet the authentic accounts by other witnesses bear out that the risen Christ used his 'all power in heaven and in earth' to appear under various forms of body, thereby to prove that he is glorified and is no longer an earthly, fleshly creature. On at least one occasion, likely two, he appeared in a form like that of the body in which he was crucified, so as to identify himself to doubting Thomas.—Luke 24:36-43, *A.R.V.*; John 20:19-30.

Due to these different manifestations Mary Magdalene mistook her resurrected Lord as a gardener. The two disciples whom he joined on the road to Emmaus did not know him till reaching the house and he disclosed himself at the meal. When he appeared in familiar form to satisfy Thomas, that disciple, now convinced, broke out with an exclamation of amazement: "My Lord and my God!" not meaning that Thomas was claiming that Jesus was Almighty God or Jehovah himself. "But these [signs] are written, that ye might believe that Jesus is the Christ, the Son of God."—John 20:28-31.

When Jesus manifested himself to seven disciples at the sea of Galilee while fishing and they came ashore to the fish breakfast he miraculously provided for them, at first "the disciples knew not that it was Jesus". But after the miracle "none of the disciples durst ask him, Who art thou? knowing that it was the Lord". (John 21:4, 12) Thereafter, when he appeared at a mountain in Galilee, "they worshipped him: but some doubted." (Matthew 28:16, 17) Years later he appeared without a fleshly body to Saul of Tarsus, the future apostle Paul; for Saul's companions saw no one, but heard the sound of the voice. Jesus miraculously permitted Saul to see some of his heavenly glory as a divine spirit. To Saul, who did not identify him by any 'print of the nails in his hands and his feet', the Lord said in reply to his question: "I am Jesus, whom thou persecutest." The vision cost Saul his eyesight for three days. Hence for the forty days after his resurrection Jesus did not appear in this way to his disciples, but in fleshly form.

Christ Jesus truly is risen. In resurrection glory he said: "I am he that liveth, and was dead; and, behold, I am alive for evermore," because clothed now with immortality. (Revelation 1: 5, 18) He is the "firstborn from the dead", the "firstfruits of them that slept". (Colossians 1: 18; 1 Corinthians 15: 20) He is the first one to be resurrected to life eternal. His resurrection is the beginning of "the first resurrection", in which his faithful disciples are promised to share. (Revelation 20: 5, 6) He is God's firm and immortal Foundation for a new and free world without end.

CHAPTER XXI

THE CHURCH OF FREEMEN

THE gates of hell did not prevail against Jehovah's greatest Martyr, "whom God hath raised up, having loosed the sorrows of hell, as it was impossible that he should be holden by it." (Acts 2:24, *Douay*) "Whom God raised up, loosing the pangs of death, inasmuch as it was not possible for him to continue held fast by it." (*Roth.*) This strengthens the declaration made to his disciples by Christ Jesus: "And upon this rock I will build my church; and the gates of hell shall not prevail against it." (Matthew 16:18) After his resurrection he announced: "Behold, I am alive for evermore, Amen; and have the keys of hell and of death." This gives promise to his disciples that, as his soul or life was not left a prey forever to *hell* or the abode of the dead, likewise the souls of his faithful followers would not be abandoned for ever to the grave. Christ Jesus has the power to release from "hell" and "death", and he declares: "Every one which seeth the Son, and believeth on him, may have everlasting life: and I will raise him up at the last day."—John 6:40.

The Rock upon which the church is founded is heavenly. It is Christ Jesus. Forty days after his resurrection to life as a heavenly "new creature" he ascended to heaven, not immediately to begin reigning, but to sit at God's right hand of power and build his church. (Acts 1: 1-9; Hebrews 10: 12, 13; 12: 2) His Father, Jehovah, is himself the great heavenly Rock, upon which all creation rests: "Proclaim the name of Jehovah: ascribe ye greatness unto our God. The Rock, his work is perfect." (Deuteronomy 32: 3, 4, *A.R.V.*) Jehovah's Son, Christ Jesus, is "the express image of his person, and upholding all things by the word of his power". As to this Son and his important place in the heavenly organization Zion Jehovah said: "Thus saith the Lord Jehovah, Behold, I lay in Zion for a foundation a stone, a tried stone, a precious cornerstone of sure foundation: he that believeth shall not be in haste." (Hebrews 1: 3; Colossians 1: 15; Isaiah 28: 16, *A.R.V.*) Upon himself as Anointed King and Son of the living God, Christ Jesus builds his royal organization, the church. The apostle Peter, who believed in the "Rock", boldly proclaimed to enemy and to church alike that Christ Jesus is the Foundation, The Rock, upon which the church of Christ is built.—Acts 4: 8-12; 1 Peter 2: 3-10.

"Church" means a congregation called out from the world for God's purpose, and as such the congregation of the twelve tribes of Israel under Moses as prophet was a "church". (Acts 7: 37, 38) The first members of the church built on Christ Jesus were taken from the "church" of such natural Israelites, or from "Israel after the flesh". On the other hand, all members of God's church in Christ become a new creation and hence are spiritual Israelites, "the Israel of God." (1 Corinthians 10:18; Galatians 6:15, 16) When Jacob, whose name God changed to Israel, blessed his twelve sons before his death, he left twelve foundation pillars upon which that typical nation of Israel might rest. When Christ Jesus was laid as the Foundation Stone in Zion he also raised up twelve foundation pillars for the organization of his church, namely, his twelve apostles, of whom Peter was one. This is symbolically pictured at Revelation 21:14: "And the wall of the city had twelve foundations, and in them the names of the twelve apostles of the Lamb." (Galatians 2:9) The final number of the heavenly church will be only 144,000, according to God's decree. Because they were foreshadowed by the faithful of the twelve tribes of Israel, therefore the church of God is likened to twelve tribes of 12,000 members each. (Revelation 7:4-8; 14:1, 3) They are under a "new covenant", mediated by the Greater Moses, Christ Jesus. The new superseded the old law covenant made with natural Israel.—Hebrews 8:6-13.

Christ Jesus, when on earth, did not put salvation of human creatures first and frantically try to convert the world. He confined his preaching and activities to the nation of Israel and told his disciples then to do likewise: "I am not sent

but unto the lost sheep of the house of Israel."
"Go not into the way of the Gentiles, and into
any city of the Samaritans enter ye not: but go
rather to the lost sheep of the house of Israel."
(Matthew 15: 24; 10: 5, 6) Had a sufficient number of the Jews abandoned the "Jews' religion"
and displayed faith in God's Word and turned
to Jesus about whom God's Word prophesied,
the entire body of the church would have been
selected from among the Jewish nation. The
Scriptures, however, foretold that it would not
be so, but that the houses of Israel would stum-
ble over Christ Jesus as the Rock and only a
remnant of natural Israel would accept him and
be built into the church upon Christ. The Lord
Jesus foreknew this by means of the prophecies,
and said to Peter: "And I will give unto thee
the keys of the kingdom of heaven: and whatsoever thou shalt bind on earth shall be bound
in heaven; and whatsoever thou shalt loose on
earth shall be loosed in heaven." (Matthew
16: 19) How, then, did Peter use the two keys?

Before his ascension to heaven Jesus said to
his disciples: "It behoved Christ to suffer, and
to rise from the dead the third day: and that
repentance and remission of sins should be
preached in his name among all nations, beginning at Jerusalem. And ye are witnesses of
these things." (Luke 24: 46-48; Acts 1: 7, 8) Ten
days after his ascension the witnessing began
on the day of Pentecost, at Jerusalem. Jesus had
said aforetime to his disciples: "Fear not, little
flock; for it is your Father's good pleasure to

give you the kingdom"; and he took his then
faithful apostles into the Kingdom covenant
with himself. (Luke 12: 32; 22: 28-30) At Pentecost it was due time for other Jews to be given
the opportunity to be taken into the covenant for
the kingdom of heaven. How would this opportunity be opened up to such Jews? By the "key
of knowledge"; and this knowledge would be
imparted by preaching.—Luke 11: 52; Acts
2: 21; Romans 10: 11-17.

On the day of Pentecost heaven let loose the
opportunity, and Peter used the first 'key of the
kingdom of heaven' and let loose. That day,
while the apostles and other disciples were assembled together in Jerusalem a sound came
from heaven, and God's spirit or invisible force
was poured out upon the faithful disciples. They
were begotten by the Father's power and were
anointed for the Kingdom by his spirit. This
definitely was their commissioning to preach or
bear witness to the Kingdom. Due to the demonstration made by all those disciples' speaking
in foreign languages, a crowd of Pentecost cele-
brators from many lands and tongues gathered
outside. Then Peter, the receiver of the Kingdom keys, rose up and preached to them Christ
the King, and concluded, saying: "For David is
not ascended into the heavens: but he saith
himself, The LORD said unto my Lord, Sit thou
on my right hand, until I make thy foes thy
footstool. Therefore let all the house of Israel
know assuredly, that God hath made that same
Jesus, whom ye have crucified, both Lord and

Christ." (Acts 2: 34-36) So starting off the Kingdom witness, Peter used the first of the "keys", and thousands were that day admitted into the Kingdom privileges. "Then they that gladly received his word were baptized: and the same day there were added unto them about three thousand souls." Then they engaged in house-to-house preaching activity, being well received by the people.—Acts 2: 41, 46, 47.

The prophecy of Daniel 9: 26, 27 indicates that a half of a week of years, or three and a half years, passed after this Pentecost. During that time the conversion to Christianity was restricted to Jews and Samaritans, as Jesus had said: "Be witnesses unto me, both in Jerusalem,

and in all Judæa, and in Samaria," before going
to the uttermost parts of the earth. (Acts 1: 8)
For that length of time heaven bound the Kingdom privilege down to these and away from the
Gentile nations in general; hence Peter was
bound from any use of the second of the Kingdom "keys".

The time limit was at last reached. Down till
then only a remnant of the Jews, together with
some Samaritans, had acted on the Kingdom
opportunity. Then heaven loosed the privilege
to the Gentiles, and Peter was released from
restrictions for this service. Forthwith he used
the second key. Did God send him to Rome to
use it? No; but to an Italian who had been con-
verted from heathenism to faith in Jehovah God
and who was living in Caesarea on the Mediterranean seacoast, about seventy miles from
Jerusalem. God sent him a vision of an angel
who bade Cornelius to send for Simon Peter,
who was then at Joppa not far away. Just about
the time that Cornelius' messengers arrived God
sent a vision to Peter showing that the way was
now open for other nations than Jews, and so
Peter returned with the messengers to Cornelius' home. Then Peter preached to him and his
assembled kinsmen and friends concerning the
Christ or Anointed Jesus: "And we are witnesses of all things which he did, . . . And he
commanded us to preach unto the people, and
to testify . . . through his name whosoever believeth in him shall receive remission of sins."
—Acts 10: 1-43.

Did heaven confirm what Peter was doing with the second "key of knowledge"? "While Peter yet spake these words, the holy spirit fell on all them that heard the word. And they of the circumcision [Jews] that believed were amazed, as many as came with Peter, because that on the Gentiles also was poured out the gift of the holy spirit. For they heard them speak with tongues, and magnify God." Thereafter Cornelius and other Gentile believers were baptized, not with John the Baptist's baptism, which was for Jews, but "baptized in the name of Jesus Christ". (Acts 10: 44-48, *A.R.V.*) Thereby believers from among the Gentiles were taken into the covenant for the Kingdom. Now Peter had finished his exclusive work with the "keys of the kingdom of heaven". There was no need for him to have a successor to such work, and God has not appointed or raised up any successor. The door remains open to the Gentiles.—Acts 14: 27; 1 Corinthians 16: 9.

Why did Jehovah God use Simon Peter and visit these non-Jews with his Kingdom favor? After Peter, or Simeon, had made a report on this the apostle James said: "Simeon hath declared how God at the first did visit the Gentiles, to take out of them a people for his name." (Acts 15: 7-14) That is the purpose of the "new covenant", namely, to take out and bring forth such a people. The Christians from among the Gentile nations as well as those from among the Jews must be together a "people for his name", that is, God's name, which is Jehovah. There was now no racial or national distinction; all must be one in Christ their Head, an undivided church, without schism. "For as we have many members in one body, and all members have not the same office; so we, being many, are one body in Christ, and every one members one of another." (Romans 12: 4, 5) "For as many of you as have been baptized into Christ, have put on Christ. There is neither Jew nor Greek, there is neither bond nor free, there is neither male nor female: for ye are all one in Christ Jesus. And if ye be Christ's, then are ye Abraham's seed, and heirs according to the promise." (Galatians 3: 27-29) "Wherefore, henceforth know we no man after the flesh: yea, though we have known Christ after the flesh [before being resurrected as a spirit], yet now henceforth know we him no more [after the flesh]. Therefore if any man be in Christ, he is a new creature: old things are passed away; behold, all things are become new."—2 Corinthians 5: 16, 17; also 1 Corinthians 12: 12, 13, 18, 27.

Jesus is the Head member of the church. The other members constitute the church body. "And he is the head of the body, the church." (Colossians 1: 18; Ephesians 1: 22, 23) To the members of Christ's church-body it is written: "That ye would walk worthy of God, who hath called you unto his kingdom and glory." (1 Thessalonians 2: 12) Since God's kingdom under Christ is heavenly and flesh and blood cannot inherit it, how may human creatures find entrance into it?

By the following steps outlined in the Scriptures:

Being conceived in sin and shapen in iniquity and being hence under condemnation from birth on, there must be a making right or justification of the human creature first, to relieve him of divine condemnation. This is accomplished after the human creature shows his faith, not only by believing in Jehovah as God and in Christ Jesus as the ransom sacrifice for sins. Additionally he must confess to being bought by Christ Jesus' sacrifice and must make a full and complete consecration of himself to God, to be His and to do His will forever. The believer symbolizes his consecration by baptism in water. The opportunity being open for the Kingdom and also a part with Christ Jesus in the "covenant by sacrifice", Jehovah God justifies the human creature and counts him as possessing the right to human life. That human life right, however, is at once sacrificed that the consecrated one may be taken into the "covenant by sacrifice". God begets the justified one by his Word (symbolized by water) and by his spirit, and thus brings that one forth as a spiritual son of God. This acknowledged son of God manifesting faithfulness, God calls him to the Kingdom and takes him into the covenant for that Theocratic Government and then anoints him with his holy spirit. By such anointing the consecrated one is baptized into the "body of Christ".

If you will read the scriptures below[1] in their order you will see for yourself that the above is the Scriptural order.

All thus anointed are in line for the Kingdom. Although yet in a body of flesh, they are a "new creation". They must now copy their Head and King Christ Jesus and bear witness to God's kingdom in the manner he did. They must maintain their integrity toward God and keep covenant with him through all the suffering of reproaches and persecution, even unto death. They are not "saved" to life eternal as soon as they believe and start following Christ Jesus, but only after proving faithful to death. They must give all diligence to make their calling and election sure. If before death they turned aside and proved unfaithful, they would prove deserving of everlasting destruction. But for them to endure faithfully to the end means their ultimate salvation. The Scriptures of truth listed below prove these facts correct.[2]

Such are not yet immortal; otherwise they could not keep the "covenant by sacrifice" and die the death of faithfulness and be made conformable to Christ's death. By their integrity and loyalty till death they have a part with Christ Jesus in the vindicating of his Father's name. Therefore God will give "to them, who

[1] Romans 4 : 24, 25 ; 5 : 1, 9, 12, 16 ; 8 : 1, 33 ; James 1 : 18 ; John 3 : 3, 5 ; 1 Peter 1 : 3 ; Titus 3 : 5-7 ; 1 Corinthians 1 : 9 ; 2 Thessalonians 2 : 14 ; 2 Corinthians 1 : 21 ; 1 John 2 : 20, 27 ; Romans 6 : 3, 4 ; 1 Corinthians 12 : 12, 13.

[2] 2 Corinthians 5 : 17 ; 1 Peter 2 : 21 ; Romans 8 : 16-18, 28-30 ; 2 Timothy 2 : 11, 12 ; 2 Peter 1 : 4-11 ; Hebrews 10 : 38, 39 ; Romans 1 : 31, 32 ; Revelation 2 : 10 ; Matthew 10 : 22 ; 24 : 13.

by patient continuance in well doing, seek for glory and honour and immortality, eternal life." —Philippians 3: 10, 14; Romans 2: 6, 7.

When do they receive immortality? Those who die before the setting up of the kingdom of God and the coming of the King to the temple must sleep in death, unconscious, inactive, awaiting those events. First at the arrival of the King at the temple for judgment do the sleeping members of Christ's body or church receive the "crown of life". Speaking of the resurrection of the church-body the apostle Paul writes: "It is sown a natural body; it is raised a spiritual body. . . . Behold, I shew you a mystery: We shall not all sleep, but we shall all be changed, in a moment, in the twinkling of an eye, at the last trump: for the trumpet shall sound, and the dead shall be raised incorruptible, and we shall be changed. For this corruptible must put on incorruption, and this mortal must put on immortality. So when this corruptible shall have put on incorruption, and this mortal shall have put on immortality, then shall be brought to pass the saying that is written, Death is swallowed up in victory." (1 Corinthians 15: 42-54) The members of Christ's body are given a spiritual resurrection, to heavenly life in the spirit, in the Kingdom.

The remnant thereof who are yet on earth in the flesh when the King comes to the temple must fulfill the covenant by sacrifice by faithfulness to death. However, they do not sleep in death, but are instantly "changed" into the heavenly likeness of their present King and Head. (1 John 3:2; Colossians 3:1-4) The "gates of hell" do not prevail against God's church on the Rock.

The apostle Paul warned that immediately after his death a falling away of men from the true faith and into religion would occur. The apostle John warned of the same effect of Satan's work. (Acts 20:29-31; 2 Thessalonians 2:1-3; 1 John 2:18-23) The apostle Peter said of such ones: "Promising freedom to them, they themselves being all the while slaves of corruption; for by whom one hath been defeated, by the same hath he become enslaved." (2 Peter 2:1-3, 19, *Roth.*) It was even so. Less than a hundred years after John died there arose a man named Tertullian (A.D. 155-222), who taught there is a trinity of three persons of one substance in one God. So centuries after him a religionist wrongfully inserted the text at 1 John 5:7 to give seeming Bible support to such a doctrine.[1] Then Augustine (A.D. 354-430) used his powerful influence to fasten the pagan doctrine of "immortality of human souls" upon the religious congregations, contrary to the Bible doctrine of Christ's ransom sacrifice. On such basis other blasphemous errors were introduced and adopted, such as eternal torment of souls in a fiery hell, Purgatory, prayers for the dead, the mass, etc.

---

[1] Kenyon's *Handbook to the Textual Criticism of the New Testament*, page 270 and footnote; also page 133, ¶ 3, and page 138, ¶ 4. Note *Diaglott* and *A.R.V.* as to 1 John 5:7, 8.

CHAPTER XXII

"THE TIME OF THE END"

MPEROR Constantine, as pontifex maximus of the Roman Empire, called the first ecumenical council, at Nicaea (or Nice) in Asia Minor, in A.D. 325. He was unbaptized at the time, and in the following year (326) he ordered the execution of his oldest son and then his wife. Constantine meddled in the reputedly "Christian" council. He decreed that the "trinity" doctrine should thenceforth be the faith of the religious community. He backed it up by the sword of the state. The Nicean council gave way to the rule that the state might use its secular arm to bring professing "Christians" of the Roman world-empire into line with the newly codified belief. It marked the development of the so-called "state church". It laid the foundation for the establishment of "organized religion" which has been miscalled "Christendom".

In the parable of the wheat and the tares Christ Jesus foretold this production of multitudes of imitation Christians. He likened them to tares. Then he explained: "He that soweth the good seed is the Son of man; the field is the world; the good seed are the children of the kingdom; but the tares are the children of the

wicked one; the enemy that sowed them is the
devil; the harvest is the end of the world; and
the reapers are the angels. As therefore the
tares are gathered and burned in the fire; so
shall it be in the end of this world." (Matthew
13: 24-30, 36-43) Under such picture language
Jesus predicted the showing up and separation
of the counterfeit Christians from the real ones,
followed by the destruction of the hypocritical
religionists. This parable the clergy have used
to teach that our literal earth and the sun, moon
and stars will be destroyed by universal fire.

As further support to such an interpretation
of the "end of the world", the religionists quote
Jesus' words: "Till heaven and earth pass, one
jot or one tittle shall in no wise pass from the
law, till all be fulfilled." "Heaven and earth
shall pass away, but my words shall not pass
away." (Matthew 5: 18; 24: 35) To this are added the words of the apostle Peter: "But the
heavens and the earth, which are now, by the
same word are kept in store, reserved unto fire
against the day of judgment and perdition of
ungodly men. But the day of the Lord will come
as a thief in the night; in the which the heavens
shall pass away with a great noise, and the elements shall melt with fervent heat, the earth
also, and the works that are therein, shall be
burned up. Seeing then that all these things
shall be dissolved, what manner of persons
ought ye to be in all holy conversation and godliness, looking for and hasting unto the coming
of the day of God, wherein the heavens, being

on fire, shall be dissolved, and the elements shall melt with fervent heat?" (2 Peter 3: 7, 10-12) Say the religionists: 'The world's end in Noah's day was by literal water, and so the end of this world will be by literal fire, consuming all material things, and leaving only the spiritual things to remain.'

Such "private interpretation" of prophecy fails to consider that, whereas the water of the Flood was literal, the literal earth was not destroyed, and the sun and stars were not even touched by the Flood nor were their fires put out. It is placing far too much importance upon puny mortal man to insist that, because of Adam's fall and the wickedness of his descendants, God the Creator will destroy his wonderful handiwork of earth, moon, sun and stars, and stellar nebulae, which He spent countless millenniums of time in creating. Man is unimportant. God could easily have wiped out the unfaithful pair in Eden and started a new and perfect race.

"Behold, the nations are as a drop of a bucket, and are counted as the small dust of the balance: . . . All nations before him are as nothing; and they are counted to him less than nothing, and vanity." Jehovah will not destroy his glorious handiwork, the earth, for the sake of all such nations, but will destroy the nations instead, that his handiwork may be fit for occupancy by his righteous servants. "He hath established it, he created it not in vain, he formed it to be inhabited." (Isaiah 40: 15-17; 45: 12, 18) "Thus saith the LORD, The heaven is my throne, and the earth is my footstool." It is to this footstool that Christ Jesus has taught his disciples to pray for God's Theocratic rule to come, saying: "Thy kingdom come. Thy will be done, as in heaven, so in earth."—Isaiah 66:1; Luke 11:2.

Although many scripture texts indicate there will be a display of much literal fire upon the earth and in the atmospheric firmament about the earth at the final end of "this world", the Scriptures are nonetheless plain that "the earth abideth for ever", and that there will be survivors safely carried through this world catastrophe as surely as Noah and his family were carried through the end of the old world. The ungodly pre-Flood world consisted of the visible earthly organization of humankind and the wicked heavenly organization of demons which controlled corrupt humankind. Such were the "earth" and the "heavens" that made up the "world that then was", and that perished in the flood.—2 Peter 3:6.

The superficial appearance of our literal earth was greatly changed by the addition of the flood from the fallen water canopy, but upon this same earth another visible organization of ungodly men was built up. It dates particularly from the time of the founding of Nimrod's kingdom at Babel, or Babylon, and it has spread over all the earth. This human, visible organization of religion, commerce and politics makes up the symbolic "earth", and men think it will endure just as long as our earthly planet does.

Our planet earth is surrounded by an invisible air mass, which is the "firmament" or expanse of atmosphere extending up about one hundred miles higher than man. In like manner the symbolic "earth" has invisible spirit powers in control of it, namely, the demons under Satan the Devil. This organization of wicked spirits with Satan as their prince is both higher than man and unseen to him. Hence that demon organization constitutes the "heavens" with relation to man's present earthly organization. Man on earth can no more get rid of these demonic "heavens" than man can by airplane or rockets or other means get up above the air envelope which is about our earthly globe and in which man breathes. God alone can and will deliver humankind from such demon powers of control.

The symbolic "heavens and the earth which are now" make up "this world" and its "elements" and "works". Christ Jesus said: "My kingdom is not of this world." He repeatedly called Satan the Devil "the prince of this world". —John 18: 36; 12: 31; 14: 30; 16: 11.

The world's destruction as described by Peter applies to the symbolic "heavens" and "earth". Hence the "fire" which shall dissolve and burn up the invisible and visible parts of Satan's world must be symbolic rather than literal. Since literal fire is destructive of combustible things and purifies away the dross, so the "fire" in which this present world passes away "with a great noise" pictures the destruction which God in his hot wrath brings upon Satan's mighty

organization, visible and invisible, thereby puri-
fying the universe of wicked demons and wicked
men.

It is written: "Our God is a consuming fire."
(Hebrews 12: 29) This God says to religious
"Christendom", which misrepresents Christianity and brings reproach upon God's name:
"Therefore wait ye for me, saith Jehovah, until
the day that I rise up to the prey; for my determination is to gather the nations, that I may
assemble the kingdoms, to pour upon them mine
indignation, even all my fierce anger; for all
the earth shall be devoured with the fire of my
jealousy." (Zephaniah 3: 8, *A.R.V.*) To the
great Babylonish organization under the unfaithful Lucifer God says: "And I will punish
the world for their evil, and the wicked for their
iniquity: . . . Therefore I will make the heavens to tremble, and the earth shall be shaken
out of its place, in the wrath of Jehovah of hosts,
and in the day of his fierce anger." (Isaiah
13: 1, 11-13, *A.R.V.*; 14: 4, 12) The world's end
will be by an act of God.

It is clear, therefore, that the destruction of
this demon-ruled "world" does not mean the destruction of the earth which Jehovah God was
"six days" in preparing for man's habitation.
How, then, shall we know when we are at the
end of the world? By signs, by evidences or
proofs visible and perceptible to our senses.
Said Jesus in his astounding prophecy on the
end of the world: "So likewise ye, when ye shall
see all these things, know that it is near, even

at the doors." (Matthew 24:33) "So likewise ye, when ye see these things come to pass, know ye that the kingdom of God is nigh at hand." (Luke 21:31) The establishment of the kingdom of God marks the end of Satan's world, for Jesus said that his Messianic kingdom is not a part of this Satanic world.

Daniel, chapter four, showed that God's kingdom would not be set up until the end of the "seven times" of the Gentile nations under their invisible overlord Satan. Because of the controversy over Jehovah's supremacy and universal domination God delegated to Satan the Devil a limited period of time. In that period God's adversary would have uninterrupted rule over the world. Such period without interruption by God would terminate with the end of the "seven times" of the Gentile powers. Its end must therefore mark the end or consummation of Satan's world of uninterrupted rule. The Greek text of the Bible uses the word *aion* (eon) to designate Satan's uninterrupted rule which must end when the "seven times" run out. Those "seven times" ended in the fall of A.D. 1914.

However, the end of Satan's *aion,* or uninterrupted rule, does not mean the destruction at once of his organization visible and invisible. It simply means that the "time of the end" has begun for his organization. Daniel 11:40 predicted what would occur "at the time of the end". From then on the demonic-human organization of Satan would move rapidly to its end in utter destruction. That is the *final* end of Satan's world organization, which organization the Greek Bible text calls the *kosmos* (translated "world"). As to such *final* end Daniel's prophecy says: "At the time appointed the end shall be." (Daniel 8:19; 11:27) It is Jehovah God who had appointed the day and hour of such *final* end, respecting which Jesus said: "But of that day and hour knoweth no one, not even the angels of heaven, neither the Son, but the Father only." (Matthew 24:36, *A.R.V.;* Mark 13:32) These words, by the way, prove that Jesus is not one in person with his Father. In order to discern that the *final* end is soon upon us Jesus stressed the need to watch the signs of the times. Jehovah God knows the appointed time, and by the signs he gives us warning, that we may take the proper course and not be overtaken in a state of sin at that day and hour.

When Christ Jesus ascended to heaven and into God's presence the "seven times" had over 1800 years yet to go. Naturally he had to wait at God's right hand until the time to begin reigning and taking action against Satan's world organization (or *kosmos*). When the period of Satan's uninterrupted rule ended, then God would empower Jesus to proceed against the enemy organization. The prophecy of Psalm 110:1, 2 must be fulfilled: "Jehovah saith unto my Lord, Sit thou at my right hand, until I make thine enemies thy footstool. Jehovah will send forth the rod of thy strength out of Zion: rule thou in the midst of thine enemies." (*A.R.V.*) "But he, when he had offered one sacrifice for sins for ever, sat down on the right hand of God; henceforth expecting till his enemies be made the footstool of his feet." (Hebrews 10: 12, 13, *A.R.V.*) Thus the end of Satan's uninterrupted rule must mark the "beginning of sorrows" upon his world organization.

Have we passed that "beginning of sorrows", and are we now approaching the *final* end of Satan's organization (*kosmos*)? The answer to that question is of the utmost importance and deserves the most serious consideration. Satan the Devil is invisible; and, since likewise God's kingdom is invisible, it being heavenly, what proof have we that the "seven times" and Satan's uninterrupted rule ended in A.D. 1914 and that Jehovah's Theocratic Government by Christ was set up at that time? Jehovah's great Prophet, Christ Jesus, foretold the visible proofs or signs.

Jesus had just predicted the destruction of Jerusalem and its temple. So several of his disciples came to him privately and put this question to him: "When shall these things be? and what shall be the sign of thy coming, and of the end of the world [*aion*]?" (Matthew 24: 3; Mark 13: 3, 4) Jesus then briefly foretold events to precede the end of Satan's uninterrupted rule and the birth of God's kingdom, and then added: "But the end is not yet." What, pray, would mark the beginning of sorrows at the end of the Devil's unhindered rule of humankind? Jesus answered: "For nation shall rise against nation, and kingdom against kingdom: and there shall be famines, and pestilences, and earthquakes, in divers places. All these are the beginning of sorrows. Then shall they deliver you up to be afflicted, and shall kill you: and ye shall be hated of all nations for my name's sake."—Matthew 24: 7-9.

The year A.D. 1914, in which the "seven times" ended, marked the beginning of World War I, a war different from previous wars in that regimentation of whole nations and kingdoms for war purposes was there instituted. Famine and food shortages afflicted the world, and it was necessary to organize relief for stricken areas in order to prevent revolution and anarchy. Pestilence broke out, notably the so-called "Spanish flu". In just a few months that plague, raging from the frigid polar regions to the equatorial tropics, laid low in death many more millions than the four and a half years of World War I did. Earthquakes, for example, the one which struck Japan in 1923 and killed 99,331 persons, added to the destruction and human misery; and more such seismic disturbances of the earth have been recorded in these few years since 1914 than in all previous history of man. During all this time hatred was expressed by *all* worldly nations against Jehovah's people by persecution upon them for preaching Christ's kingdom.

World War I was not from God. Jehovah's covenant people had nothing to do with it. It was, though, the visible, tangible proof that Jehovah by his now enthroned King had taken due action against Satan's invisible organization, whose uninterrupted rule had then expired. It was evidence to men that Jesus' prophecy had been fulfilled: "The powers of the heavens shall be shaken." (Matthew 24:29; Luke 21:26) It meant that Jehovah had now commanded his King: "Rule thou in the midst of thine enemies." It proved that Christ Jesus did so and took action against the invisible demon organization of that Old Serpent, the Devil. Sa-

tan and his demons were no longer to be tolerated unhindered in their heavenly position, and Christ Jesus, the Seed of God's "woman", made war against the demon organization. A fight ensued in heaven, unseen to mankind, and Satan and his wicked angels were defeated. They were cast out of heaven and down to the vicinity of the earth, where the visible part of Satan's organization was in the sorrows of World War I. By enabling Christ Jesus to gain this victory over his mighty enemies Jehovah God fulfilled the promise to his King to "make thine enemies thy footstool".—Revelation 12: 7-13; Psalm 110: 1.

Thus the heavens of Satan's organization were shaken out of their high position of power and no longer tolerated in the midst of God's holy heavens. That was a most maddening sorrow to Satan. His "world" (*aion*) of uninterrupted rule was at an end. The destruction of his world organization (*kosmos*) must follow shortly. That *final* end shall be at God's inescapable appointed time.

CHAPTER XXIII

MANNER OF THE KING'S COMING

MONG the meaningful events marking the "time of the end", which began in A.D. 1914, Jesus predicted this: "And the powers of the heavens shall be shaken, and then shall appear the sign of the Son of man, in heaven: and then shall all the tribes of the earth mourn, and they shall see the Son of man coming in the clouds of heaven, with power and great glory." (Matthew 24: 29, 30) This disproves that the conversion of the world to Christ and the making of the earth a fit place for him to come to is to be brought about before the *final* end of Satan's world organization (*kosmos*). Otherwise, why should "all the tribes of the earth mourn" instead of rejoice? How, then, does the King come?

That Christ Jesus would leave the midst of this world of Satan and would in due time come again, he openly declared. Comforting his disciples after he instituted the memorial of his death, Jesus said: "In my Father's house are many mansions: if it were not so, I would have told you. I go to prepare a place for you [which proves that Moses, David, John the Baptist, and others had not gone to heaven]. And if I

go and prepare a place for you, I will come
again, and receive you unto myself; that where
I am, there ye may be also." (John 14:2, 3) A
few hours later, when the Jewish high priest
demanded of him: "I adjure thee by the living
God, that thou tell us whether thou be the Christ,
the Son of God," Jesus replied: "Thou hast said:
nevertheless I say unto you, Hereafter shall ye
see the Son of man sitting on the right hand
of power, and coming in the clouds of heaven."
—Matthew 26:63, 64.

Does this mean that the King Christ Jesus
will bodily come again and appear in a fleshly
form so that all the tribes of earth will be able
to see him in the sky? Religionists who teach the
destruction of our terrestrial globe by literal
fire at the end of the world say yes. They quote
the words of the angels who appeared at the
time of Jesus' ascension to heaven: "Ye men of
Galilee, why stand ye gazing up into heaven?
This same Jesus, which is taken up from you
into heaven, shall so come in like manner as ye
have seen him go into heaven." (Acts 1:11) At
that time a "cloud received him out of their
sight". The disciples could not see him further
for the cloud which obscured him. The angels'
words, "in like *manner*," do *not* say or mean, "in
like *body*." The body in which Christ Jesus was
seen ascending heavenward was not the body
which was nailed to the tree. It was a body which
he had materialized for the time being in order
to appear to his disciples. When the cloud hid
him from their sight, then he dissolved that

body as he had done to the other bodies he assumed during the forty days previous. At his resurrection he was "made alive in the spirit", and he is now spirit and hence invisible. "And the Lord is the Spirit; and where the spirit of the Lord is, there is freedom."—2 Corinthians 3:17, *Diaglott; Roth.*

As to his "manner" of ascending, it should not escape notice that he did not manifest himself to "all the tribes of the earth", but only to his consecrated disciples. Later, on the road to Damascus when he gave a miraculous vision of his glory, it was exclusively to Saul, who became his apostle Paul. It was not to any of the religious men who were with Saul. They heard the sound of the voice, but saw no speaker. (Acts 9:7) All such was in full keeping with Jesus' words before his death: "Yet a little while, and the world seeth me no more; but ye see me; because I live, ye shall live also." (John 14:19) It is a settled Scriptural truth, therefore, that human eyes will not see him at his second coming, neither will he come in a fleshly body. When he came in flesh at his first presence among men it was a humiliation. He "made himself of no reputation, and took upon him the form of a servant, and was made in the likeness of men". The flesh was necessary in order that he might be a perfect man and provide the ransom sacrifice or sin-offering; but not so at his glorious second coming. "So also the Anointed One, having been once for all offered for the many to bear away sin, will appear a second time *without*

a sin-offering, to those who are expecting him,
in order to salvation." (Hebrews 9:28, *Diaglott;
Young*) Even to his disciples it was only during
the forty days after his resurrection, and before
his ascension to heaven, that he appeared in
fleshly form.

His second coming will accordingly be unob-
served by human eyes, except for what events
will accompany his coming as visible signs to
make his believing followers aware of his unseen presence. Describing his coming at the time
of the battle of Armageddon, the glorified Jesus said: " . . . to the battle of that great day
of God Almighty. Behold, I come as a thief.
Blessed is he that watcheth, and keepeth his
garments, lest he walk naked, and they see his
shame." (Revelation 16:14-16) A thief comes
without previous notification, unannounced,
quietly, and keeping himself unseen to those in
the house. This is further proof that Christ's
coming is invisible, as a spirit, and must be detected by signs, proofs.

All facts considered, then, the only way in
which men on the earth will see him at his glorious coming is with the eyes of understanding
or powers of discernment. This is further sup-
ported by the words at Revelation 1:7 in a
vision to the apostle John: "Behold, he cometh
with clouds; and every eye shall see him, and
they also which pierced him: and all kindreds
of the earth shall wail because of him. Even so.
Amen." As at his ascension, when he disap-
peared from his disciples' eyes behind the cloud,

so here the clouds render him invisible, but at the same time they stand as a symbol of his invisible presence. Long ago, when the Israelites were journeying through the wilderness forty years the pillar of cloud which went before them symbolized and represented the invisible presence of the Lord.—Exodus 13: 21, 22.

So, in the above prophetic text, the "clouds" symbolize the manifestations of his power whereby he makes apparent his unseen presence. He will be present before his presence is discerned first by his faithful followers who watch for his coming. In their case the "clouds" betoken his presence with showers of rich blessing for them. The world in general will not believe the announcement of his presence, but all nations will hate his true footstep followers and will "pierce" them, in this manner piercing Christ Jesus. Did he not say that what they do to the least of his brethren they do to him? Then, by the great storm of trouble and destruction which the "clouds" will let loose upon these wicked ones and unbelieving kindreds of the earth, "every eye will see," that is, will discern, him. Realizing their guilt and the penalty of destruction in store for them, they "shall wail because of him".

What, then, is the "sign of the Son of man" that he said would appear "in heaven" after "the powers of the heavens shall be shaken"? Revelation 12: 1-10 (*A.R.V.*) describes it as follows: "A great sign was seen in heaven: a woman arrayed with the sun, and the moon under her feet,

and upon her head a crown of twelve stars; and
she was with child; and she crieth out, travail-
ing in birth, and in pain to be delivered. And
there was seen another sign in heaven: and behold, a great red dragon, having seven heads
and ten horns, and upon his heads seven dia-
dems. And his tail draweth the third part of the
stars of heaven, and did cast them to the earth:
and the dragon standeth before the woman that
is about to be delivered, that when she is delivered he may devour her child. And she was delivered of a son, a man child, who is to rule all
the nations with a rod of iron: and her child
was caught up unto God, and unto his throne.
. . . And there was war in heaven: Michael and
his angels going forth to war with the dragon;
and the dragon warred and his angels; and they
prevailed not, neither was their place found any
more in heaven. And the great dragon was cast
down, the old serpent, he that is called the Devil
and Satan, the deceiver of the whole world; he
was cast down to the earth, and his angels were
cast down with him. And I heard a great voice
in heaven, saying, Now is come the salvation,
and the power, and the kingdom of our God,
and the authority of his Christ."

By thus "comparing spiritual things with
spiritual" and letting God's Word interpret itself, it becomes manifest what the *sign of the
Son of man* is. It is the evidence appearing from
God's Word and from its fulfillment that the
Kingdom of God has been born or brought forth
from God's "woman", Zion, his holy universal

organization. The purpose of the Devil's organization is to prevent or destroy the Government at its birth in A.D. 1914, at the end of the "seven times". Yet Christ Jesus, who is the "woman's" Seed, is brought forth as the "man child" in the capacity of King, and he is at once safely enthroned and commanded by Jehovah God to rule in the midst of his enemies. War immediately follows in heaven, and the Devil is ousted. Not until after Satan and his demons had been cast out, namely, not until after A.D. 1918, was this *sign* seen.[1] Then it was discerned only by those who had spiritual vision of the things in the heavens. The religionists did not see it, no more than their religious prototypes in Jesus' day saw that he was King and the kingdom was at hand. Wherefore Jesus said to them: "The kingdom of God cometh not with outward shew; neither shall they say, Lo here! or, lo there! for, behold, the kingdom of God is among you." (Luke 17: 20, 21, *margin*) The King was among them, and their selfish eyes could not discern that fact because of the lack of outward show. Likewise, the kingdom of God was born and set in action in A.D. 1914, but the religious clergy do not see or discern the sign in heaven and they choose "Caesar" as king instead. The time will come when they shall see it, but then only to mourn.

Jerusalem was the capital of Jehovah's typical Theocracy in Israel. When it began to be trodden down of the Gentiles, in 606 B.C., God

[1] See *The Watchtower*, the issue of March 1, 1925.

began fulfilling his word, "I will overturn, overturn, overturn it; and it shall be no more, until
he come whose right it is; and I will give it
him." (Ezekiel 21:27) In A.D. 1914, at the close
of the "seven times" of the Gentiles, Christ
Jesus, whose right it is to be God's King in the
true and everlasting Theocracy of heaven, came
and God gave the throne of The Theocratic
Government to him. That real Theocracy suf-
fers no treading under foot by Gentiles. Instead,
the Devil and his demons are thrown out of
heaven and all enemies of The Theocracy are
made the footstool of its King, The Seed of
God's "woman". In this way Christ Jesus came
to the Kingdom in A.D. 1914, but unseen to men.

By another prophet Jehovah had further
prophesied: "Behold, I will send my messenger,
and he shall prepare the way before me: and
the Lord, whom ye seek, shall suddenly come to
his temple, even the messenger of the covenant,
whom ye delight in: behold, he shall come, saith
the LORD of hosts." (Malachi 3:1) When Jesus
rode the ass into Jerusalem and went to the
temple and cast out the money changers and
commercial vendors and then offered himself
as King to the Jewish nation, it was a half of a
week of years, or three and a half years, after
his anointing with God's spirit to be King and
to preach, "The Kingdom of heaven is at hand."
That was merely a small-scale or miniature fulfillment of Malachi's prophecy. The major or
complete fulfillment is in the great "day of Jehovah", which began in A.D. 1914. When, there-

fore, does the great King-Priest, like Melchize-dek, come to the temple?

Bear in mind that the fall of A.D. 1914, when Christ Jesus received the Kingdom, parallels or corresponds with his anointing for the kingship at Jordan, in the fall of A.D. 29. Since he came to the temple three and a half years thereafter, then three and a half years after the fall of A.D. 1914 marks the time when he came to the temple as King. After that "Christendom" must come under judgment as to whether she would accept him as King or choose "Caesar" (worldly politics) instead. This agreement between the

minor and the major fulfillment of Malachi's
prophecy fixes the spring of A.D. 1918 as the
time when the King Christ Jesus came to the
temple. This harmonizes also with the fact that
in the fourth year of Solomon's reign, or less
than four years after he was anointed and enthroned, Solomon came to the temple foundation and began building it. Christ's coming to
the temple in 1918 was entirely unexpected, even
to his devoted faithful followers. The truth of
his coming then was first discerned by the Scriptures and by the fulfillments of prophecy after
the event, namely, first in 1922.

All power in heaven and in earth has been
given to the glorified Christ Jesus. For a divine person like him a personal bodily coming
to earth is not necessary in order to fulfill the
prophecies and promise of his second coming.
The Bible speaks many times of Jehovah's coming down to earth, not meaning, however, that
he literally leaves his heavenly throne and bodily comes down and stands upon our small
planet. "Do not I fill heaven and earth? saith
Jehovah." (Jeremiah 23: 24, *A.R.V.*) Whither-
soever Jehovah turns his notice and attention
and thither directs his power of operation, there
in effect he is present or makes a visit. Likewise
with Christ Jesus, "the image of the invisible
God." He works even as his Father does. Once
he healed a nobleman's son by remote control,
without coming near the nobleman's house, Jesus being then in Cana and the dying child in
Capernaum. (John 4: 46-54) At another time

he cured the sick servant of a Gentile centurion in like manner at a distance from the centurion's house. (Luke 7:1-10) He healed the demonized daughter of a Syrophoenician woman by likewise sending forth his power through space. —Mark 7:24-30.

Before ascending to heaven he said to his disciples: "Lo, I am with you alway, even unto the end of the world." (Matthew 28:20) He would be with them, not bodily, but by his continual help and care and guiding power. So when he comes to the temple in 1918, he does so by directing his attention to the temple work to be done and then applying his power. His presence there, first discerned by his watching disciples, is not kept secret. Like the lightning which shines from one quarter of the heaven to the other, so the Lord causes the enlightening information on his coming and presence at the temple to be shone abroad by his disciples to all on earth.—Matthew 24:27; Luke 17:24.

In the light of this Scriptural revelation we must understand 1 Thessalonians 4:15-17: "We which are alive, and remain unto the coming [Greek text: *parousia;* presence] of the Lord, shall not prevent them which are asleep. For the Lord himself shall descend from heaven with a shout, with the voice of the archangel, and with the trump of God: and the dead in Christ shall rise first: then we which are alive and remain shall be caught up together with them in the clouds, to meet the Lord in the air."

This comforting scripture proves that, as
Christ Jesus was resurrected from the dead
seven days after presenting himself as King at
Jerusalem's temple, he will, by God's power,
raise from the sleep of death those faithful
Christians sleeping in death at his coming to
the temple. Since Christ's church-body is "sown
a natural body; it is raised a spiritual body",
the resurrection of such sleeping ones was to
life in the spirit. Hence it was invisible to human eyes, as when Jesus himself was resurrected. They are now with him at the temple,
that is, in the condition of unity with him in the
place invisible to human eyes, which place is
symbolized by the "air".—Contrast Ephesians
2: 2.

Those spirit-begotten Christians who die
faithful after he comes to the temple do not need
to sleep in death awaiting his coming. At death
they are "changed, in a moment, in the twinkling
of an eye", from human to spirit. (1 Corinthians
15: 51, 52) The remnant yet alive on earth after
the Lord's arrival at the temple are "caught up"
or separated from this worldly organization.
Amid the evidences of his blessed presence
("clouds") they are brought into the temple condition of unity with him, the condition not out-
wardly discerned by natural men. There they
must await their "change" after their work on
earth is done. Concerning this more appears on
following pages.

CHAPTER XXIV

FREEDOM-LOVING WITNESSES

MONG other signs which Christ Jesus detailed as due to appear during the "time of the end" and after "the powers of the heavens shall be shaken" is this: "And he shall send his angels with a great sound of a trumpet; and they shall gather together his elect from the four winds, from one end of heaven to the other." (Matthew 24: 31; Mark 13: 27) Inasmuch as the gathering is by command of the reigning King and by means of his angels, this work cannot be blocked by governments on earth even though they may ban the work and may decree that the gathered elect ones are "an illegal organization". That Jehovah's King would have angelic servants engaged at work when he exercises his royal functions at the temple, he makes clear, saying: "When the Son of man shall come in his glory, and all the holy angels with him, then shall he sit upon the throne of his glory: and before him shall be gathered all nations." (Matthew 25: 31, 32) Such angels do not have to be seen by men in order to do their work of gathering.

Christ Jesus is God's Elect One for the Kingdom. "Behold my servant, whom I uphold, mine elect, in whom my soul delighteth; I have put

my spirit upon him; he shall bring forth judgment to the Gentiles." (Isaiah 42:1) Matthew
applies this prophecy to God's beloved Son.
(Matthew 12:15-21) The fact that God designates him as his *servant* shows that the Son is
not "equal in power and glory" with the Father,
but that Jehovah God is the Supreme Power,
and that He and Christ Jesus his Son constitute
together "the Higher Powers". (Romans 13:1)
The members of the church-body of the Great
Servant are with him in the covenant for the
Kingdom and accordingly are elect with him.
"Elect according to the foreknowledge of God
the Father, through sanctification of the spirit,
unto obedience and sprinkling of the blood of
Jesus Christ." (1 Peter 1:2) Why should he
gather together the elect remnant of his body
yet on earth at his coming to the temple in
A.D. 1918?

The need for gathering indicates that the
faithful ones of his elect had been scattered as
a consequence of World War I. This was due to
"Christendom's" persecution of them, as Jesus
forewarned, saying: "Then shall they deliver
you up to be afflicted, and shall kill you: and ye
shall be hated of all nations for my name's sake.
And then shall many be offended, and shall be-
tray one another, and shall hate one another.
And many false prophets shall rise, and shall
deceive many. And because iniquity shall
abound, the love of many shall wax cold. But he
that shall endure unto the end, the same shall be
saved." (Matthew 24:9-13) Such persecution

during the war period reached its climax in the year 1918, at the time of the Lord's coming to the temple for judgment and before the World War had ended. In the United States the hatred, which was fanned by the religionists, vented itself in the mobbing and imprisoning of Jehovah's covenant people and the banning of their literature; and the co-operation of these Christians in America with Jehovah's people in foreign lands was broken up. Under the great stress and trial of their integrity only a remnant kept faith and held true to their covenant obligations to the Lord and hoped for a reopening of His work on earth.

Of whom was this remnant composed? True spiritual Israelites. They had dedicated themselves to the Most High God and were then brought by Him into the new covenant to be a "people for his name" and also into the Kingdom covenant with "the King of kings, and Lord of lords". Impelled by a love of the truth they began to assemble together, particularly from about the year 1878 forward. Realizing the bondage to superstition, religion and priestcraft in which all "Christendom" lay bound, they made a break for freedom and came out from all religious sects, Catholic, Protestant, Jewish, and others. They gathered together freely to discuss and be instructed in the truths which the Lord's great "Messenger of the covenant" then began to make known. In July, 1879, the magazine *The Watchtower* began to be published in this behalf, and in 1884 the Watch

Tower Bible and Tract Society was incorporated and chartered in the state of Pennsylvania. The truths they learned from the storehouse of truth, the sacred Bible, they published to others in many lands and languages, by books, free tracts, free public lectures, and all other valid means.

Thousands became free by the truths exposing the falseness of such religious doctrines as a fiery hell of conscious torment of human souls, Purgatory, divine ordination of clergymen, trinity, etc. The clergy of all denominations were disturbed and embittered. They conspired among themselves to overthrow this educational work and prevent the people from learning the truth and getting free of their power. Then came 1914 and the outbreak of world war. The religious clergy used this emergency to lay false charges against these publishers of truth and freedom, and succeeded in having their public activities practically stopped in all nations.

Nevertheless, the greatest work of Jehovah's covenant people was yet to be done. The "time of the end" had begun in A.D. 1914, the Devil's world-organization was doomed and was heading toward its final end, and the people were in danger of destruction in the coming "battle of that great day of God Almighty". According to God's rule of action prior to the Flood and also Jerusalem's destruction in 606 B.C. and again in A.D. 70, he would warn the people of the impending world catastrophe and give them an opportunity to escape perishing with the nations.

The Kingdom had been established as the "new heavens" in 1914, and it must be advertised. Lovers of truth and righteousness must be shown the way to flee to the Kingdom for deliverance and salvation.

Jesus prophesied that this work must be done. Immediately after foretelling the World War and the persecution of his faithful elect ones he stated distinctly what work they must do without fail after that world struggle. His word is both a prophecy and a command, namely: "And this gospel of the kingdom shall be preached in all the world for a WITNESS unto all nations: and then shall the end come."—Matthew 24:14.

For Jesus' own faithful testimony on earth even to a martyr's death he was honored with the title "The Amen, the faithful and true witness". (Revelation 1:5; 3:14; 19:11) As his Father's Elect Servant it was incumbent upon him to see that the Kingdom witness was given before the final end of Satan's oppressive organization. He had cast the invisible part of that wicked system out of heaven and down to the earth, and the prophecy was now in effect: "Woe to the inhabiters of the earth, and of the sea! for the devil is come down unto you, having great wrath, because he knoweth that he hath but a short time." (Revelation 12:12) It is at the most but a short time until the decisive battle at the earth is fought in which the seven-headed dragon organization is wiped out. God's kingdom will triumph, and man's only hope of salvation is in it. The woe-stricken people must receive witness.

For these urgent reasons the mighty King Christ Jesus broke the bonds of his faithful remnant of the elect after his arrival at the temple: "to open the blind eyes, to bring out the prisoners from the prison, and them that sit in darkness out of the prison house." (Isaiah 42: 1, 6, 7; 49: 9) He used his angels in gathering the dispersed elect ones, and this by the loud, wide-sounding proclamation of the establishment of the Kingdom, like the "great sound of a trumpet". He gathered these elect by bringing them into unity with himself at the temple, by making known his presence at the temple for judgment and setting forth clearly before them God's will and his work for them before the *final* end. He revealed to them that the issue is God's supremacy and name.

Then the commission of the Christians according to their anointing received at the temple was made clear. "Ye are my witnesses, saith Jehovah, and my servant whom I have chosen; that ye may know and believe me, and understand that I am he: before me there was no God formed, neither shall there be after me. I, even I, am Jehovah; and besides me there is no saviour. I have declared, and I have saved, and I have showed; and there was no strange god among you: therefore ye are my witnesses, saith Jehovah, and I am God." (Isaiah 43: 10-12, *A.R.V.*) After long and hard years in which Jehovah used them in this commissioned work in the face of international hatred and persecution, the elect remnant perceived that God had conferred upon them a "new name". It is different from all the abusive, contemptible and unscriptural names which the enemies were calling them. Such "new name", which God's own mouth named, was and is "Jehovah's witnesses". (Isaiah 62: 2; 65: 15; Revelation 2: 17) Fearlessly and joyfully they received the name unto themselves in July, 1931, and let it be known to all the nations. They continue trying to live up to that God-given name.

During World War I those spiritual Israelites came physically under the power of the Babylonish political systems of this world. It was as when the typical Israelites of old experienced the desolation of their land and were carried off captive to Babylon for seventy years. In A.D. 1918 the spiritual Israelites yielded to the world's political interference in their Christian activities. They withdrew from their public educational work largely because of the religious doctrine which still prevails, namely, that the political officials of Satan's visible organization are the "higher powers" to whom all Christian souls are to be subject, as commanded at Romans 13: 1. By such perversion of Scripture the religious Hierarchy in control have been able to act as the "spiritual advisers" of the political powers and to use the arm of the state to take away and suppress freedom of speech, of press, of assembly, and of worship of God. Such religious misapplication of Scripture con-

cerning the "higher powers" has long caused the
ignorant bondage of professing Christians to
worldly officials at the expense of the interests
of God's work and of true freedom.

After the Lord's coming to the temple and
freeing the faithful remnant of spiritual Israelites from captivity to modern-day Babylon he
began to open their eyes gradually to the truth.
In 1929 the clear light broke forth. That year
The Watchtower published the Scriptural ex-
position of Romans chapter 13. It showed that
Jehovah God and Christ Jesus, rather than
worldly rulers and governors, are "The Higher
Powers" and that the Christian souls must
"obey God rather than men"; and that "every
ordinance of man" to which they must submit
is every Scriptural ordinance of men who are
servants within God's organization under the
King Christ Jesus. (1 Peter 2:13) This revelation of vital truth freed the spirits of God's
consecrated people as never before.

Such truth enabled them to remain as "the
Lord's freeman", even though physically falling
into the clutches of worldly officers and being
imprisoned and reduced to the condition of
bond-servants or slaves. Armed with such truth
they could hold fast their unqualified allegiance
to God and not bow their necks in servitude to
any parts of Satan's organization, religious,
commercial, or political. This truth made them
realize their God-sanctioned freedom to push
on with his "strange work" of witnessing to his
Kingdom, regardless of all the opposition and

all the 'mischief framed by a law' against them. (Psalm 94: 20-22) To them it is written: "You indeed, brethren, were called to freedom"; and they do not use this freedom for selfish gratification of the flesh with the worldly pleasures, but for the loving service of God and the proclamation of his name and Messianic kingdom. —Galatians 5: 13, *Weymouth; Diaglott; Rotherham.*

The remnant of Jehovah's witnesses endeavor to spread the spirit of freedom throughout the entire earth. This they do by the spread of the truth as contained in God's written Word. Their Leader, Christ Jesus, said: "If ye continue in my word, then are ye my disciples indeed; and ye shall know the truth, and the truth shall make you free." By continuing in his word and by being doers of the word as his disciples, they have, by God's grace, come to know the truth. They have come to the freedom enjoyed by the true Christians in the days of the apostles. It was Christ's apostles who told the worldly rulers: "Whether it be right in the sight of God to hearken unto you more than unto God, judge ye. For we cannot but speak the things which we have seen and heard. . . . We ought to obey God rather than men."—Acts 4: 19, 20; 5: 29.

So now Jehovah's witnesses refuse to sacrifice God's gift of freedom. They continue to speak the things they see in His Word despite all demonic and human efforts at interference. They follow the example of Christ Jesus and his apostles as to the manner of speaking the Kingdom message, by going from house to house as well as in public places, not shunning to declare the whole counsel of God. Like the apostle Paul they may say: "I kept back nothing that was profitable unto you, but have shewed you, and have taught you publicly, and FROM HOUSE TO HOUSE, testifying both to the Jews, and also to the Greeks." (Acts 20: 20, 21, 27; also 2: 46; 5: 42; Luke 9: 4-6; 10: 5-9) Because this is not the easy-going "orthodox way" of religion's clergy to preach, whose way requires the people to come to religious edifices to hear preaching from a pulpit, the religionists look upon the educational activities and message of Jehovah's witnesses as a "strange work". They do not heed the warning that this "strange work" precedes and will be followed immediately by Jehovah's "strange act" at Armageddon.—Isaiah 28: 21.

Many sincere persons continue under bondage to "organized religion" because their clergy have mistaught them to think that "Christendom's" religion and Christianity are the same thing. In due time the exposure of this came out. In 1928 this statement was published and spread throughout "Christendom": "Satan is the god of this world, and therefore the nations of the world can not properly be designated as Christian nations. THERE IS NO SUCH THING AS A CHRISTIAN RELIGION, BECAUSE TRUE CHRISTIANITY IS NOT A RELIGION." (The book *Government,* page 139, ¶ 1; published 1928) This truth was made more prominent from 1936 forward, and the religionists everywhere manifested great indignation

at this exposure and at the public pronouncement that "religion is a snare and a racket".
Both sixteen centuries of history till now and
the present way of religion back up the foregoing statements as true.

The remnant of Jehovah's witnesses are comparatively few and weak in themselves, as during all past centuries. Hence they are feared
only because of the mighty truths they possess
and fearlessly proclaim under commission from
God. Vicious endeavors are made by religionists
to destroy them and their message of Christian
freedom. Revelation 12:13, 17 makes it plain
that the remnant of Jehovah's witnesses are the
main target of the attacks by Satan and his demons. It is with the demons, and not with creatures of flesh and blood, that the remnant
wrestle and fight, having their "loins girt about
with truth" and flashing the "sword of the spirit, which is the word of God".—Ephesians
6:12-17.

Satan's wicked design is to regiment all the
people of the earth under a totalitarian form
of world government and thereby hold all men
in bondage, ignorant of freedom-giving truth,
and away from Jehovah God and his kingdom
of the new world of righteousness. To this end
he used religionists to promote the establishment of Fascism in 1922 and of Nazism in 1933,
working together with Vatican City by concordats. In Germany the Nazi dictator at once suppressed Jehovah's witnesses as a "subversive
organization" and broke up their meetings.

Eventually 6,000 of them were thrown into concentration camps, isolated and distinguished from others by a violet badge, and most brutally treated. Still they remain free in spirit, refusing to come into bondage to totalitarian rule. Also in democratic lands, Jehovah's witnesses must resist totalitarian-religious aggressions and fight for freedom of worship.

CHAPTER XXV

"MEN OF GOOD-WILL"

HE march to complete freedom is on! Nothing that the desperate organization of Satan in its "last days" does can halt the forward march. At the head of the procession is the irresistible Leader to whom the Lord God points, announcing: "Behold, I have given him for a witness to the peoples, a leader and commander to the peoples. Behold, thou shalt call a nation that thou knowest not; and a nation that knew not thee shall run unto thee, because of Jehovah thy God, and for the Holy One of Israel; for he hath glorified thee. Seek ye Jehovah while he may be found; call ye upon him while he is near."—Isaiah 55: 4-6, *A.R.V.*

When the Lord's appointed Leader came to the temple in 1918 he found the covenant people of Jehovah in grievous captivity within the gates of modern-day Babylon. He gave the command: "Go through, go through the gates; prepare ye the way of the people; cast up, cast up the highway; gather out the stones; lift up a standard for the people." (Isaiah 62: 10) The stones which impede the march over the highway of truth must be removed; the standard of Kingdom truth, which is the standard of freedom, must be held aloft for all captives to see and follow it unto the security, prosperity and peace of God's kingdom by his Son. Before the King's coming to the temple the war in heaven was fought out and Satan the Devil was given a great fall from his lofty heavenly seat of power. Now his organization, great Babylon, faces destruction in the final war of Armageddon. Those who would live as God's freemen under his Theocratic Government must at once make a break for liberty, heeding the heavenly warning-call:

"Fallen! fallen! is Babylon the Great, and hath become a habitation of demons and a prison of every impure spirit and a prison of every impure and hated bird; because by reason of the wine of the wrath of her lewdness have all the nations fallen, and the kings of the earth with her did commit lewdness, and the merchants of the earth by reason of the power of her wantonness waxed rich. . . . Come forth, my people, out of her, that ye may have no fellowship with her sins, and of her plagues that ye may not receive."—Revelation 18: 1-4, *Rotherham*.

Nations, kings, and merchants, all having ties and connections with religious Babylon, are doomed to overthrow with her. Many sincere persons of good-will toward God and his kingdom are held captive to Babylon, not knowing the truth which shows them the way of escape. To continue in Babylon means to die slaves, giving moral endorsement and support to her

sins and therefore tasting with her the plagues
from the hand of God. His kingdom is the only
refuge to which to flee from destruction at the
final end.

At the human birth of the Savior who was to
be the King of that Theocratic Government a
great heavenly host appeared praising God and
saying: "Glory in the highest unto God! and on
earth peace, among men of good-will." (Luke
2: 14, *Roth.*) Now the Kingdom has been established in the heavens, and the choice must be
made between that Righteous Government and
worldly Babylon. Only those who forsake Babylon as doomed and who fearlessly come out and
demonstrate their good-will toward Jehovah
and his kingdom enjoy God's peace that passes
all human understanding in this restless and
distressed world. Such enjoy freedom from fear,
now, when there is "upon the earth distress of
nations, with perplexity; the sea and the waves
roaring; men's hearts failing them for fear,
and for looking after those things which are
coming on the earth: for the powers of heaven
shall be shaken".—Luke 21: 25, 26.

Those who gather out the stumbling-stones of
religious errors and traditions of men and who
lift up Jehovah's standard of truth are not the
enemies of the people, Catholic, Protestant,
Jew, or pagan. When the apostle was branded
by the religionists as dangerous to the people's
interests, he asked: "Am I therefore become
your enemy, because I tell you the truth?"
(Galatians 4: 16) He warned that in this world

the precious liberty would ever have to be safe-
guarded jealously and fought for against all
Babylonish encroachments. Having exposed the
religious "fifth column" of that day, he wrote:
"My action was on account of the false brethren
secretly introduced, who had stolen in to spy
out the freedom which is ours in Christ Jesus,
in order to enslave us again. Not for an hour
did we give way and submit to these, that the
gospel might continue with you in its purity."
—Galatians 2: 4, 5, *Weymouth*.

Since 1918 the religious "fifth column" has in-
filtrated itself among all democratic and liberal
nations and is sneakily intruding upon the
rights, privileges and immunities of lovers of
democracy. Its ultimate aim is to enslave the
people and crush the truth of God's kingdom
message. Therefore the words of the apostle
ring out with compelling force in these peril-
ous times: "For freedom did Christ set us free:
stand fast therefore, and be not entangled
again in a yoke of bondage." (Galatians 5: 1,
A.R.V.) The fight against religious encroachment and for freedom to worship Jehovah must
go on as in the time of Judge Jephthah.

Jephthah's daughter, his only child, was first
to come out of his house and praise Jehovah God
for the victory in pushing the totalitarian Am-
monite aggressors back and out of the domain
of Jehovah's typical Theocracy. (Judges 11: 34-
36) During these recent days a class of people
of like mind and action as Jephthah's daughter
have been manifesting themselves. This has

Jephthah's daughter comes forth first to meet him.—Chap. 25

Free men though in a Nazi concentration camp.—Chap. 24

been particularly so since 1938. In that year the Theocratic rule and procedure were put in operation within the visible organization of God's covenant people on earth who are under a greater fighter than Jephthah, namely, Christ Jesus. The class like Jephthah's daughter have been growing up since Christ's coming to the temple. They have observed the remnant of His body members preaching "this gospel of the kingdom in all the world for a witness unto all nations" and have observed the religious opposition and persecutions these endure in all lands. They have marked, too, how the faithful remnant refuse to give in to the encroachment on their liberty as servants of the Most High God, but beat back those religious-political enemies of freedom of worship and victoriously carry on declaring the day of God's vengeance against Babylon and comforting all that mourn. Particularly since the outbreak of total war in 1939 has this fight for the liberty of worship of Jehovah waxed most fierce, but his witnesses triumph by Christ Jesus over all opposition. At this the present-day class like Jephthah's daughter greatly rejoice, and they hail Jehovah's Judge and King, Christ Jesus, and take their stand on his side. He offers them to God, as Jephthah offered up his daughter, and sets them to work with his temple company.—Revelation 7:15.

To these persons of good-will the great Life-giver does not grant hopes of life in heaven and a place *in* the Kingdom, The Theocratic Government. The hope of life on the earth in the new

world is set before these. It is the Father's good
pleasure to give the Kingdom to the "little flock"
of Christ's body members, but as for these people of good-will the Good Shepherd says: "And
other sheep I have, which are not of this fold:
them also I must bring, and they shall hear my
voice; and they shall become one flock, one shepherd." (John 10:16, *A.R.V.*) These who become
the "other sheep" hear the Good Shepherd's
voice in the Kingdom message proclaimed by
Jehovah's remnant. They recognize the message
as genuine Bible truth, and they come to Christ
Jesus as their Leader, Guide and Redeemer.
Through his meritorious sacrifice they give
themselves in full consecration to Jehovah God
to do His will and serve His kingdom ever thereafter. Like their Leader they publicly symbolize
their heart-act of consecration to God by being
baptized in water. God's will now for his consecrated ones is to declare His name throughout
all the earth and to publish the good news of
His kingdom. Hence the "other sheep" join with
the remnant of the "little flock", because these
are doing exactly that work. Thereby both com-
panies "become one flock" under "one shepherd".
The remnant are of the temple class, having
been gathered to Christ Jesus as "living stones"
of the temple under him, the Chief Corner
Stone. Thus in joining with the remnant, the
"other sheep" serve at God's temple, as did
Jephthah's daughter.

Continuing faithful in their integrity toward
God, the "other sheep" will form the "great mul-

titude" foreseen at Revelation 7: 9-17. In that vision the apostle John, after seeing the gathering of the 144,000 members of the twelve tribes of spiritual Israel, then says: "After this I beheld, and, lo, a great multitude, which no man could number, of all nations, and kindreds, and people, and tongues, stood before the throne, and before the Lamb, clothed with white robes, and palms in their hands; and cried with a loud voice, saying, Salvation to our God, which sitteth upon the throne, and unto the Lamb. . . . These are they which came out of great tribulation, and have washed their robes, and made them white in the blood of the Lamb. Therefore are they before the throne of God, and serve him day and night in his temple: and he that sitteth on the throne shall dwell among them." With such freedom of worship the freedom from fear and freedom from want also become their portion: "They shall hunger no more, neither thirst any more; neither shall the sun light on them, nor any heat. For the Lamb, which is in the midst of the throne, shall feed them, and shall lead them unto living fountains of waters: and God shall wipe away all tears from their eyes."

This vision guarantees that there shall be an earthly class that will be carried alive through the world's final tribulation foreshadowed by the Noachian flood. Jesus' prophecy on the end of the world included this comparison: "For just as the days of Noah, so will be the presence [Greek text: *parousia*] of the Son of Man."

(Matthew 24: 37, *Roth.; Diaglott; A.R.V.,* margin) During the antediluvian presence or *parousia* of Noah not only was there great self-indulgence on the part of the people, together with great violence in the earth, but there was also a preaching of righteousness by Noah, together with his building of the ark at Jehovah's command. Noah's three sons, together with their wives, responded to Noah's preaching and joined with him in building the great boat. Is it now as in Noah's days? No answer is better than the facts.

The King's presence or *parousia* began in 1914, and then his appearing or *epiphaneia* at the temple came in 1918. Since then the Greater Noah, Christ Jesus, has been building the Theocratic organization of security and preservation. He has also caused a preaching of righteousness and a declaration of the coming of God's wrath to be done by his remnant of the elect throughout the earth. The selfish people of the world have gone on in their pursuits and violence has increased in the earth, but the lovers of righteousness have taken the Kingdom message to heart. Many have come, and an unnumbered multitude will yet come, out from doomed Babylon, to seek refuge and safety under Jehovah's Theocratic Government and to put themselves in subjection to its King. Thereby they are baptized unto the Greater Noah, Christ Jesus. (1 Peter 3: 20, 21) They become loyal companions of His remnant in the giving

of testimony to the nations, and share their sufferings.

Seven days before the deluge broke upon the "world that then was" Jehovah notified Noah and his sons and the wives to get into the completed ark and bring the animals in with them. The entering of the Lord's "other sheep" into the "one flock" under the "one shepherd" is now

taking place. This is one of the most certain
visible signs or evidences that 1914 marked the
end of Satan's uninterrupted rule or *world*
(*aion*) and that the final end of his organization invisible and visible is drawing near. The
"other sheep", together with the remnant, take
heed to their course to keep themselves unspotted from this world, lest "that day come upon
you unawares. For as a snare shall it come on
all them that dwell on the face of the whole
earth. Watch ye therefore, and pray always,
that ye may be accounted worthy to escape all
these things that shall come to pass, and to
stand before the Son of man". (Luke 21: 34-36)
There is no other way for them to escape destruction at the hands of Jehovah's Executioner
in the oncoming world disaster.

Noah's days and presence (or *parousia*) were
not over with at the end of the flood, but he and
the other flood survivors went forth from the
ark into the cleansed earth and worshiped Jehovah God in perfect freedom and peace. The
words of the divine mandate to multiply and fill
the earth were then heard, and Noah's sons and
their mates were privileged to obey that mandate to a miniature fulfillment thereof. In these
corresponding days of the presence or *parousia*
of the Son of man, and after the terrific baptism
of fiery destruction upon the wicked world at
the final end, the remnant and the "other sheep"
will come forth from God's provided covert of
safety and preservation. They will have obeyed
His command: "Before the day of Jehovah's

anger come upon you. Seek ye Jehovah, all ye
meek of the earth, that have kept his ordinances; seek righteousness, seek meekness: it
may be ye will be hid in the day of Jehovah's
anger." (Zephaniah 2:2, 3, *A.R.V.*) They will at
once devote themselves to the worship of their
divine Savior and Preserver, without any fear
of molestation or interference.

Then will come an unspeakably joyful reward
to the "great multitude" of the Lord's "other
sheep", foreshadowed by Noah's sons and their
wives. To them will be issued the divine mandate to multiply and fill the earth with righteous
offspring. The righteous invisible overlord,
Christ Jesus, will be in full control and will become their "everlasting Father". Their regener-
ation to perfection of human life will then begin.
Because of their faith and obedience to God
with unbroken integrity they have been counted
righteous. Hence they will beget and bring forth
their offspring in righteousness. Paradise will
be restored to the earth and be made earth-wide,
and this shall be the everlasting abode of faithful men and women.—Isaiah 9:6; Matthew
19:28.

CHAPTER XXVI

"ABOMINATION OF DESOLATION"

HE proclamation of the good news that God's kingdom has been established and will stand for ever was foretold by Jesus. It was to be done by those who should be hated of all nations for his name's sake. (Matthew 24: 9, 14) Inasmuch as the proclaimers are abominable in the nation's sight, so also is the good news they proclaim abominable, because the news glorifies Jesus' *name* or office as King. The worldly nations refuse to have any king but "Caesar". Hence the proud course that the nations adopt in the face of the proclamation of God's kingdom through Christ is abominable to Jehovah God. "Every one that is proud in heart is an abomination to Jehovah: though hand join in hand, he shall not be unpunished." "He that justifieth the wicked, and he that condemneth the righteous, both of them alike are an abomination to Jehovah."—Proverbs 16:5; 17:15, *A.R.V.*

Long ago, in the typical Theocracy, when King David had made the hill of Zion his capital and brought the sacred ark of the covenant of Jehovah into the tent he pitched there, Mount Zion became holy to Jehovah and he inspired

David to write these words: "The earth is Jehovah's, and the fulness thereof; the world, and
they that dwell therein. . . . Who shall ascend
into the hill of Jehovah? and who shall stand in
his holy place? He that hath clean hands, and
a pure heart; who hath not lifted up his soul unto falsehood, and hath not sworn deceitfully."
(Psalm 24:1-4, *A.R.V.*) Do "Christendom's"
rulers and governors measure up to those divine
requirements? Secular and religious history answers no! even though the ruler of Vatican City
"blessed" the rebellion against Spain's republic
in 1936 and called the false-swearing traitor to
democracy a "Christian gentleman". The rulers
and governors who turn away their ears from
hearing the good news of God's established kingdom and who at the same time make religious
prayers and sacrifices to Him do not meet his
requirements. Instead, "he that turneth away
his ear from hearing the law, even his prayer
is an abomination. The sacrifice of the wicked is
an abomination to Jehovah; but the prayer of
the upright is his delight. The way of the wicked
is an abomination to Jehovah; but he loveth him
that followeth after righteousness."—Proverbs
28:9; 15:8,9, *A.R.V.*

Ancient Mount Zion with its holy ark of the
covenant and with its anointed king who "sat
on the throne of Jehovah" as his Theocratic
representative was the "holy place". Its king
had to meet the Lord God's holy requirements.
Mount Zion as the "holy place" typified the kingdom of God. Christ Jesus ascended into that

holy place of the Messianic kingdom because he perfectly met the divine requirements; and his Father gave him the right thereto in A.D. 29 at his anointing. He gave him the Kingdom in A.D. 1914, at the end of the "seven times". Christ's lowly footstep followers keep their hands clean and unspotted from this world of politics, commerce and religion and keep their hearts pure in devotion to God's Righteous Government. These ascend with their Head, Christ Jesus, into the royal hill of the great King of Eternity and are permitted to stand as approved in the holy place of his kingdom as "heirs of God, and joint-heirs with Christ Jesus". (Revelation 2:10; 3:21; 14:1; 20:4, 6) By following the requirements stated at 2 Peter 1:5-11 they make their calling and election sure. At their resurrection out of death they are granted an abundant entrance into the heavenly kingdom.

The apostle Paul, who was in the Kingdom covenant, spoke of professed Christians who wanted to set aside the searching requirements and to run ahead and start reigning before God's time, right down here on earth without Christ Jesus. He reproved these proud, self-exalting ones, saying: "Now ye are full, now ye are rich, ye have reigned as kings without us: and I would to God ye did reign, that we also might reign with you. . . . For the kingdom of God is not in word, but in power."—1 Corinthians 4:8-20.

Such attempt by professing Christians to ignore the Lord's rules and time and to establish themselves as kings in the Lord's name and without his Anointed King is an attempt to ascend the hill of Zion and to stand in the holy place. It is antichrist, because it is a setting up of a counterfeit kingdom of God in the place and stead of the true kingdom of Jehovah's Christ. It is confusing and blinds mankind to the truth. It prevents their belief and hope in God's power to erect his promised Government, and hence leads to destruction. It brings contempt and reproach upon God's name and kingdom. It is all an abomination of desolation in God's sight. For this cause it is said to "Christendom", as it was said to unfaithful Jerusalem: "Behold, your house is left unto you desolate." (Matthew 23:38) She is not a holy place.

The prophet Daniel foretold the setting up of just such an "abomination that maketh desolate" after A.D. 1914, in the "time of the end". (Daniel 11:31; 12:11) Christ Jesus declared that the fulfillment of Daniel's prophecy would follow World War I and would be one of the proofs of the end of the world (*aion*), and that the abominable thing would be stood up in spite of the preaching of the good news of the Kingdom. Hence it would be showing the height of disdain and disbelief for the glad message. Immediately after foretelling the preaching of the Kingdom gospel in all the habitable earth for a witness to the nations Jesus said: "When ye, therefore, shall see the abomination of desolation, spoken of by Daniel the prophet, stand in the holy place, (whoso readeth, let him understand:) then let

them which be in Judæa flee into the mountains."
(Matthew 24: 15, 16) "But when ye shall see the
abomination of desolation, spoken of by Daniel the prophet, standing where it ought not, (let
him that readeth understand,) then let them that
be in Judæa flee to the mountains."–Mark 13: 14.

Do we have this added proof today that the
final end will soon overtake Satan's organization, including "Christendom", and that it is
therefore high time to flee to God's "mountain"
of the Kingdom and take refuge under it? Honest examiners of the facts will admit that we
do. As far back as its issue of June, 1880,
(page 6) *The Watchtower* pointed forward to
the ending of the "seven times" of the Gentiles
in 1914. After that date was reached, and World
War I came, proving that it was the time for the
Messianic rule to begin and all human governments to yield their power and control to the
Rightful Ruler, the testimony to this effect was
pressed with greater force and publicity than
ever by Jehovah's people. The answer of the nations of "Christendom" to the testimony· these
witnesses gave was hatred, unbelief, persecution, imprisonment, banning of their literature
and stoppage of their Christian work. In fact,
the work of Jehovah's consecrated people was
left like the "two witnesses" or "two prophets"
symbolically pictured at Revelation 11: 3-10.
"And when they shall have finished their testimony, the beast that ascendeth out of the bottomless pit shall make war against them, and
shall overcome them, and kill them." A few days

afterward the 'dead witnesses' were revived and work was resumed.

Shortly after the World War ended in 1918 the remnant of the faithful witnesses of the Lord were revived and gathered together for his service. Then the testifying to the reign of God's Son went forward with increased zeal and vigor. The governments of "Christendom" observed it with astonishment. At the Peace Treaty conference at Versailles, France, in 1919, a league of nations was proposed and urged upon the nations, especially by the American president in attendance. The proposal was adopted and incorporated into the Peace Treaty, and the treaty was thereafter submitted to the governments of the victorious Allies. The United States Senate refused to ratify the treaty with a league of nations included.

While the League issue was being threshed out both at the Peace Conference and in the legislative chambers of governments the religious clergy of "Christendom" preached in favor of this international organization and its Permanent Court of International Justice as the only means for maintaining world peace, security, and prosperity. On May 9, 1919, the so-called "Council of the Federation of Churches of Christ in America" came out with a report advocating the League and blatantly declaring: "The League of Nations is the political expression of the Kingdom of God on earth." The pope of Rome tried to get atop the League as a most opportune vehicle to ride, but failed.

On January 16, 1920, the League of Nations held its first meeting, at Geneva, Switzerland.

That was the first manifestation and establishment of the predicted "abomination of desolation". It was a counterfeit kingdom of God, a presumptuous substitute for the government of "the Prince of Peace". The clergy of America tried for years with might and main to shove the United States into it, and an American association called "League of Nations, Incorporated" urged American entry, saying, "In a world as dark as this, why blow out the only light there is?" To this blasphemous makeshift for the divine Government which descends from God out of heaven "Christendom" pinned her hopes. At length 57 nations had joined this super-national government. By rejecting the message concerning the end of the Gentile times and the establishment of the Messianic kingdom, "Christendom" rejected Christ as King and worshiped a creature of her own hands as the image of his kingdom. But it was in fact not an image of that divine Government. The typical Theocracy in the days of King David and Solomon was a prophetic pre-imaging of the Rule of Jehovah God by his Son. "Christendom's" monstrous creation was an "image of the beast". (Revelation 13:14, 15) She set it up over earth, which is the Lord's, to take the place of Jehovah's Theocratic Government. Hence she made it to stand "where it ought not". Where is that? "In the holy place," in the place and stead of God's Theocratic rule by his Messiah. What an "abomination" indeed!

The League was definitely not the Rule of "the Lion of the tribe of Juda". Being a collective organization of over fifty governments of the Devil's world, and incorporating representative parts of the seven world-powers which held successive world dominance from ancient Egypt down till the "time of the end", the League of Nations is likened in the Scriptures to a "scarlet coloured beast, full of names of blasphemy, having seven heads and ten horns". Interpreting this symbolic vision to provide a key for its understanding, God's angel said: "There are seven kings: five are fallen, and one is, and the other is not yet come; and when he cometh, he must continue a short space. And the beast that was, and is not, even he is the eighth, and is of the seven, and goeth into perdition." (Revelation 17: 3, 10, 11) When the "seven times" of the Gentiles ended, in 1914, the seventh "king" or dominating world power had come. Profane history identifies it as the Anglo-American world imperialism, the bulwark of Protestantism.

Since the seven-headed "beast" is the eighth ruling creature and is of the seven, being composed of them and incorporating them, it is the prophetic picturization of the League of Nations. Being full of names of blasphemy, this royal-colored beast is not of Jehovah's origination. It is of the "god of this world", and is antichrist. It blinds men to the truth and keeps them in bondage to the mimic god and away from Jehovah and his glorious kingdom. Those wondering at it and admiring it, heedless of

God's warning Word, will not gain life in the new world. (Revelation 13:8) Jesus said: "That which is highly esteemed among men is abomination in the sight of God."—Luke 16:15.

The sight of the "abomination of desolation" standing contrary to divine law in the place that is "holy" or set apart for God's Righteous Government is a sign, Jesus said; a sign that the great tribulation is dangerously near. It is a signal to flee with utmost haste out of the danger zone. In the January 1, 1921, issue of *The Watchtower* the League of Nations was pointed out both as the "image of the beast" and as the "abomination that maketh desolate". From then on Jehovah's witnesses used every means of publicity to call public attention to the danger signal, the desolating abomination, and to sound the alarm for the people to flee out of Babylonish "Christendom" and all other parts of Satan's visible organization and to take refuge in the mountain of God's organization. The Lord's "other sheep" heeded the warning and fled to his Theocratic mountain, which shall never be moved. They join in sounding the warning. As the features of the "abomination" become more and more distinct, the flight of the "other sheep" speeds up.

The seven-headed "abomination" was patched together for the preservation of the peace and security of the world that Satan the Devil might continue his domination thereof. Concerning its fortunes the prophetic account says: "The beast that thou sawest was, and is not; and shall ascend out of the bottomless pit, and go into perdition: and they that dwell on the earth shall wonder, whose names were not written in the book of life from the foundation of the world, when they behold the beast that was, and is not, and yet is." (Revelation 17: 8) The time when this "peace and security" beast "is not" is when it has descended into the "bottomless pit" or the abyss of inaction, inoperativeness and frustration of its announced purposes. In 1928 the worldly governments, including America, endeavored to reinforce the "peace and security" armor of the League by producing the Paris Peace Pact outlawing war. But such human devices did not prevent the fulfillment of divine prophecy. Because the papal Vatican could not get astride this League "beast", which was dominated by Protestant Britain, the papacy promoted totalitarian movements in order to forge a so-called "sword of the church" and to remake the League and alter its form to suit papal designs for world domination.

In harmony with its ambitious scheme the Vatican established itself as a political state in 1929, known as "Vatican City". It signed concordats with the totalitarian dictators, and it welcomed to the papal court the representatives of all countries, including Japan, that turned totalitarian after the Nazi-Fascist pattern.

As a result totalitarian aggression began, without any reproof or condemnation from the Vatican. In September, 1939, total war broke out. Thereafter more than thirty members (the

majority) of the League of Nations became actively involved in the struggle between totalitarian and democratic political powers, symbolized
in Daniel 11: 40-43 as war between the Rome-
controlled "king of the north" and "the king of
the south" under Anglo-American control.
Thereby the essential functions of the League of
Nations and its Permanent Court of Arbitration
were forced to suspend operations, and the
seven-headed "beast" took a fall down into the
bottomless pit or abyss, but not to stay down.

The prophecy says that the international
"collective security" beast will "ascend out of
the abyss" and "shall be present". (Revelation
17: 8, *Diaglott; Roth.*) This must come at the
close of the total war and at the international
effort then to restore peace and security. Even
during the dark hours of the total war the re-
vival of such a mechanism of international co-
operation was widely and soberly discussed, especially among the United Nations, and an international police force was proposed to safeguard the peace and enforce the decrees of the
"beast". Hence the beast must have horns, and
the Revelation prophecy shows it has "ten",
which is a complete all-embracing earthly number. This police force will encompass the earth,
but particularly "Christendom", as foreshadowed by unfaithful Jerusalem, who rejected
Christ Jesus as King and whose house was left
unto her desolate. During the global war the
earth was encompassed with armies. It was
deemed necessary also to continue thus encom-

passing the globe with armies permanently
after the total war as a protective device against
aggressors and disturbers of man-made peace.
The scheme is pushed under the seemingly good
pretext of maintaining the "Four Freedoms";
but, contrary thereto, the prophecy shows that
great political pressure and regimentation will
be applied to the people to make all support the
political-religious "new world order".

It is written: "As many as would not worship
the image of the beast should be killed. And he
causeth all, both small and great, rich and poor,
free and bond, to receive a mark in their right
hand, or in their foreheads: and that no man
might buy or sell, save he that had the mark, or
the name of the beast, or the number of his
name." (Revelation 13: 15-17) Though this had
a measure of application before the scarlet-
colored beast, which is the "image of the beast",
went into the abyss, it will apply still more so
after the scarlet beast ascends out of it. This
beast has learned quite a few totalitarian tricks
during the total war, and it will not unlearn
them or discard them in the postwar "new
order".

The "peace and security" beast ascends out
of the abyss, but not to freedom, for a blood-
drunk "woman" gets on the beast's back and
rides it and reigns over it as mistress. Writes
the apostle John: "I saw a woman sit upon a
scarlet-coloured beast, full of names of blasphemy, having seven heads and ten horns." The
"woman" does not have any nauseating feelings

at riding this "abomination of desolation". She
herself is described as "having a golden cup in
her hand full of abominations and filthiness of
her fornication: and upon her forehead was a
name written, MYSTERY, BABYLON THE GREAT,
THE MOTHER OF HARLOTS AND ABOMINATIONS OF
THE EARTH."—Revelation 17: 1-5.

The "woman" is the "great whore" having international relations. She symbolizes Satan's
offspring, namely, "organized religion." Its
most blasphemous and deceptive and powerful
expression on earth is the religion of "Christendom" under the dominance and lead of the
Roman Catholic Hierarchy. With so many dis-
cordant selfish elements making up the postwar
association of nations, Babylonish religion under the Vatican's leadership will serve as the
binding tie, but only for a time. The Vatican will
act as a supranational power over the postwar
confederacy of nations. She will assume to medi-
ate between God and man and thereby insure
the blessings from on high upon the international agency of control and stability.

The "woman" will ride the "abomination of
desolation", and will call the arrangement the
"restoration of the Kingdom of Christ on earth".
Thereby "Christendom" will make the abomination to stand once again "where it ought not",
"in the holy place." Because of this blasphemous
anti-Christ abomination, "Christendom" will
bring irreparable desolation upon her own self
first, and upon all nations of the earth shortly
thereafter, at Armageddon.

CHAPTER XXVII

FINAL WAR FOR FREEDOM

HE final war will come as a most sudden and complete surprise. Christ Jesus likened it to the descent of the flood upon a rainless earth in Noah's days, and also the descent of fire and brimstone from heaven upon the cities of Sodom and Gomorrah in Lot's day, at a day and hour when the worldly peoples were at their eating, drinking and normal selfish activities. (Luke 17: 26-30) Nevertheless, the appearing of the 'desolating abomination in the holy place' is an unerring proof that the unknown day and hour of the beginning of the final war is dangerously near. In view of world developments there is no time to delay further one's flight to the "mountains" of God's handiwork, his kingdom. Take your stand immovably for Jehovah and his Theocracy now. Why? Jesus' prophecy answers: "For then shall be great tribulation, such as was not since the beginning of the world to this time, no, nor ever shall be. And except those days should be shortened, there should no flesh be saved: but for the elect's sake those days shall be shortened."—Matthew 24: 21, 22.

In order to induce humankind to worship the idolatrous "abomination of desolation", postwar "Christendom" will urge the people to take sanctuary in that man-made structure for freedom of religion and freedom from want and fear. Contrariwise, God's Word of truth exhorts us: "Neither fear ye their fear, nor be in dread thereof. Jehovah of hosts, him shall ye sanctify; and let him be your fear, and let him be your dread. And he shall be for a sanctuary." (Isaiah 8: 12-14, *A.R.V.*) It is gross folly to put trust in "Christendom". In her refusal of God's kingdom she is foreshadowed by rebellious Jerusalem with her temple, to whom Jesus said: "Your house is left unto you desolate." Like Jerusalem, so "Christendom" is doomed to desolation, after the beast or "peace and security" creature gets out of the abyss of total war. Jesus so foretold, saying: "And when ye shall see Jerusalem compassed with armies, then know that the desolation thereof is nigh."–Luke 21: 20.

In the postwar "new order" Jerusalem's modern counterpart, "Christendom," will surround herself with armies of an international police force for her continued world domination. The Roman Catholic Hierarchy will attempt to act as the spiritual police force of the entire earth. "Christendom" will then feel she can cry "Peace and safety". This international police force, or the stationing of order-preserving armies according to the mutual understanding between allied nations, will be for the maintenance of the "abomination of desolation" in the "holy place". Hence those armies will be really maintained against God and his kingdom. And *when you see this*, said Jesus, then you may be certain that "Christendom's" astounding "desolation" is nigh. Religion will not save her.

Organized religion will lead all nations directly into the final war with God and his Anointed King. It will thereby bring desolation and perdition upon all nations. In proof, note the course of the scarlet beast after the "woman" Babylon seats herself on its back after it gets out of the abyss. "And the beast that was, and is not, even he is the eighth, and is of the seven, and goeth into perdition. And the ten horns which thou sawest are ten kings, which have received no kingdom as yet; but receive power as kings one hour with the beast. These have one mind, and shall give their power and strength unto the beast. These shall make war with the Lamb, and the Lamb shall overcome them: for he is Lord of lords, and King of kings: and they that are with him are called, and chosen, and faithful." (Revelation 17:11-14) Organized religion is thus seen sanctioning a blasphemous anti-Christ arrangement and will therefore suffer perdition with the "beast" she rides.

Since religion and the beast try to dominate the earth to the exclusion of "the Lord of lords, and King of kings", she and the beast persecute those on the side of His kingdom, namely, the "called, and chosen, and faithful" with Him. These are the remnant of Jehovah's witnesses who insist that Christ Jesus is the Rightful Ruler and who proclaim Jehovah's Government by

Christ. Organized religion and her beastly political pet prove beyond contradiction that they fight against God and Christ, not only by striving to rule in the stead of Christ Jesus himself, but also by trying to overthrow the work of Jehovah's anointed witnesses on earth and to silence their Kingdom testimony. (Matthew 25:40; Acts 5:39) Before the ten horns of the seven-headed beast turn upon her in retribution, organized religion will turn the horns against Jehovah's witnesses and will ride the beast in a final savage charge against them.

Therefore "Christendom" will use her postwar "new order" and her encompassing armies (Jesuitic as well as military) for the suppression of the Kingdom message. She will claim it is treasonable and disturbing and unsafe to the postwar rule. Jehovah, however, will not permit his "strange work" by his witnesses to stop until it is finished and all his "other sheep" are gathered out from this world and are safe in the "one fold". Then he will permit the "woman" and the beast seemingly to triumph as if having stopped the work. (John 19: 11) Only at that stage of developments will "Christendom" astride her beastly abomination cry out that at last in the fullest sense she has peace and security. What next? Jehovah's faithful witnesses know what then to expect: "For yourselves know perfectly that the day of the Lord so cometh as a thief in the night. For when they shall say, Peace and safety; then sudden destruction cometh upon them, as travail upon a woman with child; and they shall not escape. But ye, brethren, are not in darkness, that that day should overtake you as a thief." (1 Thessalonians 5: 1-4) "Christendom's" religious machinery for permanent peace will fail disastrously. Her prophecy concerning its destiny will prove false.

"Christendom" is being pushed irresistibly into that course which spells horrifying desolation for herself and the rest of Satan's visible organization. How can that be? Because by religion she has exposed herself to the demons under Satan, "the prince of the demons." By the demons she and all rulers of the inhabited earth are being gathered into a conspiracy and a lineup against the only lawful ruler of the earth, which is the Lord's. The demons are the invisible part of Satan's great dragon-organization. The revelation of the unseen things unveils

this: "And I saw coming out of the mouth of
the dragon, and out of the mouth of the beast,
and out of the mouth of the false prophet, three
unclean spirits, as it were frogs: for they are
spirits of demons, working signs; which go forth
unto the kings of the whole world, to gather
them together unto the war of the great day of
God, the Almighty. (Behold, I come as a thief.
Blessed is he that watcheth, and keepeth his garments, lest he walk naked, and they see his
shame.) And they gathered them together into
the place which is called in Hebrew Har-
Magedon."—Revelation 16:13-16, *A.R.V.*

Har-Magedon, or *Armageddon,* means "mountain of the assembly of troops". It is derived
from the Hebrew words "har" meaning "mountain", and "gadad" meaning "to troop". (*Davies*)
At Micah 5:1 God's organization Zion is addressed as follows: "Now gather thyself in
troops [*gadad*], O daughter of troops: he hath
laid siege against us: they shall smite the judge
of Israel with a rod upon the cheek." It is upon
his holy capital organization of Zion that Jehovah God enthrones his King, Christ Jesus, and
it is against that Kingdom organization that the
nations and rulers of the earth under demon
control now tumultuously gather together in
order to unseat Jehovah's Anointed King and
so exercise the dominion themselves without any
restraining bands. On this anti-Christ movement Psalm 2:1-6 says: "Why do the nations
rage, and the peoples meditate a vain thing?
The kings of the earth set themselves, and the

rulers take counsel together, against Jehovah, and against his anointed, saying, Let us break their bonds asunder, and cast away their cords from us. He that sitteth in the heavens will laugh: the Lord will have them in derision. Then will he speak unto them in his wrath, and vex them in his sore displeasure: Yet I have set my king upon my holy hill of Zion."—*A.R.V.*

Scripturally interpreted, then, the place "Armageddon" does not mean a literal place named "Megiddo" in Palestine. It refers to Jehovah's kingdom, to which his Ruler, Christ Jesus, has come, with his heavenly troops for the war against Satan's world-organization. These troops he used in throwing Satan and his demons out of heaven. At his coming to the temple he raises the sleeping saints and unites them with himself in heavenly glory. The faithful remnant yet on earth he gathers to himself into the temple condition of unity with him and of fellowship with him in God's service. This has been accomplished since A.D. 1918, therefore, and God's covenant people now stand at Armageddon, awaiting the final war. For years since then they have observed the gathering of the nations against God's King and kingdom. "When the Son of man shall come in his glory, and all the holy angels with him, then shall he sit upon the throne of his glory: and before him shall be gathered all nations." (Matthew 25: 31, 32) Concerning the gathering of the wicked nations the question is raised: "Shall the throne of wickedness have fellowship with thee, which [throne] frameth mischief by statute? They gather themselves together against the soul of the righteous, and condemn the innocent blood."—Psalm 94:20, 21, *A.R.V.*

Because the approaching battle will be fought at the holy place of the assembly of God's troops, *Armageddon,* therefore the "battle of that great day of God Almighty" is commonly called "the battle of Armageddon", or, for short, simply "Armageddon". There, at the Lord's side, is the place of security and preservation to which his "other sheep" must flee, even though it is under assault by the enemy. There they must join the remnant of the "little flock" of 'called, chosen and faithful' ones in singing the praises of Jehovah God and his kingdom in defiance of the foe.

At the day and hour chosen by God, his King begins the final battle against Satan and his demons at the earth and all nations on earth. The conflict that follows is no mere fight on this planet between democratic forces and totalitarian powers, a mere international struggle. It is a combat between God's organization under Christ Jesus and Satan's invisible and visible organization. The two opposing line-ups are symbolically described at Revelation 19:11-21. The Hebrew books of the Bible record many battles which Jehovah fought with miraculous exhibitions of power against the violent enemies of his covenant people. Those battles foreshadowed his marvelous victory at Armageddon. "Then shall Jehovah go forth, and fight against those nations, as when he fought in the day of battle." (Zechariah 14: 3, *A.R.V.*) Jehovah's witnesses on earth will have no part in the violence of that battle. Why not? "For the battle is not yours, but God's."—2 Chronicles 20: 15.

Because "Christendom's" desolating abomination will then be standing presumptuously in the holy place God will cause desolation to be wreaked upon her. He will strike confusion into the enemy ranks. The hitherto docile political and commercial powers will awake to realize how organized religion has befooled them. They will take vengeance upon the religious organization. "And the ten horns which thou sawest upon the beast, these shall hate the whore, and shall make her desolate and naked, and shall eat her flesh, and burn her with fire. For God hath put in their hearts to fulfill his will, and to agree, and give their kingdom unto the beast, until the words of God shall be fulfilled." (Revelation 17: 16, 17) Organized religion's desolation will thus come first.

Desolation of the oppressive political powers and greedy commercial traffickers and false guides of humankind will come next. Their destruction will be permanent as if by being "cast alive into a lake of fire burning with brimstone", and all humankind who have disregarded the divine warning to flee to the side of God's kingdom will be destroyed with them. (Revelation 19: 19-21) Jeremiah's prophecy, chapter twenty-five, foretells that not a nation will escape drinking the cup of the deserved divine wrath, and that "the slain of Jehovah shall be at that day from one end of the earth even unto the other end of the earth". (*A.R.V.*) Jesus declared that except those days of the final tribulation should be shortened for the elect's sake, no flesh should be saved. By the proclamation of the Kingdom message since the Lord's coming to the temple in 1918 Jehovah God has shortened the final tribulation, and all flesh that is approved by him will be saved through the battle of Armageddon and survive in the new world to follow.

Last of all, at Armageddon, Jehovah's King of the new world will crush the Serpent Satan and his demon "seed", who have been cast out of heaven and down to the earth. "And he laid hold on the dragon, the old serpent, which is the Devil and Satan, and bound him for a thousand years, and cast him into the abyss, and shut it, and sealed it over him, that he should deceive the nations no more, until the thousand years should be finished: after this he must be loosed for a little time." (Revelation 20: 1-3, *A.R.V.*) Aforetime, when Satan and his demons stirred up the religionists to have Christ Jesus killed and he lay in the depths of death, God's Word said: "Say not in thy heart, Who shall ascend into heaven? (that is, to bring Christ down:) or, Who shall descend into the abyss? (that is, to bring Christ up from the dead)." From this text, at Romans 10: 6, 7 (*A.R.V.*), it is understood, therefore, that the abyss into which Satan the Devil is cast for a thousand years is the same condition as that in which Christ Jesus was for three days, namely, death.—Hebrews 2:14.

Such is the great day of Jehovah's vindication; "in the which the heavens shall pass away with a great noise, and the elements shall melt with fervent heat, the earth also and the works that are therein shall be burned up." (2 Peter 3:10) Hidden in the protecting shadow of God's hand, his faithful remnant, together with their loyal companions of the "other sheep", will look forth and behold this glorious, yet terrifying, demonstration of Jehovah's power through Christ Jesus. They will rejoice in this vindication of God's holy name.—Isaiah 26:20, 21; Habakkuk 2:14; 3:2-16.

CHAPTER XXVIII

PRINCES OF A FREE EARTH

EVERTHELESS we, according to his promise, look for new heavens and a new earth, wherein dwelleth righteousness." This is the glorious outlook which the God of truth gives to those who trust in his Word of promise. The realization of that promise will far exceed in grandeur and blessedness all that our eyes of faith can now visualize.—2 Peter 3:13.

The apostle John, after seeing in symbolic scenes the destruction of "the heavens and the earth which are now", writes: "And I saw a new heaven and a new earth: for the first heaven and the first earth were passed away; and there was no more sea. And I John saw the holy city, new Jerusalem, coming down from God out of heaven, prepared as a bride adorned for her husband. And I heard a great voice out of heaven saying, Behold, the tabernacle of God is with men, and he will dwell with them, and they shall be his people, and God himself shall be with them, and be their God. And God shall wipe away all tears from their eyes; and there shall be no more death, neither sorrow, nor crying, neither shall there be any more pain: for the former things are passed away. And he that sat upon the throne said, Behold, I make all things new. And he said unto me, Write: for these words are true and faithful."—Revelation 21:1-5.

Political and religious promises to build a new and finer and free world by men's hands are therefore ridiculous and presumptuous. They prove that the promisers forget God and hold his Word as untrue. But it will be their so-called "new order" that will pass away at Armageddon, and God's Word will stand vindicated as true. The new world of righteousness will be fashioned by Almighty God through his Master Workman, The Word, Christ Jesus. "For, behold, I create new heavens and a new earth; and the former things shall not be remembered, nor come into mind. But be ye glad and rejoice for ever in that which I create; for . . . the new heavens and the new earth, which I will make, shall remain before me, saith Jehovah." —Isaiah 65:17, 18; 66:22, *A.R.V.*

By the enthronement of his King at the end of the "seven times" in A.D. 1914 the great Creator created the "new heavens", the capital organization of his universe. The "war in heaven" that followed ended in the overthrow of the wicked heavens of Satan and his demons, although the destruction of those wicked creatures was not carried out at once after their debasement to the earth but awaits the final end of Satan's organization at Armageddon. The "new heavens" are symbolized by the "new Jerusalem" which descends from heaven. That is, it extends its power down from heaven to the earth for the creating of a new governing organization symbolized as "the new earth". The "new Jerusalem" rules in the midst of its enemies until Armageddon is fought out and the enemies are destroyed. The Righteous Ruler of the "new Jerusalem" is the Lamb of God: "And I saw a great white throne, and him that sat on it, from whose face the earth and the heaven fled away; and there was found no place for them." (Revelation 20: 11; 3: 21) Then the King and the city, which represents his 'bride, the wife of the Lamb', reign as the "new heavens" over the cleansed terrestrial globe, and the establishment of the "new earth" takes place. Who will compose that new earthly organization?

The "new earth" will be the official visible representatives of the invisible heavenly Ruler, the new righteous Overlord over humankind. The Lord's "other sheep" are being gathered into the "one fold" first since the "new heavens" were created, and hence will not be made the earthly representatives of their invisible Overlord, even though they survive the great tribulation at the world's end. The office of representatives will be granted to faithful men who preceded Jesus' earthly ministry in the flesh. Such men were privileged to foreshadow him and his faithful course and sacrifice by their own deeds of faith and devotion to God. Many of them were in the human line of descent down to his birth in the flesh, being thus his forefathers according to the flesh. Having served as Jehovah's witnesses and as prophetic representations of Jehovah's coming King, they will again serve as his trust-worthy representatives on earth under the Kingdom actually established. That is no unjustified discrimination against the "other sheep" and is no cause for complaint by them. Everything is of God's mercy and loving-kindness, and is for the glory of him who does all things according to his own unselfish will.—Romans 9: 14-16; 11: 29.

One of those faithful men of old prophesied of the destruction of the totalitarian world arrangement, pictured by the king of Assyria and his princes. He then said: "Behold, a king shall reign in righteousness, and princes shall rule in judgment. And a man shall be as an hiding place from the wind." (Isaiah 31: 6-9; 32: 1, 2) Christ Jesus, "the Son of man," will reign as King in Zion, the "new Jerusalem"; and the 144,000 members of his church-body "shall be priests of God and of Christ, and shall reign with him a thousand years". (Revelation 20: 4, 6) They reign with him in the invisible heavens, but the faithful men of old will rule in judgment on the earth under the Kingdom. They receive their life from Christ Jesus the King. When put in official position on earth, they will as the King's sons be "princes" visible to humankind. This is definitely stated in Psalm 45, which is addressed to God's King.

After a description of the King's queen, 'the wife of the Lamb,' and then of her virgin companions, the Lord's "other sheep", Psalm 45: 16 says to the King: "Instead of thy fathers shall be thy children, whom thou mayest make princes

in all the earth." Among such ones are Moses
and John the Baptist, both of whom died before
the day of Pentecost and hence were not begotten of the spirit. Accordingly, in proof that
these foremost prophets of old will not reign
with Christ in heaven but will be princes on
earth inferior to the Kingdom, Jesus said:
"Verily I say unto you, Among them that are
born of women there hath not risen a greater
than John the Baptist: notwithstanding, he that
is least in the kingdom of heaven is greater than
he."—Matthew 11: 11.

Where are those future "princes" now? Not
in any imaginary place called "limbo", neither
in heaven. They are dead, in *Sheol,* or *hell,* the
place of unconsciousness and non-existence in
death. Faithful Jacob expected to go there, and
thought that his beloved son Joseph was there
also. According to Genesis 37: 35 Jacob said:
"I will go down to my son into HELL, mourning."
(*Douay Version*) Or, "I will go down to SHEOL
to my son mourning." (*A.R.V.*) Or, "I will go
down into the GRAVE unto my son mourning."
(*Auth. Ver.*) Also patient Job, while being tormented with bodily afflictions by the Devil,
prayed to go to the dead's abode, saying: "Who
will grant me this, that thou mayst protect me in
HELL?" (Job 14: 13, *Douay*) Or, "Oh that thou
wouldest hide me in SHEOL!" (*A.R.V.*) Or, "O
that thou wouldest hide me in the GRAVE!" (*A.V.*)

The transfiguration scene in the holy mountain, in which Moses and Elijah appeared talking with Jesus, does not deny the fact that they

are dead. Jesus said that what his disciples saw there was a "vision"; just as John, when receiving the Revelation, saw visions in which he himself talked and also saw and heard others speaking. But such visions were not realities. (Matthew 17:9; Acts 12:9) Had the prophets Moses and Elijah actually been raised from the dead and appeared in fleshly bodies in that transfiguration scene, then it would have denied the Scripture truth that Jesus Christ is "the first-begotten of the dead". (Revelation 1:5; Colossians 1:18) Some time before that transfiguration Jesus plainly said: "No man hath ascended up to heaven, but he that came down from heaven, even the Son of man." (John 3:13) And with this fact Peter agreed on the day of Pentecost.—Acts 2:34.

Such men of old need a resurrection. This they expected to receive through the woman's Seed who should bruise the Serpent's head. The apostle Paul writes to the Christians in the covenant for the kingdom of heaven and gives them a narrative account of those faithful men of old, from Abel to John the Baptist. He tells of their refusal to compromise and bargain their way out of suffering, and adds: "And others were tortured, not accepting deliverance; that they might obtain a better resurrection." (Hebrews 11:35) Though not sharing in the reward of the "first resurrection" with the "kingdom of heaven" class, yet they do obtain a resurrection better than that of the remainder of redeemed humankind. Why? Because they kept covenant

with God and maintained their integrity against
the Devil, and thereby they have "done good".
Hence Jesus said they come forth to a "resurrection of life". In their awakening out of death
they will come forth as perfect men and to the
station of "princes in all the earth".—John
5: 28, 29.

They could not, however, receive this resurrection before Christ's coming to the temple,
at which time the "dead in Christ" must rise
first. On this matter the apostle writes to Christians called to the heavenly calling and to the
"first resurrection" and says to them: "And
these all, having obtained a good report through
faith, received not the promise: God having provided some better thing for us, that they without us should not be made perfect." (Hebrews
11: 39, 40) Now that the King has come to the
temple and resurrected the sleeping saints and
gathered his faithful remnant into the temple
condition of unity with him, there is hope that
these faithful men of old may be resurrected in
the near future. Some Scripture texts and prophetic dramas suggest that they may be raised
to life before the battle of Armageddon and may
meet the faithful spiritual remnant and with
them see the mighty battle and the glorious victory of which they prophesied. The Revelation
concerning the destruction of Satan's "woman",
Babylon, says: "Rejoice over her, thou heaven,
and ye saints, and ye apostles, and ye *prophets;*
for God hath judged your judgment on her."
(Revelation 18: 20, *A.R.V.*) The faithful rem-

nant have a hope that, like as Joseph met his aged father Jacob before the seven years of famine in Egypt were up, so they may have the joy of welcoming these faithful prophets and witnesses of old back from the tomb before this dire period of spiritual famine ends at "the battle of that great day."—Genesis 46: 26-30.

Christ Jesus is the Foundation of the new world of righteousness. "And his name shall be called Wonderful Counsellor, The mighty God, The everlasting Father, The Prince of Peace. Of the increase of his government and peace there shall be no end." (Isaiah 9: 6, 7) When he raises those ancient witnesses from the dead by giving them life and thus becoming their "Everlasting Father"; and when, after Armageddon, he installs them in office as "princes in all the earth", then the "new earth" as well as the "new heavens" will have come indeed. That new world will be established that it cannot be moved for ever. Hence the divine command is now given: "Say among the nations, Jehovah reigneth: the world also is established that it cannot be moved: he will judge the peoples with equity. Let the heavens be glad, and let the earth rejoice; let the sea roar, and the fulness thereof; let the field exult, and all that is therein; then shall all the trees of the wood sing for joy before Jehovah; for he cometh, for he cometh to judge the earth: he will judge the world with righteousness, and the peoples with his truth." —Psalm 96: 10-13, *A.R.V.*

CHAPTER XXIX

THE THOUSAND-YEAR REIGN

LIMPSES of life on earth in the new world of righteousness are graciously given in the Scriptures of truth. After a victory song such as Moses and the Israelites sang on the east shores of the Red sea after Jehovah had engulfed the hosts of Pharaoh in destruction, the "great multitude" of the Lord's "other sheep" will receive instructions what to do. "For out of Zion shall go forth the law, and the word of Jehovah from [the new] Jerusalem; and he will judge between many peoples, and will decide concerning strong nations afar off," at the battle of Armageddon. The Armageddon survivors will convert the instruments of mortal combat of the destroyed nations to purposes glorifying God. "And they shall beat their swords into plowshares, and their spears into pruning-hooks; nation shall not lift up sword against nation, neither shall they learn war any more. But they shall sit every man under his vine and under his fig-tree; and none shall make them afraid: for the mouth of Jehovah of hosts hath spoken it. For all the peoples walk every one in the name of his god; and we will walk in the name of Jehovah our God for ever and ever."—Micah 4: 2-5, *A.R.V.*

360

The prophecy of Ezekiel, chapters 38 and 39, supply a vivid account of the final, all-out warfare of Satan's organization under his chief spirit-prince Gog against Jehovah's faithful remnant of spiritual Israelites and their companions at Armageddon. With an awe-inspiring demonstration of almighty power the Most High God destroys the wicked spirit and human enemies and vindicates his name. "And my holy name will I make known in the midst of my people Israel; neither will I suffer my holy name to be profaned any more: and the nations shall know that I am Jehovah, the Holy One in Israel." (Ezekiel 39:7, *A.R.V.*) Then the prophecy describes how God's surviving people will dispose of the bloodstained combustible instruments of the enemy and will dispose of their bones scattered about and thus cleanse the earth.

The God of righteousness and holiness will no more curse the ground. Paradise will not be restored earth-wide immediately, but the Lord's "other sheep" will go ahead with subduing the earth under divine guidance and blessing. "Truth shall spring out of the earth; and righteousness shall look down from heaven. Yea, the LORD shall give that which is good; and our land shall yield her increase." "Then shall the earth yield her increase; and God, even our own God, shall bless us." (Psalms 85:11, 12; 67:6) With no wars to ravage the land the earth will speedily become a Paradise, just as Jesus foretold in his comforting words to the friendly thief on the tree alongside him: "Verily I say

unto thee this day: With me shalt thou be in
Paradise." (Luke 23:43, *Roth.*) In this blessed
earth under Kingdom rule the "great multitude"
of "other sheep" from all nations will enjoy
peace and fellowship with the faithful men of
old, the princely representatives of the kingdom
of heaven. (Matthew 8:11; Luke 13:28, 29) In
obedience to the divine mandate these righteous
children of "The everlasting Father, The Prince
of Peace", will marry and bring forth children,
not for trouble and death-dealing war, but to fill
the earth. They will rear them with complete
freedom from fear and "bring them up in the
nurture and admonition of the Lord". (Isaiah
65:20-25; Ephesians 6:4) There will be no overcrowding of the earth. Just how long the filling
of the earth to a comfortable extent will require
is not stated. It was 427 years from the Flood to
God's covenant with Abraham, and long before
that covenant the typical fulfillment of the divine mandate by Noah's sons was accomplished.

The truth concerning the divine mandate was
revealed in 1938. Now a question arises respecting those of the Lord's "other sheep" who die before the battle of Armageddon. Many of these in
totalitarian Nazi-Fascist lands have died as
faithful martyrs for Jehovah's name's sake, and
many in other lands have died for other causes,
but all standing the test of faithfulness and pre-
serving their integrity toward God and his
Theocracy. Will these have a part in the carrying out of the divine mandate in the new world?

It suggests itself as reasonable that, God having held this hope before them, and they having died faithful and blameless to him, he would not deny them the privilege of the divine mandate. Concerning God's judgment Christ Jesus said: "He gave him authority to execute judgment, because he is a son of man. Marvel not at this: for the hour cometh, in which all that are in the tombs shall hear his voice, and shall come forth; they that have done good, unto the resurrection of life; and they that have done evil, unto the resurrection of judgment."—John 5: 27-29, *A.R.V.; Douay.*

The faithful witnesses and prophets of ancient time have an early resurrection to life because they have done good and passed judgment with God's approval. Those "other sheep" who since the Lord's coming to the temple for judgment prove their integrity to God and die faithful have likewise "done good" and hence appear to be in line for a "resurrection of life". Since 1918 Christ Jesus on his throne at the temple has been judging the nations and dividing the people as "sheep" and "goats". He pronounces favorable judgment upon the "sheep" and ushers them into life everlasting under the Kingdom. The "other sheep" do not come into judgment with the rest of humankind, who have "done evil". Reasonably, then, such "other sheep" as die faithful under judgment test before Armageddon is fought to the finish will be favored like the faithful men of old and will receive an early resurrection 'unto life' and before the divine mandate is completely fulfilled. This will privilege them to share in that joyful hope and service. Such favor to the resurrected "other sheep" will not be contrary to Matthew 22: 28-32. It will be no part of the coming forth of the unjust unto a "resurrection of judgment" because such unjust ones have "done evil".

It is written, at Proverbs 10: 7: "The memory of the just is blessed: but the name of the wicked shall rot." The place of the rebellious wicked is not in the memory of God, but is in Gehenna, symbolized by the "lake which burneth with fire and brimstone", where Almighty God destroys both their body and soul. (Matthew 10: 28, *A.R.V.*, margin; Revelation 21: 8) Their everlasting death is not due to condemnation and death inherited from Adam, but is for personal, willful wickedness against God. Hence their death is called "the second death", to distinguish it from that which is inherited. For such reason they are not spoken of as "in the tombs" or "in the graves", which is to say, in the memory of God as having an opportunity for redemption by Christ's blood. They cannot "escape the judgment of Gehenna". (Matthew 23: 33, *A.R.V.*, margin) Therefore God will not remember them in the time of "resurrection of the dead, both of the just and unjust". (Acts 24: 15) He will remember the redeemable ones like the thief who, before dying unjust upon the tree, asked that he be remembered by Jesus in the Kingdom.

The divine mandate will be carried out in proof that God's word does not return to him void but that his purposes are never frustrated or defeated. Thereafter the rest of the dead in the graves will hear the voice of the King and come forth to the "resurrection of judgment".

The symbolic vision of that resurrection reads: "I saw the dead, small and great, stand before God; and the books were opened: and another book was opened, which is the book of life: and the dead were judged out of those things which were written in the books, according to their works. And the sea gave up the dead which were in it; and death and hell [(*margin*) death and the grave] delivered up the dead which were in them: and they were judged every man according to their works. And death and hell were cast into the lake of fire. This is the second death. And whosoever was not found written in the book of life was cast into the lake of fire."—Revelation 20: 12-15.

They do not come forth all in a twenty-four–hour day or to a judgment day of twenty-four hours' length. The reign of Christ is a thousand years long, and it provides sufficient time in which to judge them according to the works they perform on earth after awakening out of death. The apostle Peter speaks of the "day of judgment and perdition of ungodly men" and says: "But, beloved, be not ignorant of this one thing, that one day is with the Lord as a thousand years, and a thousand years as one day." (2 Peter 3: 7, 8) At that, this judgment day is not as long as one of God's creative days. It comes during the last thousand years of the "seventh day", the day of God's sabbath or rest.–Genesis 2: 1-4.

These, that have "done evil" due to being conceived in sin and shapen in iniquity during this present life, will not come forth to a reward, but according to God's mercy through Christ the Ransomer. They will not come forth to take part in the divine mandate, because that will have been completed by the Lord's "other sheep". Hence to these the words of Christ Jesus apply, at Luke 20: 34-38. There he says that Abraham, Isaac and Jacob live in the purposes of God, which is proof that there will be a resurrection of them and others. "And Jesus said unto them, The sons of this world marry, and are given in marriage: but they that are accounted worthy to attain to that world, and the resurrection from the dead, neither marry, nor are given in marriage: for neither can they die any more: for they are equal unto the angels; and are sons of God, being sons of the resurrection." —*A.R.V.*

This does not mean they attain to immortality. The angels are not immortal, but are subject to Christ Jesus, who has been rewarded with immortality. Man is a "little lower than the angels"; and hence being "equal unto the angels" means that these resurrected humans do not marry. (Psalm 8: 5) By obedience and faithfulness during the judgment day they are regenerated by Christ Jesus, "The Everlasting Father." Then God approves and justifies them and grants them the right to everlasting life in the Paradise on earth. Therefore they cannot justly "die any more", because they continue faithful. They attain to "that world", the new world, a "world without end". God guarantees them endless life and protects their right to it. They do not attain unto this justification and life-right till the end of the thousand years of Christ's reign. As it is written: "But the rest of

the dead lived not again until the thousand
years were finished."—Revelation 20: 5.

Christ Jesus the King, having been entrusted
with the "keys of hell and of death", discharges
his responsibility with them. He releases those
in hell by awakening the dead, and then upon the
worthy and obedient ones he undoes the effects
of the death which passed upon all men because
of the sin by the one man in Eden. In this way
he destroys "death and hell", casting them to
their destruction or abolition in the "lake of fire
burning with brimstone". "For he must reign,
till he hath put all enemies under his feet. The
last enemy that shall be destroyed is death."
This is by God's power and by God's appointment of him to that mission. (1 Corinthians
15: 25-27) Then the effects of Adam's sin, which
brought a heritage of death to his descendants,
will have been obliterated completely and for
ever. In this respect "there shall be no more
death, neither sorrow, nor crying, neither shall
there be any more pain: for the former things
are passed away".—Revelation 21: 4.

Those who die during or at the end of the
thousand-year judgment day will perish, not
because of an inheritance of death, but because
of self-chosen disobedience and wickedness and
rebellion against Jehovah and his reigning
King. When these are executed by Jehovah's
righteous Judge Christ Jesus, their deserved
destruction in Gehenna will not occasion any
sorrow, crying or pain on the part of the righteous ones who support Christ's righteous judg-

ment. Such rebels experience the "second death", destruction as in a "lake of fire". They do not go down into the hell of which Christ the Judge has the key, but into Gehenna, "everlasting punishment," because the "second death" means everlasting destruction.—Matthew 25:46.

Upon those who come forth "unto a resurrection of judgment" the final judgment test comes at the end of the thousand years. Then "Satan shall be loosed out of his prison, and shall go out to deceive the nations which are in the four quarters of the earth, Gog and Magog, to gather them together to battle: the number of whom is as the sand of the sea. And they went up on the breadth of the earth, and compassed the camp of the saints about, and the beloved city: and fire came down from God out of heaven and devoured them. And the devil that deceived them was cast into the lake of fire and brimstone".—Revelation 20:7-10.

The thousand years of confinement in the abyss does not reform Satan or cause his salvation. Though his head was bruised by the Seed of God's "woman" at the battle of Armageddon a thousand years previous, he is still defiant toward God and is bent on overturning Jehovah's Theocratic Government, "the beloved city" or "new Jerusalem". The covetous desire for universal domination still moves him to the attack on the Government and its subjects on earth and its princely representatives. During his detention in the abyss the earth has been free of religion or demonism. The truth has had

full sway on earth, and has made the people free
from the bondage of error and of sin, and free
from fear and want.

Following his unchangeable tactics, Satan the
Devil tries to reintroduce religion on earth and
hence goes forth to deceive, to deceive everyone,
if possible, to the four corners of the earth.
"Gog and Magog" picture a farthermost extrem-
ity of the earth. The searching test of integrity
will be upon all such, without exception. Those
who yield selfishly to the deception, forsaking
truth, shall suffer destruction in Gehenna.
Those who keep integrity toward God and his
"beloved city" will prove that God can put men
on earth who remain true and faithful to him
under the wily test of Satan the Devil. They receive the gift of the right to everlasting life.

Satan will fail again, and Jehovah God will
receive this final vindication. The wicked one
will be cast, not into an abyss, but into everlasting destruction in Gehenna, where he and his
false and beastly organization will remain in
abhorrence "for ever and ever". (Revelation
20:10; Ezekiel 28:19) The righteous One, Jehovah's beloved Son Christ Jesus, shall reign in
life immortal and will forevermore reflect the
light and glory of his Father to all creatures
that live. Truth will have triumphed, and the
freedom of the new world will continue un-
diminished and without end.

CHAPTER XXX

FREEDOM NOW!

HIS vision of a free world without end is to be credited to Jehovah God alone. It has been made plain by his reigning King at the temple, Christ Jesus. Its marvelous details are written down in His "word of truth". The brightening light that is now shed upon its sacred pages, illuminating them, is proof that we are in the "time of the end", the time when the meaning of the Bible's pages should be unsealed to those running to and fro through them.—Daniel 12:4.

By the spending of your time and effort to apply your mind to the study of the vision you have bought much truth. (Proverbs 23:23) Do not now sell such truth at any price this world and its "new world order" can offer. The truth is your most precious possession, for it is the truth that makes you free. The freedom that Christ Jesus the Great Master promised to the disciples of truth is not freedom as a civilian of this world. The freedom as a citizen of any nation of this world is now greatly endangered. It is fast being swallowed up in totalitarian rule, and will pass away completely in that identical postwar arrangement which the creators thereof hold forth as the stronghold of the

"Four Freedoms". All deceived thereby will be bitterly disillusioned.

The freedom which the truth through Christ bestows upon you endures for ever. If you continue in His word, no human or demon power can take the true freedom away from you. It is a foretaste of that new world from God's hand, in which "the creation itself will be emancipated from the slavery of corruption, into the freedom of the glory of the children of God. For we know that the whole creation groans together and travails in pain together till the present time". With your possessing the truth and living according to its light, your freedom begins now.—Romans 8: 21, 22, *Diaglott.*

Those of the world who boast of its freedoms are slaves without being aware of it or without honestly acknowledging it: slaves of sin. They are the slaves of error, superstition and religion. They are the slaves of the invisible, superhuman demons who rule the darkness of this world, and no discoveries of "science falsely so called" can make these spiritistic forces subject to human control. The world is organized sin and error; it is rebellion against God organized and is hopelessly under demon domination. "The friendship of the world is enmity with God. Whosoever therefore will be a friend of the world is the enemy of God." (James 4: 4) It can never be a free world. Its friends are bound up with it, to suffer the wrath of God upon it and to die chained to it at its destruction.

Dictatorial and totalitarian powers may take away from you your personal liberty and your civic freedoms, but they can not take from you the freedom wherewith the truth makes you free. The truth makes you free from sin, fear, religion and demon rule. The truth makes you free to serve Jehovah God and to follow his Christ. In that course lies the way to everlasting life in the new world of righteousness. The truth frees you from credulity, uncertainty and instability: "that we henceforth be no more children, tossed to and fro, and carried about with every wind of doctrine, by the sleight of men, and cunning craftiness, whereby they lie in wait to deceive; but speaking the truth in love, may grow up into him in all things, which is the head, even Christ."—Ephesians 4:14, 15.

Having now begun, you must continue in Christ's word. You must be a doer of it, keeping the law of truth. "He who looks intently into that which is the perfect law of freedom, and continues in it, not becoming a forgetful hearer, but a doer of its work, this man will be blessed in his deed." (James 1:25, *Diaglott*) If you have the truth, God grants you the liberty to publish it to others. The preservation of the truth and of liberty is not by keeping it to yourself, but by telling it out that others "may recover themselves out of the snare of the devil, who are taken captive by him at his will". (2 Timothy 2:25, 26) To hold fast the truth, you must "walk in truth", which means to make progress in it and to live in harmony with the righteous precepts of God's Word of truth.

The greatest truth is that of Jehovah's kingdom and the vindication of his holy name by it. His Son, the King, fearlessly proclaimed the truth of that kingdom and he remained free, bowing in servitude to none but God. To enjoy freedom you must do likewise. Seek companionship with those who study the truth and who then publish it. Join with them in boldly proclaiming the Kingdom truth. They are the only free people on the earth, and made so by the God of liberty. Sing forth the praises of Jehovah God and his King and kingdom, and fight for and enjoy the liberty of His new world.

HOW TO STUDY THIS BOOK

HE truths of the Word of God to which this book calls attention are of such importance now to you that you should fix them inerasibly in your heart and mind. This you can do by studying this book regularly with your Bible, "the holy scriptures, which are able to make thee wise unto salvation through faith which is in Christ Jesus."—2 Timothy 3:15.

You can make such a study privately by yourself. However, it would be more stimulating to you and more broadening to your mind, and also unselfish, if you associated others with you in this vital study. The wise proverb says: "Iron sharpeneth iron; so a man sharpeneth the countenance of his friend." "Two are better than one; because they have a good reward for their labour."—Proverbs 27:17; Ecclesiastes 4:9-12.

Are you a father or mother or a member of a family? Why not, then, conduct a study within the family circle? Or, if there are no family associates, why not invite a friend or neighbor to join you in this most profitable and exciting digging for truth?

The publishers of this book have provided a valuable question booklet for students. It contains a question or set of questions on each paragraph herein in its order, which questions faithfully direct the searching mind to the vital points or key thoughts of each paragraph. Also after each question you are furnished one or more Scripture texts to help you find further proof of what is in the paragraph: "comparing spiritual things with spiritual." (1 Corinthians 2: 13) This avoids all private interpretation.

If studying by yourself, first read the paragraph in *"The Truth Shall Make You Free"*. Then test how much thereof you remember and whether you have grasped the essential things by reading the question or questions on the paragraph in the booklet and seeking to answer out of your own mind. Read next in your own Bible the texts that are cited (but not quoted) in the paragraph, and then the texts given in the booklet after the questions. Reason out what connection they have with the matter in the paragraph, and how they give Bible support and illumination thereto. Having thus treated one paragraph, proceed to the next, and so on for an hour. Do this regularly each week, and mark with joy how you grow in knowledge and understanding.

If, however, you form a study group with others, the foreword of the question booklet outlines how best such a group study may be carried on. To promote such group and private studies the question booklet, herewith illustrated, of 64 pages and neatly bound, is offered to all students on a contribution of 5c a copy. Remit to

THE WATCH TOWER
117 Adams St., Brooklyn 1, N. Y.

INDEX TO SCRIPTURES CITED

Chief Office and Official Address of

WATCH TOWER BIBLE & TRACT SOCIETY
WATCHTOWER BIBLE AND TRACT SOCIETY, INC.
INTERNATIONAL BIBLE STUDENTS ASSOCIATION
is
124 Columbia Heights, Brooklyn 2, N. Y.

Address of factories and publishers:

America,	117 Adams St.,	**Brooklyn 1, N. Y.**
Argentina,	Calle Honduras 5646-48,	**Buenos Aires**
Australia,	7 Beresford Rd.,	**Strathfield, N.S.W.**
Brazil,	Caixa Postal 1319,	**Rio de Janeiro**
British Guiana,	5 Croal St.,	**Georgetown, Demerara**
Chile, Avda.	Buenos Aires 80 (Blanqueado),	**Santiago**
China,	Box 1903,	**Shanghai**
Cuba,	Padre Varela 55,	**Habana**
Denmark,	Sondre Fasanvej 54,	**Copenhagen-Valby**
England,	34 Craven Terrace,	**London, W. 2**
Finland,	Vainamoisenkatu 27,	**Helsinki**
Greece,	Lombardou 44,	**Athens**
Hawaii,	1228 Pensacola St.,	**Honolulu**
India,	167 Love Lane,	**Bombay 27**
Jamaica, B. W. I.,	151 King St.,	**Kingston**
Java,	Post Box 59,	**Batavia Centrum**
Mexico,	Calzada Melchor Ocampo 71,	**Mexico, D.F.**
Norway,	Inkognitogaten 28, b.,	**Oslo**
Philippine Islands,	1736 M. Natividad,	**Manila**
South Africa,	623 Boston House,	**Cape Town**
Straits Settlements,	Post Box 566,	**Singapore**
Sweden,	Luntmakaregatan 94,	**Stockholm**
Switzerland,	Allmendstrasse 39,	**Berne**
West Africa,	71 Broad St., Box 695,	**Lagos, Nigeria**
Yugoslavia,	Dalmatinska ul. 59,	**Beograd**

All communications for literature should be addressed
Watch Tower Bible & Tract Society, at the above
addresses respectively.

THE NEW WORLD describes human history from perfect man's original world through the present and into the righteous new world. It also explains the reason of human suffering till now and its complete removal, by clearing up with modern detail the entire prophetic drama of Job.

THE NEW WORLD is bound in peach-colored cloth, gorgeously embossed with title and design. It contains 384 pages of reading text, a scripture index, a subject index, and artistic illustrations in color. Mailed, postpaid, to any address, on your contribution of 25c a copy.

CHILDREN is grand reading for all who desire life eternal as children of the King amid the delights of the glorious new world. Its style is very simple, with a great deal of narrative, but it is education of the highest and most urgent kind today.

CHILDREN comes in sky-blue binding, with gold title and cover embossing, bearing 384 pages beautifully illustrated in color, and a convenient index of subjects. Mailed, postage prepaid, to any designated address, on a 25c contribution.

WATCHTOWER   117 ADAMS ST.   BROOKLYN 1, N. Y.

The Emphatic Diaglott

With the *Diaglott*, you do not need to know Greek. The name *Diaglott* means "through the tongue"; that is to say, through the original language of the Scriptures from the gospel of Matthew to Revelation you can get at the true and original sense of such Scriptures. How does *The Emphatic Diaglott* make this possible? Note the illustration below:

ΑΠΟΚΑΛΥΨΙΣ
A REVELATION
THE APOCALYPSE.

ΚΕΦ. α'. 1.	CHAPTER I.
¹'Αποκάλυψις 'Ιησοῦ Χριστοῦ ἦν ἔδωκεν A revelation of Jesus Anointed, which gave αὐτῷ ὁ Θεός, δεῖξαι τοῖς δούλοις to him the God, to point out to the bond-servants αὐτοῦ ἃ δεῖ γενέσθαι ἐν of himself the things it behooves to have done with	1 A Revelation of Jesus Christ, which GOD gave to him, to point out to his SERVANTS the things it is necessary to have done

With the above arrangement you can make your own personal check on the new emphatic English translation in the right-hand column. This translation is based on the sublinear word-for-word translation, also on renderings of eminent critics, and on readings of the most ancient Bible manuscript in Greek, the Vatican Manuscript No. 1209, and other old MSS.

The Emphatic Diaglott also contains illustrative and explanatory footnotes, an abundant selection of Scripture references, a history of the Greek text, a history of the English Version, introductory information on the Greek alphabet and grammar, and a valuable alphabetical appendix of geographical and proper names, apostolic words and phrases, etc., in the Scriptures. It contains 924 pages, and is bound in blue leatherette, with title embossing in gold. Mailed, postpaid, on a contribution of $2.00 a copy.

WATCHTOWER   117 ADAMS ST.   BROOKLYN 1, N. Y.

THE 1942 WATCHTOWER EDITION OF

THE HOLY BIBLE

containing the
Hebrew and Greek Scriptures

translated out of the original tongues into the
English and being what is commonly known
as the Authorized or King James Version first
published in A.D. 1611.

It is printed in minion type, with copious marginal
references, as shown below:

PSALMS 73, 74.   *End of the wicked. Desolation of the*

20 The prayers of Dā'vid the son of Jĕs'sē are ended.

PSALM 73.

1 *The prophet, prevailing in a temptation, 2 sheweth the occasion thereof.*

A Psalm * of Asaph.

¹TRULY God *is* good to Ĭṣ'ra-el, *even* to such as are ² of a clean heart.

PSALM 73.

* Or, for.
1 Or, Yet.
2 clean of heart.
3 fat.
4 in the trouble of other men.

rant: I was *as* a beas thee.
23 Nevertheless I *am* c with thee: thou hast hol my right hand.
24 ᵇ Thou shalt guide m counsel, and ⁱ afterward to glory.
25 ʲ Whom have I in b

Observe the diacritical marks on geographical and proper names to show their correct
pronunciation in English. An appendix of
76 pages supplies you also with an Index of
Proper Names, Expressions, and Their Mean-
ings; an unusual Concordance of Bible Words
and Expressions for locating vital Scripture
texts easily; a choice selection of Bible quotations, grouped under various headings, showing God's Word on Vital Subjects; and four
maps.

THE WATCHTOWER EDITION BIBLE is 7⅞" x 5⅛" x 1⅜", in
flexible binding of maroon color. It will be sent, postpaid,
to any address, on a contribution of $1.00 a copy. Remit to

WATCHTOWER   117 ADAMS ST.   BROOKLYN 1, N. Y.

CONTINUE IN HIS WORD,
Increase Your Knowledge of the Truth,
Be Free and Keep Your Freedom

by
regularly
reading

Since its first issue, July, 1879, this courageous magazine has taken the lead in publishing the truth, free from all religious sects, political parties and commercialism. It is devoted exclusively to making clear the meaning of God's Word, the Bible, and calling attention to his loving purpose toward men and to the fulfillments of sacred prophecy in modern events and conditions, proving that Jehovah's righteous Government by Christ is at hand.

THE WATCHTOWER appears on the first and fifteenth of each month, making 24 issues a year. Each issue contains 16 pages, including a leading article with numbered paragraphs and specially prepared questions thereon at the foot of each column for use in weekly Bible-study classes the world around. In the United States the subscription rate is $1.00 a year; in foreign countries, $1.50 a year. Remit to

WATCHTOWER   117 ADAMS ST.   BROOKLYN 1, N. Y.